HOW EUROPE
MODERN WORLD

BLOOMSBURY ACADEMIC
Bloomsbury Publishing Plc
50 Bedford Square, London, WC1B 3DP, UK
1385 Broadway, New York, NY 10018, USA

BLOOMSBURY, BLOOMSBURY ACADEMIC and the Diana logo are trademarks of
Bloomsbury Publishing Plc

First published in Great Britain 2020

Copyright © Jonathan Daly, 2020

Jonathan Daly has asserted his right under the Copyright, Designs and Patents Act,
1988, to be identified as Author of this work.

Cover design: Cyan Design
Cover image © An Alchemist in His Laboratory. Oil painting by a follower of
David Teniers, the younger/Wellcome Collection

All rights reserved. No part of this publication may be reproduced or transmitted
in any form or by any means, electronic or mechanical, including photocopying,
recording, or any information storage or retrieval system, without prior permission
in writing from the publishers.

Bloomsbury Publishing Plc does not have any control over, or responsibility for, any
third-party websites referred to or in this book. All internet addresses given in this
book were correct at the time of going to press. The author and publisher regret
any inconvenience caused if addresses have changed or sites have ceased to
exist, but can accept no responsibility for any such changes.

A catalogue record for this book is available from the British Library.

A catalog record for this book is available from the Library of Congress.

ISBN: HB: 978-1-3500-2945-3
PB: 978-1-3500-2946-0
ePDF: 978-1-3500-2944-6
eBook: 978-1-3500-2947-7

Typeset by RefineCatch Limited, Bungay, Suffolk
Printed and bound in Great Britain

To find out more about our authors and books visit www.bloomsbury.com
and sign up for our newsletters.

HOW EUROPE MADE THE MODERN WORLD

CREATING THE GREAT DIVERGENCE

Jonathan Daly

BLOOMSBURY ACADEMIC
LONDON • NEW YORK • OXFORD • NEW DELHI • SYDNEY

For my teachers,
from Leonard Irish to Richard Pipes

CONTENTS

List of Maps	ix
Preface	x

Introduction: Alchemy of Civilization		1
	Historical debates	1
	Alchemy of civilization	4
	Structure of the book	12
1	**The Supremacy of Law**	17
	The early emergence of law	17
	Europe after the fall of Rome	20
	Intellectual foundations of European law	22
	The rise of European legal systems	27
2	**A Passion for Travel**	35
	Early travelers	35
	Europeans explore the world	44
3	**Tsunami of the Printed Word**	57
	The emergence of writing	57
	The printing revolution in Europe	59
	Why not China?	63
4	**Rights and Liberties**	65
	Delegation of authority in premodern Eurasian societies	65
	The emergence of liberties and immunities in Europe	68
	Urban self-government	70
	Representative assemblies	73
	The conciliar movement	75
	Christian liberties	77
	Theories of political resistance	80

Contents

5	**An Anxiety for Knowing**	**83**
	Early developments	83
	Medieval and early modern European natural philosophy	88
	Breakthroughs toward modern science	90
	Why Europe?	96
6	**The Republic of Letters**	**101**
	Intellectuals	101
	Ordinary people	106
	Synergies of practical and theoretical knowledge	116
7	**Breaking with Tradition**	**121**
	Inspired transformations	121
	War and military technology	125
	A higher status for women	128
	Breaking the power barrier	131
	A rising standard of living	133
	Conclusion	**137**
	What did Europe make modern?	137
	How did Europe do it?	141
Notes		149
Works Cited		189
Index		213

MAPS

0.1	Major cities of the world, ca. A.D. 1000	xi
0.2	Eurasia: Earth's biggest landmass	xiii
0.3	Coastline and major rivers of Europe	3
0.4	Early river valley civilizations	5
0.5	The Earth's axes	11
1.1	The spread of monasteries in medieval Europe	22
1.2	Early European universities	24
1.3	Legal systems in the world today	28
2.1	The eight circuits of the thirteenth-century Asia-centered system of exchange	37
2.2	Routes of seven fleets of Ming treasure ships, 1405–1433	39
2.3	Major trade routes of the early modern "Indian Ocean World"	41
2.4	European exploration and colonization, 15th–16th centuries	52
3.1	The spread of printing presses in Europe	61
4.1	European political divisions, 1300	67

PREFACE

One thousand years ago, a traveler to Baghdad or the Chinese capital Kaifeng would have discovered a vast and flourishing city of broad streets, spacious gardens, and sophisticated urban amenities. Paris, Rome, and London—in fact, any European city—could have fit into a corner of those great Asian metropolises (see Map 0.1). Until around 1200, the only large non-Muslim city of Western Eurasia was the Eastern Orthodox capital Constantinople. Yet by 1600, three of the five largest cities in this region were in Europe,[1] and in 1850 London dwarfed all other urban communities in history with 2.5 million inhabitants. By then, thanks to the Industrial Revolution, Europe had dramatically gained in wealth, power, and influence compared to the other great Eurasian cultures, effecting what scholars call the Great Divergence. How it occurred is the central historical conundrum of modern times.

Historians of the so-called California School, such as Kenneth Pomeranz[2] and Robert Marks,[3] agree on a rough comparability in economic performance of China and Europe (especially in the Yangzi Delta, China's most developed region, and in England) until sometime in the late 1700s or early 1800s.[4] The causes of the Great Divergence Pomeranz attributes to accidents of geology that placed large deposits of iron ore and coal in relatively close proximity in England and an accident of geography that located Europe closer to the Americas than any other Old-World region. Europe's rise to power and wealth—thanks to "coal and colonies"[5]—were thus accidental. Marks pursued this line of thinking further. "The British," he wrote, "were fortunate to develop a usable coal-fueled steam engine."[6] Peter C. Perdue, a professor of Chinese history at Yale University, has summarized the basic idea thus: "the Industrial Revolution is not a deep, slow evolution out of centuries of particular conditions unique to early modern Europe. It is a late, rapid, unexpected outcome of a fortuitous combination of circumstances in the late eighteenth century."[7] Numerous other scholars push the onset of the Great Divergence back a century or two.[8] Yet whether it began in the 1600s or the 1800s, the argument of the present book is that the Industrial Revolution, the Great Divergence, and in general the "rise of the West" were

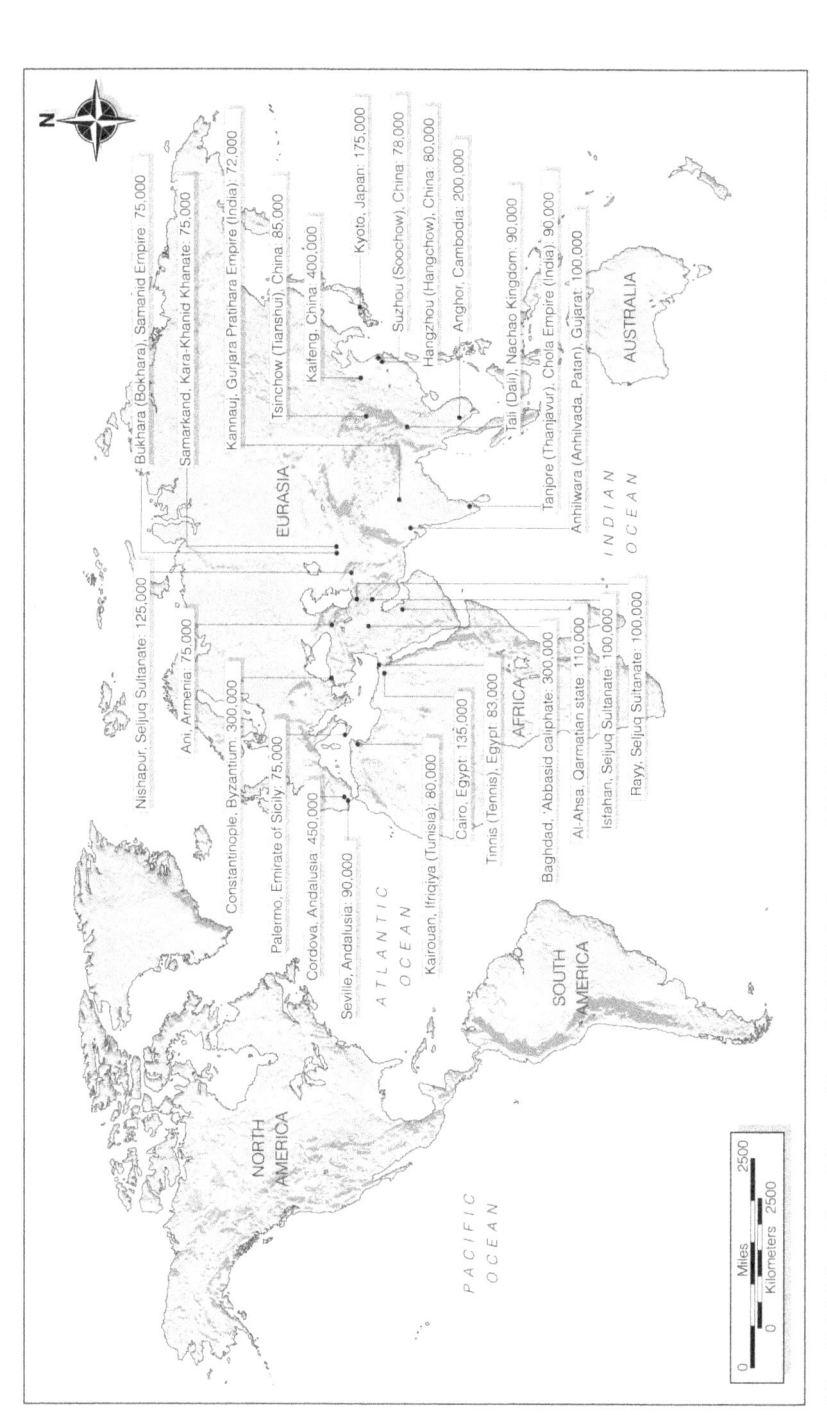

Map 0.1 Major cities of the world, ca. A.D. 1000. In the year 1000, Latin Christian Europe boasted not a single one of the world's biggest cities.

Preface

not accidental, not a stroke of luck, not unexpected, but precisely the result of "a deep, slow evolution out of centuries of particular conditions unique to early modern Europe." Not that Europe's divergence from the other great cultures was inevitable or foreordained. Contingency stalks every historical development. Rather, as I seek to show, a slow but accelerating accumulation of factors, most of them not directly engendered by material circumstances, contributed to Europe's takeoff.

It is obvious that one does not build a sophisticated machine by chance, nor does large-scale coal and iron production arise fortuitously. Human ingenuity is needed. Nor is exploiting colonies enough. Spain and Portugal imported vastly bigger quantities of gold and silver from the Americas than any other colonial powers, yet they became among Europe's least industrially and commercially developed countries. What scholars of the California School are leaving out are the invaluable contributions of thought, imagination, insight, and creativity, as if all that matters are brute strength and tonnage. Instead, this book will try to show that unleashing the power of the human mind specifically in Europe held the key to making the modern world. A key feature of this development was the unusual openness of Europeans to learning from other cultures.

What do I mean by "Europe made the modern world"? Although the Dutch Republic and England built the first modern banking and financial institutions, and the Industrial Revolution occurred first in England, by "Europe" I do not mean only its northwestern corner: nearly every other region contributed to Europe's rise. The civil law was recovered and developed in Italy. Systematic medieval philosophy and Gothic architecture arose in France. The Renaissance in painting and the plastic arts emerged in Italy. Portuguese mariners invented blue-water navigation. A German devised movable type printing. The greatest lens crafters and cartographers were Dutch. Many more countries contributed great intellectuals, scholars, inventors, and explorers. Learned societies and other voluntary associations were founded all over Western and Eastern Europe. After the Industrial Revolution began, railroads and steam engines were put into service throughout the Continent, well before these technologies caught on nearly anywhere else. Europe could not have "taken off" without continent-wide contributions.

What do I mean by "making the modern world"? I mean bringing it to life, even "midwifing" it: not creating it ex nihilo. Civilization emerged thousands of years ago in West, South, and East Asia and northeast Africa (see Map 0.2). All the early breakthroughs in culture, technology, finance,

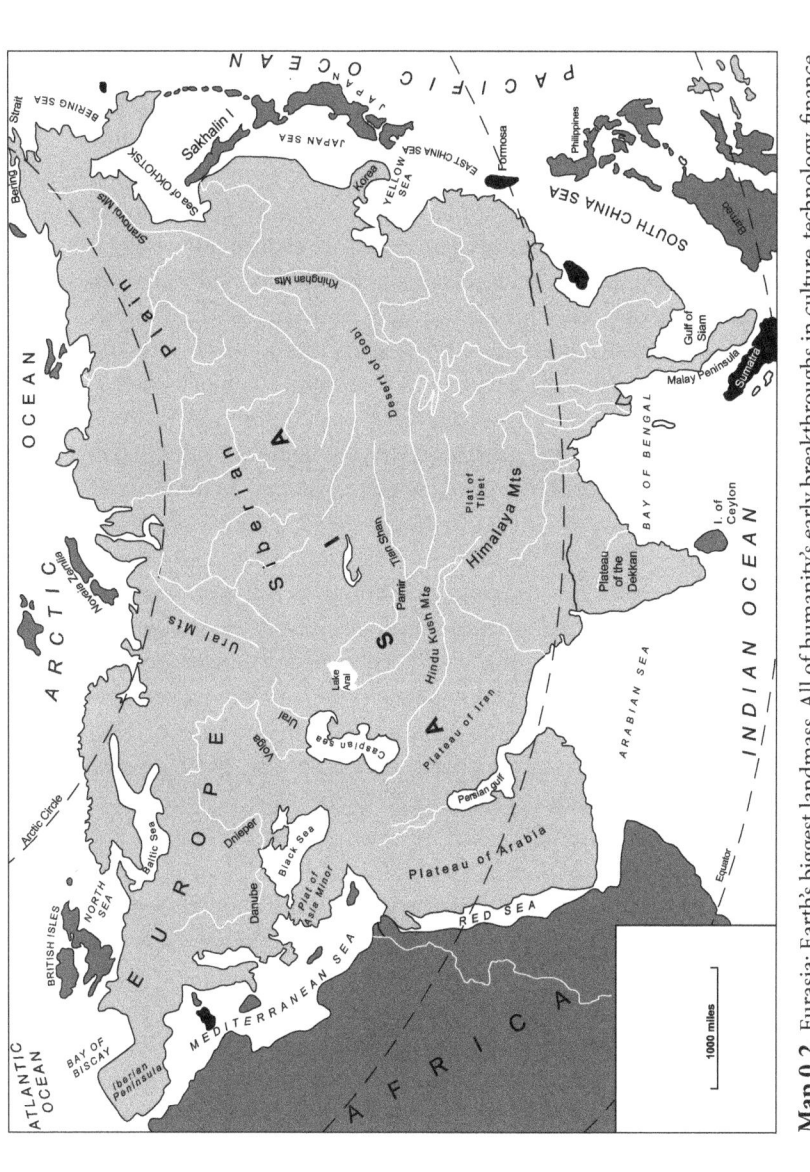

Map 0.2 Eurasia: Earth's biggest landmass. All of humanity's early breakthroughs in culture, technology, finance, trade, literacy, and religion were made in Asia and northeast Africa. Adapting these innovations contributed powerfully to Europe's development.

trade, literacy, and religion occurred there as well. Europe had nothing to do with any of them. It was, however, the eagerness of Europeans, beginning in medieval times, to learn from and incorporate achievements from around the world that made possible their success. Europeans synthesized and built upon these foundations and many others from across the globe, and then brought about massive changes in the way people think, organize society, produce wealth, exercise power, and live, engendering a way of life that we call "modern."

What do I mean by "the modern world"? I mean worldwide interconnections, embrace of and even enthusiasm for change, technology at the center of life, systematization, efficiency, prizing the individual, an explosion of rights, the ideal of female equality, representative institutions, the rule of law, and much more. Some earlier cultures introduced institutions or practices that we might call "modern." For example, Islamic law, which emerged over a thousand years ago, was able to adapt to the modern world and is used widely today (see Chapter 1). Many cultures knit together transcontinental trading networks (see Chapter 2). Likewise, in the eleventh century, artisans and entrepreneurs in Northern Song China developed what some scholars have called an early industrial revolution (see Chapter 7).

The metaphor I use to make sense of how Europe was able to "make the modern world" thanks to wide-ranging influences from around the world is alchemy. Alchemists ransacked the stores of nature in order to concoct potions of eternal life or the "philosopher's stone." All human cultures develop on this model. But some draw more widely on the advances of other cultures to produce their extraordinary amalgams. The three greatest syntheses were engineered in ancient Greece, Golden Age Islamdom, and early modern Europe. The result of each was amazing human advances, and of the third, specifically: the modern world.

Arguing that Europe made the modern world with all its positive features is not to deny the horrific ones, including vast and exploitative colonial empires, the annihilation of indigenous cultures, an especially dehumanizing chapter in the ancient practices of slavery and slave-trading, "scientific racism," and history's single most destructive armed conflict: World War II. Obviously, the devastation of culture, built environments, and lives did not foster Europe's success. Neither, presumably, could mere oppression and dehumanization. Scholars are divided about the contribution of colonialism, imperialism, and Atlantic slavery to Europe's wealth and development.[9] It seems most likely that all such evils were tragic consequences of Europeans' extraordinary aggregation of power, not their main cause. Indeed, key

Preface

elements of Europe's making of the modern world evolved gradually, beginning in the medieval era, long before the rise of colonialism and slave-based plantations. Moreover, it is the main contention of this book that ideas, concepts, practices, and other innovations of the mind—be they devised within Europe's borders or taken from abroad—contributed far more to the making of the modern world than precious metals and other commodities. Historically, fabulous wealth has been generated both honestly and squeezed from the most vulnerable without ever making the modern world. Its source must therefore be sought elsewhere. Such is the aim of this book.

For over two decades, I have taught and researched the "rise of the West." *The Rise of Western Power*[10] surveys this history in detail. The present book draws upon some of the detail and distills its basic interpretation but also develops a new approach in response to the burgeoning scholarly literature on the topic.[11] I am therefore grateful to colleagues around the world for stimulating contributions to this intellectual conversation, to my mind the most important line of inquiry in contemporary historiography.

The maps in this volume were expertly drawn by the Peter Bull Studio thanks to a generous grant from Faculty Scholarship Support Program of the Chancellor of the University of Illinois at Chicago.

I am grateful to Elinor Pearlstein, James Sack, Martin Tracey, Joaquín Chávez, Laura Hostetler, Junaid Quadri, Philip Devenish, Kaveh Yazdani, Anantdeep Singh, Timur Kuran, and Kevin Schultz for advice and insightful suggestions during this book's gestation and to Eric Brimstin, Stephen Broadberry, and Sandra de Pleijt for sharing references and unpublished work. Two anonymous reviewers provided helpful comments and criticism. The kindness of all these friends and colleagues has enabled me greatly to improve the final product, though of course any remaining errors are my own. Maddie Holder and her editorial team at Bloomsbury were encouraging, patient, courteous, and supportive.

Throughout my years of growing up, I was blessed with many wonderful teachers, including Leonard Irish in the sixth grade, H. David Matson in high school, Bernard Carnois in college, and Richard Pipes in graduate school, among many others. Each of them helped me expand my intellectual horizons, discover my passions, cultivate my abilities, become a better person, and grow into a scholar. For these gifts, I am deeply grateful.

INTRODUCTION: ALCHEMY OF CIVILIZATION

For most of human history, nearly all people lived at the edge of subsistence, had a short life expectancy, and traveled and communicated in the same ways as had their ancestors hundreds and even thousands of years before. Then, beginning roughly two hundred years ago, the world dramatically changed. In 1800, the population of no country boasted a life expectancy at birth of forty years. Today, every country surpasses that mark.[1] As a result, world population jumped from around one billion to over seven billion people. In 1800, not a single country enjoyed so much as $3,000 in per capita GDP. Now almost every country on the planet exceeds that level, with over one hundred countries besting it by three times or more. The average citizen of the world is ten times richer than his or her forebears two hundred years ago. The inhabitants of the most developed countries have seen their wealth skyrocket thirty-fold.[2] Moreover, in those same years, innumerable technological, social, political, economic, and cultural revolutions have taken place. Literacy has become all but universal. People travel by rail, road, plane, and even rocket. One-third of all humans carry in their pockets smart phones with more computing power than NASA as an agency had in 1969 when it landed two men on the moon. In 1800, medicine could cure no diseases. Now, most diseases can be either cured or mitigated. In 1800, in America, over eighty percent of the workforce was engaged in agriculture—a proportion that has fallen below two percent in recent years. In hundreds of ways human life has changed beyond recognition. Nearly all this change began in Europe. Why the change occurred and why it started in Europe are the biggest questions of modern history.

Historical debates

Scholars have advanced two chief explanations. "Eurocentrists" credit European culture, values, institutions, inventiveness, dynamism, or openness to change. "Globalists" deny any European exceptionalism, pointing instead to Europe's building on Asian foundations, exploitation of other peoples, state support for commerce, favorable geography and ecology, colonial expansion, and militarism.[3] It seems obvious that many such attributes and causes could be combined into one broad interpretation. For example, something unique about Europe's culture might have driven its peoples to become unusually exploitative or militaristic. Europeans might have built upon Asian foundations because they were exceptionally open to learning from others. Favorable environmental circumstances—such as the longest coastline of any continent (see Map 0.3)—might have combined with uncommon dynamism to raise up in Europe the world's greatest seafarers. Strikingly, however, few scholars have perceived the benefit of weaving together such a tapestry of reasons.

Globalists often present statistics showing that the standard of living in Europe before 1800 was no higher than in China or other developed countries of the time. The population growth rate, per capita income, life expectancy, agricultural output, capital accumulation—any number of material indices—can be shown to cast Europe in an unexceptional or even a negative light. As one leading globalist expressed the idea, the West "used its American money [i.e. silver from mines in South America] to buy itself a ticket on the Asian train."[4]

Yet material indices do not capture the entirety of human development. From recent history, we have a perfect counterexample. For decades after the Second World War, the Soviet Union was rated the second biggest economy in the world and the only other superpower, along with the United States.[5] Starting in the 1970s, it had more nuclear warheads than any other country. It also had a highly educated workforce and twice as many physicians per capita as the United States.[6] At the same time, however, its population lacked civil and political rights, its economy offered few finished products anyone in the developed world wanted to buy, and despite massive funding Soviet scientists won only five Nobel Prizes throughout the country's seventy-three-year existence. During those same years, American scientists received ninety-five. This juxtaposition indicates the pitfalls of purely materialistic comparisons. Moreover, in 1991 the Soviet Union simply collapsed. By 1998, Russia's world economic ranking had plunged to seventeenth place, before climbing up the rankings to a high point of eighth place in 2012 and then tumbling back down twelfth place in 2016. The "second superpower" turned out to be backward, impoverished, stagnant, and unviable.

It may well be true that the standard of living in the most advanced regions of Europe and of China around 1800 were fairly similar (though

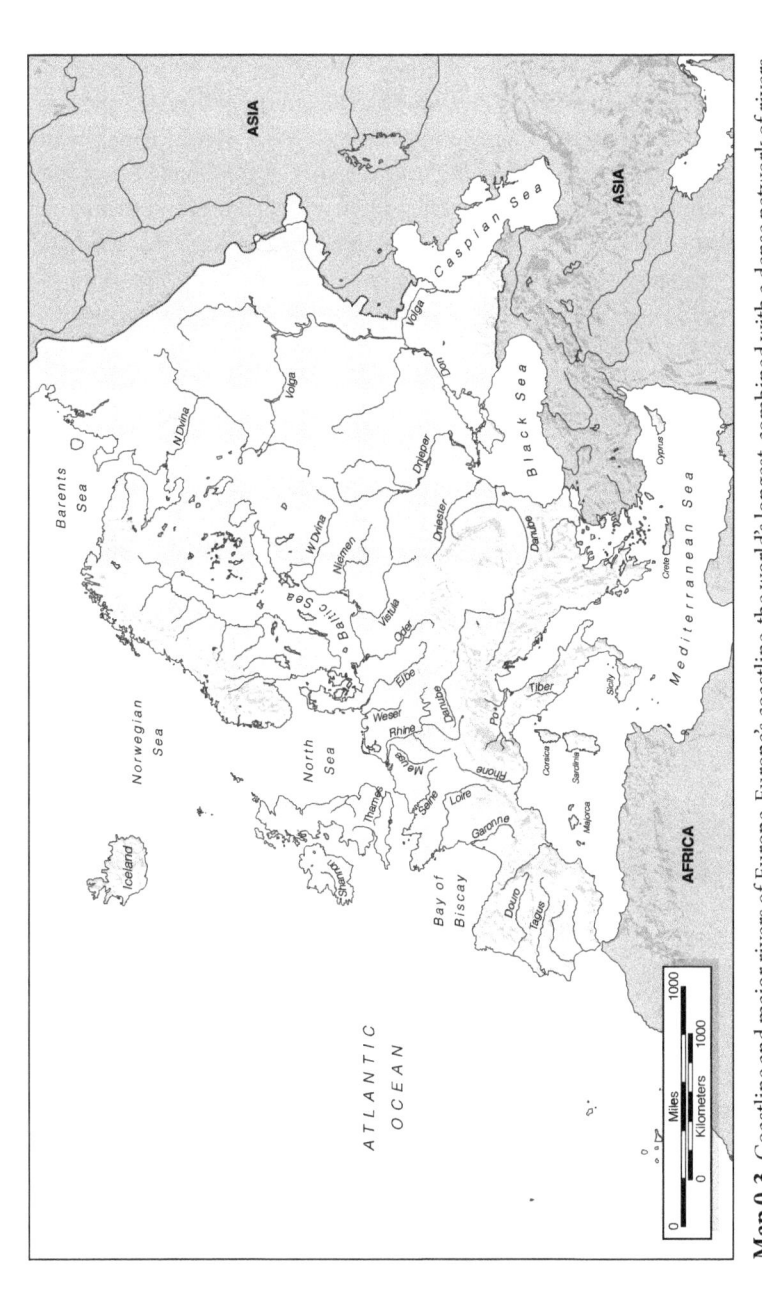

Map 0.3 Coastline and major rivers of Europe. Europe's coastline, the world's longest, combined with a dense network of rivers, gave Europeans access to efficient and inexpensive transport in the premodern era.

convincing recent research suggests they had begun to diverge as early as 1500; see Chapter 7). Yet such a comparison simply makes all the more extraordinary the achievements of Europe in the last two or so centuries, even more extraordinary than if Europe had begun to show earlier signs of accelerated development. These achievements—most of which began in Europe and then spread to its settler colonies, such as the United States and Australia, before taking root to a greater or lesser extent in every country on the planet—include representative government, the scientific method, continuous scientific advancement, modern medicine, the affirmation of human rights, the rule of law, the Olympic Games, the World Cup, movies, television, the Internet, cell phones, and social media, among many other advances. Because Europeans and their descendants brought about all these changes, and because these changes made the modern world what it is, is it not correct to say that Europe made the modern world?

We know two big facts: the world began to change dramatically roughly two hundred years ago, and most of the changes commenced and came to fruition in Europe or lands colonized by Europeans. How did this happen? The short answer is Europeans were extraordinarily open to learning from other peoples, and they gradually figured out how to unleash their own pent-up creativity. All human beings are extraordinarily creative and innovative. If left to their own devices, they will ingeniously figure out solutions to nearly any practical problem. As Aristotle understood over two thousand years ago, people in the aggregate bring more to society than any one genius, no matter how talented.[7] Painstaking observation of nature, working together, and the assimilation of environing resources, through something like an alchemical process, make human breakthroughs possible.

Alchemy of civilization

The first civilizations arose, beginning ten thousand years ago, in river valleys in Egypt, Mesopotamia, northwestern India, and northeastern China (see Map 0.4). They emerged because humans in these places figured out how to domesticate plants and animals and thus managed to settle down in specific localities, rather than following game over large expanses of territory, as humans had always done previously. This made it possible to build up cities, centers of learning, hubs of commerce, and concentrations of population. Once people were gathered together in cities, they could much more easily put their heads together and invent new technologies, establish institutions

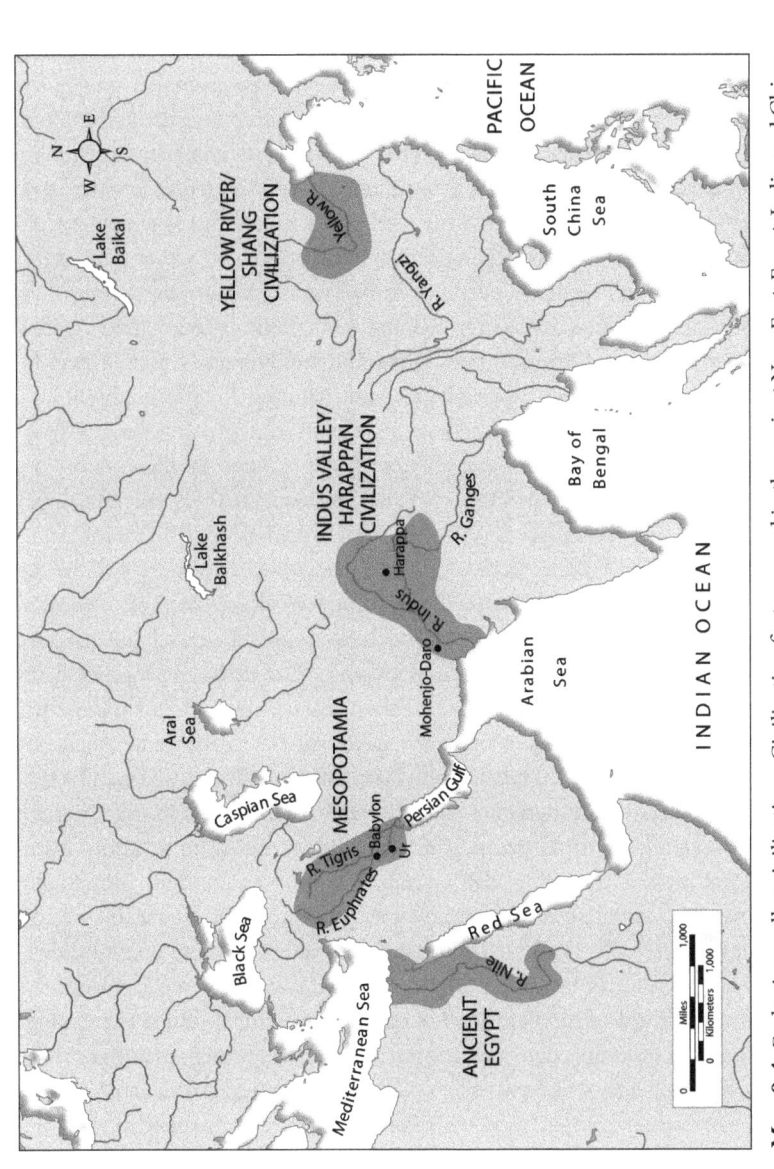

Map 0.4 Early river valley civilizations. Civilization first emerged in the ancient Near East, Egypt, India, and China.

and legal systems, explore ideas, create a wide variety of works of art and literature—in a word, to construct civilizations and to make them more and more complex, efficient, sophisticated, powerful, and influential.

Civilization first emerged from something like alchemical experimentation. Until recently, alchemists were believed to have been animated mostly by exotic and mystical designs.[8] Contemporary scholarship suggests instead that they often pursued much more specific and concrete goals and sought to achieve them by systematically experimenting with available elements and materials.[9] It is in this sense that one can liken the emergence of civilization to an alchemical breakthrough. There was no recipe, no set of laboratory notebooks to follow. Its appearance is and must remain mysterious. Yet civilization could not have arisen without meticulous experimentation, trial and error, sharing of lore and knowledge, and building up an almost infinite series of improvements. These activities came naturally to human beings.

Being alive means interacting with one's environment. All living things—from bacteria to humans—are phenomenally creative in their ability to adapt. They constantly process vast data relating to their surroundings, bodies, and mental activity and work them into an awareness of their corner of the world and their particular experiences.[10] On this basis, humans act, react, invent, build, and collaborate. Working together, human collectives—from hunter-gatherer bands to sophisticated civilizations—connect organically among themselves and with their environments in myriad ways. Even the most isolated, tiniest, least developed, and apparently most impoverished peoples on earth have learned to thrive in whatever circumstances nature has given them. Jared Diamond was astonished by the social organization, minute biological knowledge, and extraordinary powers of observation of tribal peoples of New Guinea he came to know from working among them for many years.[11] There was, in their immediate environment, no plant, animal, mineral, or other material, whose distinctive properties they did not know intimately. Members of these communities, over long periods of time, had figured out what was edible, what poisonous, what could ward off predators, what could be fashioned into jewelry, what stone could hold an edge, and countless other properties of things. They were like alchemists meticulously combining, refining, tasting, and testing all the elements to hand. The knowledge they gathered was aimed at survival. Sometimes such experimenting enabled human communities to sunder the chains of the ordinary and achieve world-changing breakthroughs.

Some forty thousand years ago, Asian mariners colonized New Guinea and Australia. Their descendants, beginning around five thousand years ago,

Introduction

peopled all the Pacific islands, sailing boldly and expertly into the void—apparently conducting the first transoceanic voyages in human history.[12] From around nine thousand years ago, indigenous people in southern Mexico figured out, through a painstaking process, how to transform a small, weedy grass, called teosinte, into modern maize, the forerunner of corn. Pennsylvania State University geneticist Nina V. Federoff has called this development, "arguably man's first, and perhaps his greatest, feat of genetic engineering."[13] Even earlier, humans began to craft works of art in various places throughout Afro-Eurasia. The most stunningly beautiful painted images known to survive are found in caves in and around the Pyrenees Mountains and date from 32,000 to 12,000 years ago.[14] Our ancestors who achieved these feats of sailing prowess, plant breeding, and stirring artistry—among many others—often worked for hundreds or even thousands of years to achieve the necessary breakthroughs of technology and skill, by sharing insights, experimenting with resources, applying diverse methods, learning from one another, and endlessly setting out into the unknown, both literally and figuratively.

Once human communities developed in the great river valleys, concentrations of people—still trying new approaches, exploring the properties of every available substance, imparting discoveries, and building up knowledge—accelerated the pace of invention. Within a few thousand years, artisans learned to ferment wine, construct wheels and plows, and smelt bronze. Functionaries devised writing systems to facilitate governance. Scholars and thinkers gradually constructed bodies of knowledge about astronomy, mathematics, law, accounting, meteorology, astrology, and many other spheres of learning. Nearly all of these early advances were made in the great centralized agrarian empires in Egypt, Mesopotamia, northwestern India, and northeastern China. Yet in time the great empires seem to have stifled creativity and innovation, by imposing strict rules, oppressive hierarchies, and authoritarian governance. Then on their margins or during times of political fragmentation bursts of extraordinary creativity brought forth radical transformations and great flights of human achievement. Three thousand years ago, for example, the Phoenicians, a seafaring people on the eastern Mediterranean, invented the world's first alphabet (see Chapter 3), which was widely adapted and seems to have promoted the flourishing of ancient Greek culture.

As people living close to nature become master knowers of their environment, and as alchemists painstakingly learn how to manipulate known materials, the ancient Greeks took everything they could find of value in their mental and intellectual environment and pulled it together into a glorious synthesis—the first major cultural synthesis in human history. This fusion included ideas, stories, concepts, myths, expertise, knowledge, skills, and methods from Egypt and the Near East, and at least indirectly from all of Afro-Eurasia. Home to a mercantile, seagoing people, one of hundreds of Greek city-states and colonies throughout the Mediterranean and Black Sea basins, Athens developed the world's first rule-governed, participatory democracy. Beginning in the 600s B.C., Greek philosophers subjected to rigorous, methodical analysis nearly every aspect of life and reality. First, they established rules of thought and speech—logic and rhetoric. Then they worked through fundamental questions of aesthetics, ethics, law, medicine, politics, faith, social relations, psychology, metaphysics, nature, and many other areas of knowledge. Other cultures had posed questions about the world, but none had ever furnished such lucid and methodical answers to them.

Greek, Egyptian, Persian, Phoenician, African, Arab, Syrian, Hindu, and Jewish scholars continued to advance learning in such Hellenistic intellectual centers as Alexandria in northern Egypt. Founded around 300 B.C., the library of Alexandria housed some 500,000 papyrus rolls gathered from the near Mediterranean world—for many centuries by far the largest library anywhere. Here Greek thinkers systematized and extended mathematical knowledge and applied Aristotelian methods to cosmology, cartography, anatomy, and physiology (see Chapter 5).

The Greek achievements were stupendous. They laid the foundations of most branches of learning and expanded human knowledge more than any other people during that early time. The contemporaneous advances in systematic learning of other ancient cultures pale in comparison. Yet the Greeks had no monopoly on creativity and perceptiveness. Around the same time thinkers, mystics, and prophets in other major and minor cultures throughout Eurasia developed most of the great religions and worldviews, including Confucianism and Daoism in China; Hinduism, Buddhism, and Jainism in India; and Zoroastrianism and Judaism in the Near East. This flourishing of new philosophical and religious approaches to the human condition and our relation to realities beyond was dubbed the Axial Age by the German-Swiss philosopher Karl Jaspers (1883–1969).[15] These regions also witnessed important scientific, technological, and intellectual breakthroughs.

Among the "Hundred Schools" that flourished during the Warring States era in China, followers of the philosopher Mozi achieved advances in logic, semantics, epistemology, ethics, mathematics, and geometrical optics (see

Chapter 5). Although the Mohist movement fell into obscurity after the Qin Dynasty unified China in the early 200s B.C., many Chinese continued to apply scientific knowledge to a wide variety of practical matters, resulting in the invention of the compass, paper, gunpowder, and printing. In addition to developing Buddhism, the world's first universal religion, ancient Indians made some significant technological breakthroughs, for example in textile production, along with fundamental and wide-ranging achievements in mathematics, like the concepts of zero and place value. Muslim scholars and thinkers accomplished the second great Afro-Eurasian intellectual synthesis beginning around 800. They melded learning from many cultures (although most of their translations from Greek were made by Syriac-speaking Christians, since few Muslim scholars knew Greek)[16] and made notable contributions to mathematics, commerce, medicine, astronomy, optics, and chemistry. The creative ferment of the Islamic world gradually declined, however, especially after the Mongol conquest of Baghdad in 1258.

Apart from the great premodern intellectual and cultural syntheses in Greece and the Islamic world, many peoples contributed extraordinary insights and innovations to human development. Again, one can think of them as alchemical achievements, involving experimentation, mental alertness, combining diverse materials, and learning from others. Take the ancient Hebrews. For over two thousand years, prophets and mystics in the eastern Mediterranean region had sought answers to questions about the universe and the meaning of life. They nearly always did so in "conversation" with other peoples, even with those of traditions and peoples alien or hostile to their own. Thus, the Hebrews adopted the story of the Flood, which had first appeared in the Sumerian *Epic of Gilgamesh*, but rejected the idea of the arbitrary gods of Egypt and Mesopotamia in favor of a loving and faithful God. This idea had one of the biggest impacts of any single idea in human history. After all, from this religious insight also emerged the two great universal monotheistic, Abrahamic religions—Christianity and Islam—to which well over half the population of the world belongs today. Not bad for a tiny and persecuted minority.

Civilization first emerged in the Middle East because that region boasted thirty-two of the world's fifty-six most productive wild grasses and four of the five major domesticable animals—sheep, goats, pigs, and cows. Peoples in other areas had to make do with one or at most several staple plants and one or two or no domesticable animals at all. Indeed, of the fourteen large domesticated animals in today's world, thirteen were indigenous to Eurasia. (Only a tiny proportion of the Earth's plants can serve as human food, and few of its animals can be domesticated.)[17] The reason why early human breakthroughs occurred almost exclusively here and then spread to Asia, North Africa, and nearby Europe had to do with population concentrations and geography. More food naturally meant more people, and more people meant more opportunities for sharing knowledge and learning from one another. Eurasia is geographically the most favored region on the planet. The movement of animals and humans is far easier along an east-west axis, because it does not require crossing climatic zones[18] (see Map 0.5). One can travel roughly 8,000 miles from the Atlantic to the Pacific Ocean without crossing into a different zone. By contrast, the east-west distances in the Americas and most of Africa are less than half as big. As a result, in both regions far fewer people were in frequent contact than in Eurasia. Such accidents of geography and climate do not determine outcomes; human agency is an essential ingredient. Yet they can make a huge difference in human development.

It is not surprising, therefore, that people outside of Eurasia made fewer breakthroughs; that they were still extraordinarily inventive is also not surprising, given humankind's innate creativity. For example, premodern people in the Americas built up complex societies and devised sophisticated cultural and intellectual innovations. The Maya in Central American devised pictographic writing from at least 500 B.C., a highly sophisticated calendar, and the concept of the numeric "zero" (before the East Indians). When Christopher Columbus arrived in the Americas, the Inca Empire of several million people was administered in part by means of a sophisticated record-keeping system of quipus, or arrangements of colored knotted strings. These strings, bound together in a variety of ways, indicated numeric values in base ten with place value and the concept of zero. Data—both numbers and labels, since places, people, and things can be identified numerically—were recorded by altering the number and type of knots, their position on the string, and the string's color.[19]

Indeed, peoples throughout the premodern world have used sophisticated mathematics and logic for keeping track of complicated family structure, navigating the high seas, devising initiation rites, contriving subtle amusements, creating beautiful adornments, myth-making, record-keeping, mapping, classification, and social organization. Most historical peoples have lacked formal mathematicians. Nevertheless, artists, craftsmen, mariners, administrators, priests, and even ordinary people could reason mathematically, sometimes at a very high level of complexity using graphs, diagrams, charts, symmetry, geometry, and arithmetic, often without reference to numbers except implicitly. Early in the twentieth century, for

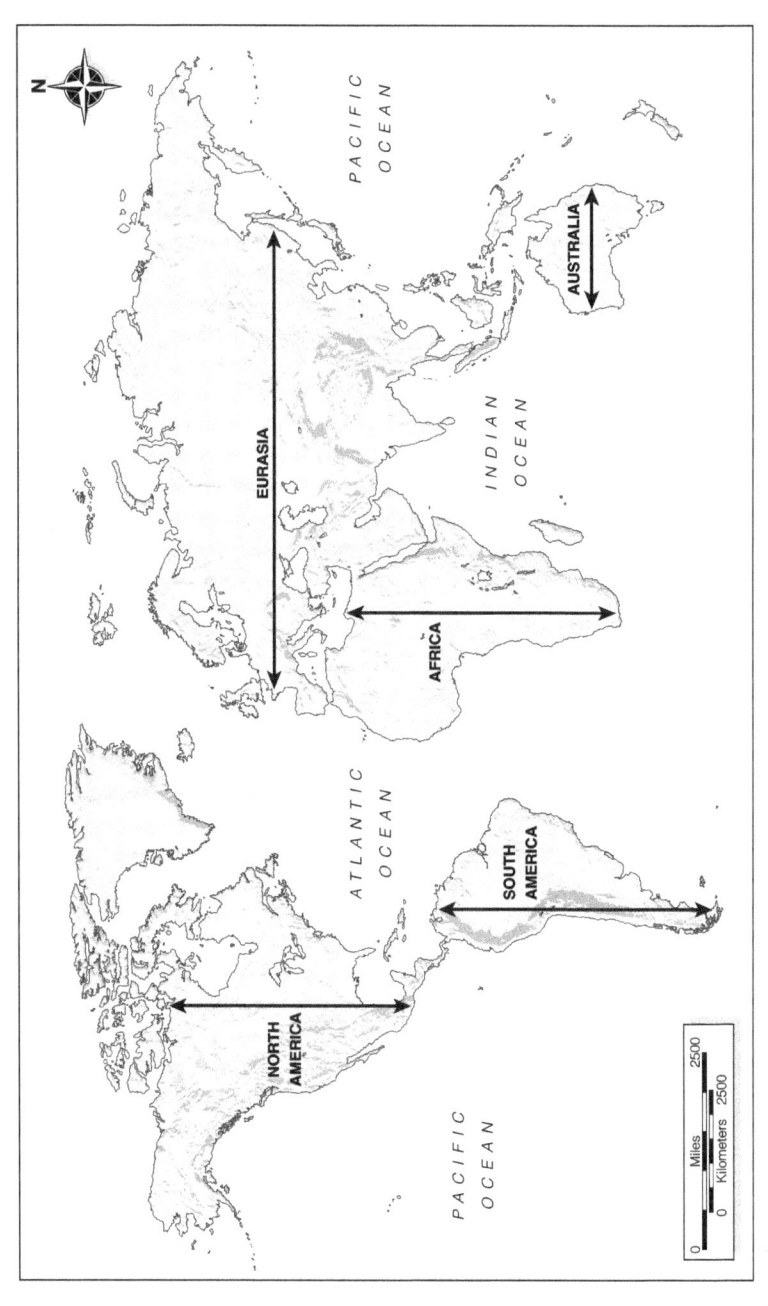

Map 0.5 The Earth's axes. Goods, ideas, and people circulate far easier along an east-west axis than on a north-south one.

example, children of the Bushoong people in the Congo Basin in central Africa challenged a European ethnologist:

> to trace some figures in the sand, with the specification that each line be traced once and only once without lifting his finger from the ground. The ethnologist was unaware that a group of people in his own culture were keenly interested in such figure tracing. And, being unfamiliar with what Western mathematicians call graph theory, he was also unaware of how to meet the challenge.[20]

Yet the exercise, involving connected planar graphs, a topic of interest to leading Western mathematicians from Leonhard Euler to Ludwig Wittgenstein and beyond, was quite literally child's play in a culture that decades ago European scholars would have dismissed as "primitive."

There are doubtless many reasons, some of them impossible to know, why various peoples flourished more than others, why some invented more technologies or created more stunning works of art. Nevertheless, there can be no doubt that all human beings create, strive to invent, benefit from sharing knowledge, delight in learning, and feel an urge to solve puzzles. All are alchemists at heart, and all cultures are the fruit of something like alchemical experimentation. The last great intellectual and cultural synthesis—the one that made the modern world and has become a continuous process—apparently took place because the European peoples, for a host of reasons, felt drawn more than any others before them to explore beyond their borders, to learn from other cultures, and to gather and channel human creativity and inventiveness from all the great Eurasian cultures. In other words, Europe, for centuries a marginal and lesser-developed region on the edges of the great Asian cultures, succeeded in making the modern world in large part because of Europeans' willingness and ability to build upon cultural foundations and achievements from around the world. The cultures Europeans developed remained extraordinarily open to learning from others, to improving upon existing patterns, and to embracing change and innovation in more and more spheres of life. Such indeed is my definition of "the modern world."

Structure of the book

This book argues that Europeans gradually built up institutions, habits, values, and patterns of life that enabled more and more people to tap into

Introduction

their inherent creativity, to try new solutions to old problems, to discover new problems to resolve, to invent, to innovate, and ultimately to transform the world. It seeks to substantiate this contention by showing that Europeans exhibited unusual characteristics for the premodern age in several spheres of human endeavor, each one examined comparatively in the following chapters. All of these areas of activity are central to modern life and therefore contributed to Europe's rise and its making of the modern world.

Chapter 1 investigates the emergence of sophisticated legal systems in Europe beginning in the Middle Ages. The resultant Roman-inspired codified, or civil, law and English common, or precedent-based, law are the two main legal systems used around the world today. The concept of the rule of law—the idea of law as above all persons, including rulers—grew up in conjunction with their emergence. It is hard to imagine a more modern and important concept for political and economic flourishing. Indeed, sophisticated law governing contracts, patents, and corporations helped stimulate a commercial revolution in Europe beginning in the Middle Ages. Moreover, the systematic methods that medieval European jurists developed for organizing and systematizing disparate sources of law were soon deployed productively in other branches of learning, including the study of nature, as universities with specialized faculties began to arise all across Europe.

Although all members of all human communities have felt drawn to wander, early modern Europeans developed a fevered interest in exploration, as discussed in Chapter 2. Ingenious navigation techniques, instruments, and vessels—borrowed, improved upon, and invented—made possible in the late 1400s the launching of Spanish- and Portuguese-sponsored seafaring expeditions into the unknown and the discovery of oceanic pathways to all the corners of the Earth. By the early 1500s, European explorers, merchants, scholars, and missionaries had begun to knit the continents and oceans together into a vast and interconnected network of economic, cultural, commercial, and intellectual exchange. Ceaseless openness to learning from other peoples—an attitude not reciprocated toward the Europeans by any other culture in the premodern era—ensured continuous and ever-accelerating development in Europe, until the entire world became linked together into our modern global systems of economic, demographic, cultural, intellectual, and scientific exchange.

Storing and sharing information in ever-more efficient ways, a crucial feature of modern society, is the subject of Chapter 3. The expansion in early modern Europe of the economy, educational opportunities, and literacy stimulated a greater demand for books than in any other cultures and drove entrepreneurs to mechanize printing. The resultant printing revolution transformed Europe and the world in ways that the earlier invention of printing in China did not. For one thing, printing presses in early modern Europe turned out scores of times more books, both in the aggregate and as separate titles, than they did in China, despite its larger population. For another, scholars and artists collaborated to produce extraordinarily detailed and accurate illustrations for technical and scientific manuals, providing a dramatic impetus to the development of technology and science. Finally, printing contributed mightily to the Protestant Reformation, which dramatically enhanced individual freedom and the concept of rights.

Rights and liberties, a precious achievement of the modern world, began gestating in medieval Europe, thanks largely to the weakness of central political authority, as argued in Chapter 4. Secular and ecclesiastical lords, monastic communities, cities and towns, and even ordinary people in the European Middle Ages customarily received grants of immunity, privilege, and right from rulers and lords seeking their support and loyalty. In time, medieval European rulers regularly summoned representatives "of the land" to discuss important matters of governance. Such representative assemblies were ubiquitous, some survived into modern times, and these served as models for parliamentary democracy around the world. Even in the church, movements arose to distribute decision-making power. All such practices and ideas contributed to theories of political empowerment and resistance that have inspired revolutions and other political change ever since.

Systematic thought and the discovery and recovery of ancient Greek, Hellenistic, and Golden Age Islamic writings on the natural world gave birth to an enterprise of nature-study in early modern Europe that steadily accumulated significant results and built up an impressive body of knowledge. The printing revolution, highly developed institutions of higher learning, and a robust tradition of intellectuals working together contributed to the emergent Scientific Revolution of the early modern era, the subject of Chapter 5. Investigations of nature occurred commonly in all major cultures but only early modern Europe engendered modern science, based on systematic inquiry, empirical research, meticulous record-keeping, collaborative endeavor, the mathematical analysis of data, extraordinary leaps of imagination, and the positing of "laws of nature."

The excitement of sharing knowledge about intellectual advances in Europe—concerning the law, literature, the arts, theology, and philosophy, including natural philosophy—fostered the development of a continuous

Introduction

web of breakthroughs and contributed to the advent of multiple intellectual spheres, in which people also exchanged information about commerce, politics, business, and other endeavors. The means of communication among intellectuals included networks of correspondence, first across Europe and then worldwide; scholarly journals to publish research findings; and learned societies focused primarily on natural philosophy but gradually also aiming to bring together intellectuals, artisans, and entrepreneurs in many fields. As classical and vocational schools multiplied in late medieval and early modern Europe, literacy and numeracy expanded more precociously than in any other world region. Newspapers, pamphlets, and lending libraries gained popularity. More and more Europeans, first in Holland and England, patronized coffeehouses, seeking camaraderie, self-improvement, debate, and knowledge. On these foundations emerged a profusion of free-standing voluntary associations devoted to nearly every conceivable endeavor. Thus, arose the Republic of Letters, the world's first public sphere, as recounted in Chapter 6. Women in Europe and America took part in this Republic in many ways: as organizers of intellectual debate in their salons, as patrons of scholarly research, and as participants in wide-ranging conversation. Never before in history had so many diverse people come together to advance learning and knowledge; to tackle social, economic, political, and cultural challenges; and to build up public and private networks and institutions—essentially creating an alternative to top-down control and governance. That alternative was modern Western society, the model for social organization around the world today.

The final chapter surveys other areas where Europeans opened important new pathways to the modern world: in art, military affairs, female emancipation, and freeing humanity from reliance primarily on muscle power. All human cultures express themselves in artistic creation. In traditional societies, once a powerful aesthetic was worked out, it set a pattern for hundreds or even thousands of years. In the early 1300s, Italian Renaissance artists broke that mold and freed themselves from traditional restraints. Over the next several hundred years, European artists vied with each other incessantly to create new approaches, styles, genres, and media. Although military technology and techniques emerged slowly throughout Eurasia, and Chinese alchemists devised an explosive powder over one thousand years ago, it was only in early modern Europe that an "arms race" enabled European explorers and conquerors to project more power abroad than any other peoples in history. These "gifts of Mars" were complemented by "gifts of Venus": contributions of women to development thanks to various forms of emancipation that transpired earlier than in other cultures. Early modern European women, especially in the northwest, achieved greater literacy and numeracy, had more opportunity for professional advancement, and enjoyed a higher status both inside and outside the home than did women in the other advanced Eurasian cultures. Finally, early modern northwestern Europeans were the first to integrate laborsaving devices and fossil fuel into their economy in a continuous pattern of development, culminating in a higher standard of living, the Industrial Revolution, and the Great Divergence.

Together these developments, with roots in the Middle Ages, enabled Europe to rise to unprecedented power and influence and to give birth to the modern world. Such is the argument in this book. But can we ever be sure what precise mix of elements made possible Europe's rise and its engendering of the modern world? Not with certainty. Historical developments are unique. Rerunning the script of history with one or other element left out, in order to test the results, is impossible. So those who argue that Europe rose primarily because of geographical accidents or exploitation of others may not be fully satisfied with the evidence and arguments presented below.

Nor will scholars be satisfied who emphasize the negative features of Europe's rise to world preeminence. Such features are numerous and grievous. They include, beyond the ones mentioned above, the obliteration of biodiversity and other forms of ecological damage, weapons of unimaginable destructive power, sophisticated tools of social control, means of rapidly disseminating misinformation in compelling forms, methods of genetic manipulation, and computer systems that may someday vie with humans for control of our planet. Of course, all of these evils are byproducts of the modern world, its dialectical flipside. Along with benefits, like vaccines for yellow fever and polio, there are drawbacks. Whether one sees more of the former or of the latter seems to depend on one's philosophy and outlook. In any event, the purpose of this book is not to judge the moral balance of the modern world but to attempt to explain its emergence.

CHAPTER 1
THE SUPREMACY OF LAW

Societies cannot function without rules to govern relations among people. When human societies first emerged, people lived close to the environment, almost completely embedded in nature. The rules governing such societies were presumably simple, learned by all, did not separate law and morality, affirmed intergenerational obligations, attributed no special importance to individuals, placed strong mutual obligations on everyone, and made no distinction between ordinary and sacred aspects of reality. The whole purpose of such rules, it seems, was to maintain social harmony, not to seek objective truth. Such legal patterns did not lend themselves to reflection, questioning, or philosophical analysis. One could not escape the rules except by leaving the society. The idea of change, moreover, was not part of the tradition. Even as more sophisticated legal concepts began to emerge, most people continued to follow the earlier traditions, or what scholars call "customary"—or even more esoterically "chthonic"—law, right down to our own times, which is how we think we know what prehistoric law was like.[1]

The early emergence of law

The law as a separate set of rules devised by officials, scribes, rulers, and other elites began to develop long after human societies first appeared—sometime during the rise of human civilization in sedentary, agriculturally based, urban cultures. The first known instance of a preserved law code was adopted by Hammurabi, a Babylonian king, nearly 4,000 years ago. This was "fiat law," which emanated from the will of the ruler. Most of the code's 282 laws concerned crimes against person and property (including slaves and livestock); many also regulated the institution of marriage. Legal traditions and formal systems of law soon emerged across Afro-Eurasia. One must assume that each such legal system was meant to affirm the ruler's authority but also to create positive conditions for the development of society. Or as Plato, an ancient Greek disciple of Socrates and a founder of the Western philosophical tradition, has an unnamed Athenian ask rhetorically in his philosophical dialogue *Laws*: "Would not every lawgiver in all his legislation aim at the highest good?"[2]

Some of the earliest legal systems to emerge resembled chthonic traditions in that law and morality were not separated and human society was deemed an organic part of the cosmos. Talmudic law, perhaps the oldest ongoing legal tradition, arose among the ancient Israelites. Instead of evolving from centuries of experience of living in community and close to nature, this tradition was understood to be directly revealed to the Jewish people by God himself, starting with Moses receiving the Ten Commandments on Mount Sinai over three thousand years ago. In the course of many centuries, a body of legal rules developed to regulate nearly all aspects of life. As in chthonic law, an individual could not readily escape the rules without rejecting the community. The early Hindu legal tradition also derived from divine revelation and also was similarly hard to separate from morality. Yet another divinely revealed legal system appeared with Islam in the early 600s. In each of these traditions, significant change was hard. Institutions could not take on a life of their own.

In China, an ancient culture and indeed the longest enduring major society today, the law evolved differently. First, the Confucian principles of harmony, stability, community-mindedness, and persuasion rather than command, deference to authority, respect for tradition, and the unity of things fostered a preference for informal conflict resolution.[3] In theory, the ruler and his officials were supposed to be guided by an underlying force of righteousness called the Way, though in practice there were no legal restraints on their power. Second, no specialized legal profession emerged. Legal experts were typically government officials, the main subject matter of whose training was the study of Confucian philosophical writings. All officials were required to acquire some legal expertise on the job; some of them, especially in central state judicial agencies, gained more specialized knowledge. Nearly all such learning concerned penal and administrative law. Third, Chinese law and justice were not purely secular. According to one scholar, "the early Ming ruling elite endowed law codes with religious meaning; religion and law were unified as indispensable components of their social practices and belief system."[4] As such, justice was conceived as restoring order and harmony and injustice as disrupting them.

Chinese codes of law aimed above all at controlling society. Penal law emphasized Confucian values.[5] For example, two of the ten gravest crimes were "unfilial behavior" and the murder of one's parents. Government officials, by contrast, were almost completely above the law. They could not even be investigated without permission from the emperor. Civil law, by contrast, was very little developed, and most commercial and civil cases were resolved informally.[6] Magistrates typically reached decisions concerning civil complaints based upon moral principles and cultural norms rather than legal statutes and codes (though recent scholarship has suggested their resort to statute law was more extensive than previously understood).[7] Amateur legal experts, who helped individuals file complaints to government officials, were not well viewed by the government and were not allowed at trial. Lawsuits were often costly in both money and dignity and so were often strenuously avoided. Complainants typically sought to resolve disputes and grievances privately, by means of oaths, rituals, animal sacrifices, lodging "indictments" in temples and before statues, and other non-legal acts.[8]

At the other end of Eurasia, over two thousand years ago, Roman jurists developed the world's first extensive and sophisticated civil law system for settling disputes among diverse peoples within a vast multiethnic empire.[9] They conceived of a law that applied to everyone, *ius gentium*. Winning acquiescence from conquered peoples was facilitated by the practice of respecting local norms and mores (customary law), so long as they did not offend Roman values. Such law was primarily participatory, with elite but amateur judges, legal experts (*iurisconsulti*), and administrators (praetors) all contributing to the system's evolution. Experts in the law elaborated precise and clear legal definitions and distinctions and composed procedural manuals, commentaries on the law, and collections of jurisprudence. Judges throughout the empire applied statute law but also had the authority both to follow and to set legal precedents. Over the centuries, they created a vast and systematic but supple corpus of law that set out most of the main branches and sub-branches of our modern legal systems today. This was the first system of law that emerged on a secular foundation—that is, not based on divine revelation—and conceptualized the law as a quasi-autonomous sphere of activity at least partially separate from both religion and state. Roman law powerfully influenced all the legal systems that emerged in the region over the next millennium: Islamic, Byzantine, European civil, and English common law.

How Europe Made the Modern World

Europe after the fall of Rome

After the fall of the Roman Empire in roughly the 400s A.D., its legal system deteriorated. In the sixth century, the Eastern Roman Emperor, Justinian, commissioned the compilation of Roman law. The resultant collection of works, the *Corpus Juris Civilis*, also gradually fell into disuse, especially in Western Europe. There during the early Middle Ages, the only continuously functioning legal and judicial system was maintained by the papacy with its tradition of canon law going back to the first century A.D. The system comprised a body of law, a hierarchy of courts, trained jurists, and professional judges.

When the Carolingian Empire collapsed in the 800s, public order broke down almost completely in Western Europe. By the year 1000, secular rulers could not assert their legal authority much farther than their private domains, or beyond a radius of at most a few dozen miles. Power fragmented among thousands of lords, some with lofty titles like duke and count but others mere possessors of castles, called castellans. Violence and lawlessness racked most regions, as public order collapsed.[10]

From this chaos and anarchy, however, emerged a truly remarkable social order, often called feudalism or feudal society. It was characterized by the development, in roughly the century after 1050, of a distinct body of feudal law.[11] One way to think of what happened is that society organized itself, taking the law into its own hands, as it were. From Carolingian times, armed horsemen came to dominate both the battlefield and social relations. Manorial estates with enserfed peasants were necessary to provide the upkeep of such combatants. It was customary for higher lords to grant their vassals such estates in exchange for service. Pledges of fealty, by both lords and vassals, cemented the relationship. This hierarchy extended from the lowliest knight to the highest lord, typically either a king or an emperor. In the eleventh century, vassals began to demand the right to pass on their estates, or fiefs, to their heirs. This demand was gradually recognized and enforced in the law throughout Europe. Simultaneously, the authority of lords to interfere in the economic and personal affairs of their vassals was legally curtailed, and many obligations of service of vassals were converted into monetary payments. These developments tended to increase the personal freedom and economic autonomy of vassals. Since all lords of vassals were also vassals of other lords (aside from kings and emperors), one can speak of growing mutuality and reciprocity of relations throughout the hierarchy. Moreover, these mutual relations were confirmed in pledges of loyalty and binding contracts. Such contracts were often compared to marriage vows. They were not as binding as the latter, because, according to the emergent feudal law, both lords and vassals had the right to dissolve the contract for any serious case of breach of faith. (Here one finds an early development in Western constitutional law of a right to political resistance; see Chapter 4.)

The rendering of justice in feudal society was also reciprocal. Every lord was by custom, and gradually also by law, empowered to hold court and decide justice for his vassals and his tenants.[12] When public order broke down before the millennium, manorial courts expanded their jurisdiction at the expense of royal courts, though to differing degrees, depending on the region of Europe. While the lord (or his steward) presided as judge, his vassals or tenants decided each case as jurors. Because the feudal hierarchy was a complex social structure, defendants could almost always appeal any judgment to a higher lord. In this way, any vassal—from knights to kings, though not mere tenants or serfs—could claim equality before the law. This notion was reinforced by the culture of litigiousness within the European upper classes. The development of feudal law was strengthened as well by the movement toward legal codification, a trend fostered by the expansion of legal training and the legal profession in the same years.[13] Feudal society thus marked a triumph of social over state power.

The breakdown of public authority emboldened church leaders to expand their power and authority, as well. For example, churchmen imposed a "Peace of God" beginning in 989 in various localities to curb fighting among lords and their looting of villages by appealing to conscience and the fear of God.[14] Violence continued, but the movement demonstrated the church's moral authority.

This authority won its biggest triumph in what came to be known as the "investiture conflict."[15] In parallel to the emergence of feudal law, persistent claims of secular jurisdiction over the church and religious affairs, including the right to appoint bishops and to dispose of steady incomes from parish churches and cathedrals, were challenged by papal reformers. A feature of the reform movement, which commenced in the mid-1000s, included seeking to purify the priesthood by forbidding priests to marry (that is, imposing clerical celibacy) and prohibiting their involvement with money, sex, blood, and weapons. There was also a push to separate and elevate the clergy from ordinary people, in part by expanding monasticism (see Map 1.1).

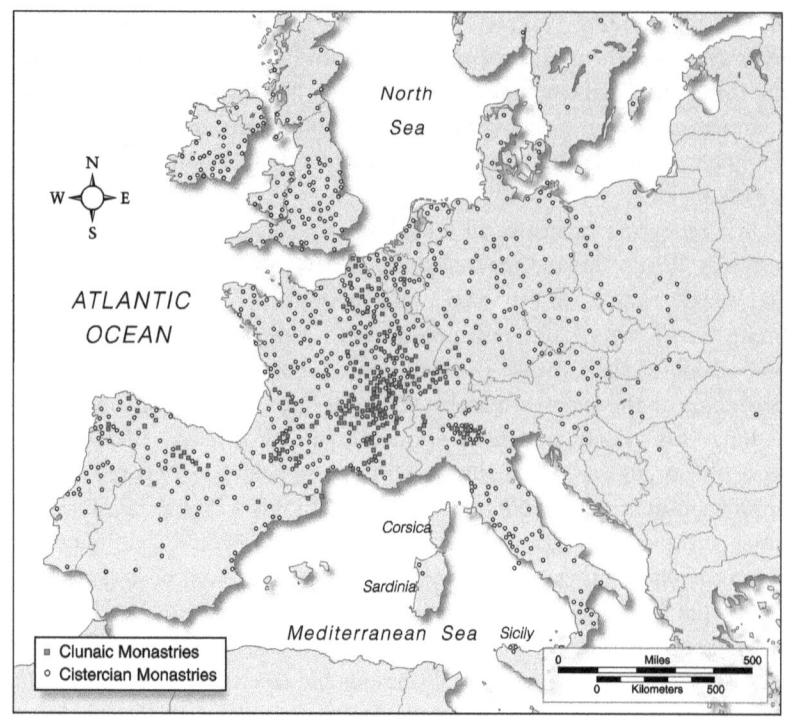

Map 1.1 The spread of monasteries in medieval Europe. With the support of the pope, monasteries quickly spread throughout Europe.

Intellectual foundations of European law

Institutionally, high church officials consolidated canon law, or the rules by which the church was governed.[16] Canon law consisted of divine law (as revealed in the Bible), pronouncements of church councils, papal letters (decretals), and episcopal statutes. Most canons were scattered in various repositories, and even legal experts could not master them. Reforming popes therefore commissioned jurists to compile and organize them. By the early 1100s, canon law had been categorized, interpreted, and applied by hundreds of jurists. Now the church could regulate minutely the life and activities of the clergy; impose and administer rules governing sacramental, moral, and religious behavior, and the commitments, practices, and offenses of the laity; and, finally, clarify its relations with secular rulers and authorities, with which the church shared many overlapping jurisdictions.

The reformers also considered it necessary to bring together, systematize, and reconcile the vast corpus of existing Roman law, including the codes of Justinian, which contained thousands of pages of case law and legal opinions. The European medieval mind, straining toward harmony, also desired to coordinate all available authoritative legal documents with the teachings of early church leaders and theologians and with the philosophical works of Christian and non-Christian thinkers.[17] European scholars wrestled with texts of Plato, Aristotle (many of them first encountered in Arabic translation), the Christian Neo-Platonists, Muslims like Ibn Sina (Avicenna), and other ancient and early medieval thinkers. The European mind was open, curious, and eager to assimilate new ideas. Yet sometimes even seemingly authoritative ideas clashed. A system of analysis and synthesis, the scholastic method, therefore, developed to bring them into harmony. The approach was called "dialectical," or dialogic, because it sought to reconcile divergent positions—ancient Greek and Roman, divine and human, religious and secular, practical and theoretical, and Islamic and Christian.[18]

The dialogic and disputational method of thinking through and demonstrating philosophical arguments seems to have first emerged in the 1050s in the remote monastery at Bec in northwestern France thanks to a chain of masters and students culminating with Anselm of Canterbury (ca. 1033–1109). In this tradition, debates about key elements of Christian theology were boldly and respectfully engaged in with non-Christians, including, according to some scholars, both Jews and Muslims. From Bec, Anselm's disciples carried the method to other centers of learning.[19] (Over the following two centuries, the scholastic method was applied to a wider range of texts, including steadily multiplying translations from Arabic.)[20]

Legal practitioners applied this method first and foremost to the Justinian texts. Europe's first degree-granting institution of higher education, the University of Bologna in Italy, was founded in 1080 specifically to study and teach such texts.[21] (Other universities followed, typically with graduate schools of theology, philosophy, and law, and some also with undergraduate schools in the liberal arts; see Map 1.2). Jurists, by means of dialectical probing, worked to systematize the vast body of Roman legal rules into a single integrated whole.[22] First, they found general principles under which these rules could be subsumed. Already in the early years of the new millennium, Fulbert, Bishop of Chartres, and his followers had distinguished between divine, natural, and positive law.[23] Second, they classified general cases as species of a common genus. Here they drew upon the system of classification developed most effectively by Aristotle.

Map 1.2 Early European universities. Systematic higher education in the Middle Ages was a pan-European phenomenon.

Among the aspects of the law to be reconciled were general principles and exceptions, justice and mercy, divine (revealed) law and positive (man-made) law, customs and statutes, and religious and secular ordinances. Within each element of these binary sets there were still more contradictions and even paradoxes to bring into consonance, for example, between God as terrible Judge and as merciful Redeemer. In synthesizing all these opposites, scholastic legal scholars demonstrated great openness to alternative points of view.[24]

The acceptance of intellectual diversity was fostered by the nature of the European university.[25] As institutions, they enjoyed autonomy from local authorities. Their members—masters and students—typically could not be prosecuted by either secular or, often, even ecclesiastical officials. The professors had almost complete authority to establish curricula, confer academic degrees, train and set the qualifications for instructors, pursue nearly any intellectual inquiry, draw upon the work of any thinker, question the assertions of most authorities, organize public disputation on a wide variety of subjects, and disagree with one another. University professors felt free to raise objections to even such central church doctrines as the existence of God and the reasonableness of the Trinity, as well as such core elements of governance as the power of princes and corruption within the church. A striking example of such critical thinking is the *Sic et Non* ("Yes and No") of the philosopher Peter Abelard (1079–1142). Drawing on the logic of Aristotle, Abelard proposed 158 questions, using the format "Must human faith be completed by reason, or not? Does faith deal only with unseen things, or not? Is there any knowledge of things unseen, or not? May one believe only in God alone, or not?"[26] His purpose was to zero in on assertions of philosophical and theological authorities that seemed to disagree or even contradict one another.

Over the following two centuries, such rational disputation became more and more systematic. The *Summa Theologica* of Thomas Aquinas (1225–1274), a professor at the University of Paris, for example, systematically analyzed hundreds of topics ranging from theology to ethics and from political theory to canon law, illuminating them with a painstaking interpretation of Greek, Roman, Christian, Jewish, and Muslim texts.[27] His dialogic method consisted in formulating a given topic, presenting numerous possible objections to his conclusion, citing one or more supporting authorities, developing his argument, and addressing the objections. Harmony was always restored, typically by showing that apparent contradictions derived from misunderstandings of either meaning or logic.

Higher schools in other cultures were different. In ancient Greece, they had been dominated by a single teacher. Islamic madrasahs were similar.[28] If the European university was a collective enterprise of co-equal professors, the madrasah was like a workshop headed by a single master.[29] Here one studied theology, history, and above all Islamic law, but not natural philosophy, logic, mathematics, or Greek texts. Knowledge was transmitted to a large extent by rote memorization of religious works and standard textbooks, and in personal interaction with a master whose legitimacy stemmed from an unbroken chain of learning down the generations. China boasted an older and more elaborate system of education. Yet the method of study also involved memorizing classic texts. True, students also received rigorous training in textual interpretation and analytical writing, but the entire system of learning aimed to prepare them for the civil service examination, the main avenue toward worldly success.

Political and legal peculiarities in Europe promoted the emergence of autonomous universities. First, political fragmentation—the absence of a unified authority—drove secular and ecclesiastical lords to compete to attract the best scholars and to provide them with favorable working conditions, such as freedom from outside interference. Second, the corporation, a legal organization grounded in Roman law, and the trust, a customary English association, were both recognized as legal entities with full juridical rights just like persons. Islamic law, by contrast, acknowledged only physical, natural persons; it denied such a status to the *waqf*, an unincorporated charitable endowment on which madrasahs were typically founded. Moreover, these so-called Islamic trusts were governed by inflexible regulations. Once established, they could not be altered, save according to rules spelled out in the founding charter. Nor could they pool resources or join together with other associations. Finally, they lacked accountability to their beneficiaries. As a result, an incorporated or chartered university enjoyed vastly more independence and influence than any madrasah, with its lone patron, no matter how eminent. Overall, medieval European universities featured many hallmarks of modern educational institutions, including relative autonomy, systematic exchange of knowledge, collegial governance, and explicit standards of training.

One of the great achievements of the legal reform movement was the compilation of canon law by the Bolognese canon lawyer and monk Gratian in the mid-1100s. He analyzed thousands of canons, reconciling and systematizing them by creating a legal framework based on theological and philosophical doctrine and Roman law. Gratian organized the canons, in his *Concordance of Discordant Canons*, from the noblest and most supreme, divine law, to the humblest and most subordinate, customary law.[30] On this spectrum, canon law was deemed superior to princely law, though natural law (what is inherently just according to human reason and conscience) stood above both. A revolutionary aspect of Gratian's understanding of natural law was his insistence that "princes are bound by and shall live according to their laws."[31] Such thinking resonated in secular law codes of the time. For example, the widely circulated and oft-republished Germanic *Sachsenspiegel* (early 1200s) affirmed that "God is Law itself; therefore, justice is dear to him."[32]

In other words, the law was seen to stand above rulers and officials. They could change old laws if they followed legal procedure but could not disregard them. Within Gratian's framework, all existing and conceivable law either had its place or, if it contradicted divine, natural, or ecclesiastical law, was rejected. Obviously, Gratian's treatise augmented the authority of the church, as interpreter and enforcer of divine and canon law. In fact, canon law, as the actual functioning legal system of Europe's most sophisticated polity, the Church of Rome, influenced the study and evolution of secular law—royal, urban, feudal, manorial, and commercial.[33] The second half of the twelfth century witnessed the publication of books on legal procedure, both Roman and canon; treatises on criminal law; and law codes and monographs on specific branches of local secular law in the various polities of Western Europe. By the early 1200s, Europe had authoritative, hierarchically organized law courts, both ecclesiastical and secular, staffed by a highly regarded profession of university-trained lawyers.[34]

The religious reform movement of this time also indirectly led to the development of two of the most important legal systems of the modern world: European civil (or codified) law and English common law. The primary method for determining guilt or innocence in criminal justice in early medieval Europe was the trial by ordeal. This took many forms. A suspect might be thrown into a lake. The idea was that God would not allow an innocent person to drown. In other cases, a suspect would be forced to retrieve a red-hot iron from a fire. Again, it was supposed that God would shield an innocent person from burns. The trial might involve combat, in which a plaintiff would have to fight a defendant (or their proxies). The winner of the fight would also win the judicial contest. In each of these cases, judges and the public expected God to adjudicate by proving guilt or innocence. The ecclesiastical reformers were troubled, however, by two things. First, a priest was obligated to give his blessing to each judicial ordeal. In this way, he was associating himself with activities that often resulted in maiming and killing people. As noted above, the reformers wanted to shield priests from involvement with death, destruction, and the shedding of blood. Second, church reformers also argued that the ordeals "tempted God."[35] Throughout the 1100s, reformers denounced and sought to root out the judicial ordeal. By the end of the century, it had largely disappeared from Western European jurisprudence.

The rise of European legal systems

What took its place were two sophisticated legal systems, the common law in England and civil law on the Continent, modern legal systems more widely used today than any others thoughout the developed world (see Map 1.3).

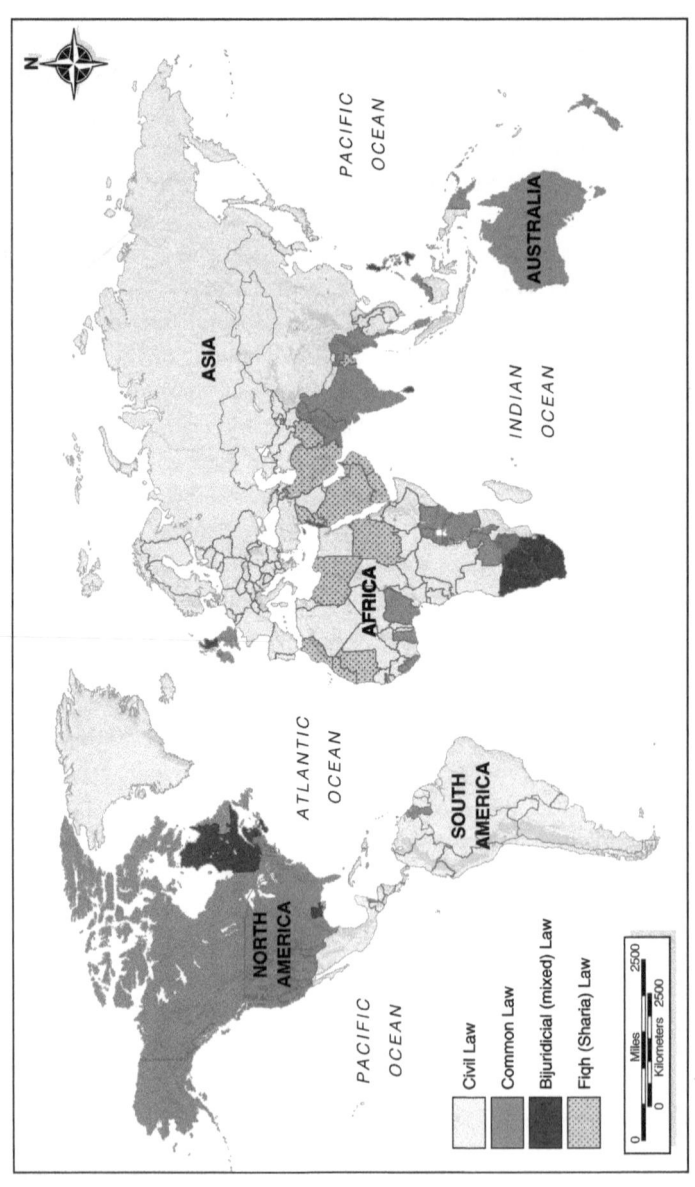

Map 1.3 Major legal systems in the world today. Emerging in the European Middle Ages under the influence of Roman law and customary legal practices, civil law on the Continent and common law in England are by far the most widespread legal systems in today's world.

It is ironic that deeply religious reformers of the Church of Rome should have contributed to the emergence of legal systems both separate from the church and conceived of as man-made rather than based on Revelation. On the European Continent, highly trained professional lawyers and judges developed rules of investigative procedure, including "judicial torture." Its purpose was to elicit confessions from all parties, especially the accused. Professional judicial officials with specialized training became the key factfinders and adjudicators.

English common law began to emerge when Henry I (r. 1100–1135) appointed traveling royal judges who earned a reputation for fairness. Over the next several decades, Henry and his successors issued writs, which defined the limits of royal judicial authority: no writ, no jurisdiction. The main role of judges was to make sure that a given case conformed to the requirements of the writ, while the verdict was handed down by a jury of free men. Since most jurors were illiterate, the proceedings had to be oral. Argumentation had to reflect customary law. Common law judges enjoyed the authority to issue decisions based on their interpretation of both writ and preceding judgments (precedents, or case law). Thus, the legal system in England was a cross between official royal law and age-old popular jurisprudence.[36] English feudal courts conducted by landowners continued to function in parallel and adjudicated entirely according to customary law. (Family law was in the jurisdiction of ecclesiastical courts.) The number of writs multiplied over time but never exceeded eighty (the writ of Habeas corpus, or freedom from arbitrary detention, became a cornerstone of Western jurisprudence). In the civil law tradition, by contrast, the law was spelled out in much greater detail and sophistication. It has been argued that the development of English common law was strongly influenced through dynastic and administrative connections between the Kingdoms of England and Sicily, where the court of King Roger II (1095–1154) "resembled that of a Fatimite caliph with its harem and eunuchs."[37] If this argumentation is correct, it would be another example of the openness of Europeans to outside influences.

Europe's law courts limited the power of rulers, even if they did so in different ways. In the words of one scholar, whereas the common law in "England replaced the voice of God with the voice of the people, the Continent moved toward replacing the voice of God with the voice of the bureaucracy."[38] In both cases, agents independent of both monarchs and ecclesiastical authorities exercised important governmental functions.

What is especially striking about both legal systems was their conceptualization of the law as outside of nature, separate from cosmic reality, unmoored from tradition, and at least partly isolated from morality and religion. As Harold Berman observed, the law was conceived as having "its own autonomous character, disembedded from other social, economic, political, and religious institutions and processes."[39] Adjudication of legal cases was to be decided on the Continent on the basis of expert legal study and procedural rules, and in England on the basis of common sense and reason. The modern mentality values such guiding principles, but they were unusual in earlier times. Most peoples throughout the world judged by custom, according to ideals of harmony, by strict religious doctrines, or by some combination of these principles. The most sophisticated legal system outside of Europe, Islamic sharia, differed in significant ways from civil and common law. Trials and judicial decisions were conducted orally, and little written documentation was presented or maintained. Plaintiffs had fewer recourses to competing jurisdictions. Sharia was considered to be derived from divine revelation.[40] Law in the Christian world, however, was developed by practitioners, typically without reference to Revelation, theology, or even religious principles. In other words, European law was beginning to anticipate modern practices already in the Middle Ages.

A variety of courts and systems of law continued to function across Europe, including ecclesiastical, manorial, royal, urban, and private. The expansion of royal control over justice in both England and on the Continent generally reined in, but did not immediately abolish, these courts, which therefore continued to limit the authority of rulers. In medieval England, moreover, important new courts emerged, including commercial and the Admiralty (or maritime) courts. (The jurisdictions of all these courts were later folded into the royal courts.)

The diversity of courts had an important political effect. People could contest the laws of one jurisdiction by fleeing to another. Thus, no political authority was absolute. Each one limited and checked the power of the others. To some extent, competition among the various legal systems in medieval Europe fostered the emergence of both the idea and the practice of the supremacy of law. Likewise, the modern concept of the separation of powers grew in part out of this competition of separate legal jurisdictions in medieval Europe.

Why did such modern concepts as the rule of law and of rulers under the law not emerge in the other great premodern cultures? Joseph Needham, the pioneering historian of Chinese science and technology, provided some insight into this question through his analysis of Chinese conceptions of the law.[41] He concluded that practitioners of the various philosophical schools, in particular Confucianism and Daoism, shied away from positive law, which they viewed with suspicion because it might lead to excessive litigiousness to the detriment of informal reconciliation, was inordinately restrictive, and would tend to diminish the authority of political elites. Nor did the concept of a "law of nations" develop, since the Chinese people were not seen as needing to coordinate their legal system with those of any other people. Finally, in Chinese legal thought there never arose an idea of what medieval and early modern European thinkers called natural law and conceived of as laws of nature imposed by a rational creator-lawgiver. Instead, the cosmic order was conceptualized in China as harmonious and cooperative thanks to its internal constitution and the specific natures of all existing things. Of course, the law played important roles in Chinese society, but it lacked the deep philosophical underpinnings and intellectual centrality that characterized its place in European thought and practice.

Another important medieval European innovation was, as mentioned above, the concept of "legal," "corporate," or "fictive" persons. European jurists, drawing on Roman and canon law, recognized corporate institutions as persons, attributing to them all the rights of an individual to own property, testify in court, bring lawsuits, and conduct any legal or other business, yet without the normal limitation on human longevity: such institutions could in principle persist indefinitely. Many guilds, universities, religious communities, and cities obtained this legal designation. Indeed, one scholar has recently argued that "late medieval polities were, to a surprising degree, self-governed, political corporations."[42] A similar concept also emerged within the common law (possibly in partial imitation of the above-mentioned Islamic *waqf*).[43] Like a corporation, a trust had the legal rights of a person in perpetuity. Yet unlike a corporation one did not need official permission to create a trust. The English formed trusts for charitable purposes, to bequeath assets to heirs other than first-born sons, to shelter wealth on behalf of women, and to create a broad array of institutions.[44]

In no other major culture of the time did the concept and practice of corporate or fictive persons emerge: only actual persons in the Islamic world, China, and India could be treated as persons for legal purposes, and thus such partially autonomous institutions as corporations and trusts could not form.[45] This meant that it was harder to pool resources, shelter them from the state, build economies of scale in the private sector, and coordinate activity independently from government.[46] Such endeavors would of course become central to European economic success in the modern age—and to the modern world itself.

From the late eleventh to the early thirteenth centuries, key elements of modern commercial law also developed in Europe, many evolving from earlier Greco-Roman, Byzantine, and Muslim practices.[47] Among them were rules governing secured credit, joint ventures, monetary penalties for breach of contract, negotiability of credit instruments, bankruptcy, bills of lading, bills of exchange, maritime insurance contracts, patent law, trademarks, and deposit banking, among many others. In this era, merchants gained more responsibility for determining legal procedure and rendering justice, since like urban communities they, too, enjoyed autonomy from royal, ecclesiastical, and other systems of justice. Two scholars who have carefully investigated correlations between the development of legal studies and economic growth in 209 European cities in the medieval era concluded that "the medieval economic rise of Europe owes much to the rise of law as a rational and systematic scholarly discipline that strengthened individual values over customary duties and generated superior rules of conflict resolution."[48] Europe benefited from having no universally applicable legal system rooted in custom and religious tradition. Its legal theorists and practitioners could therefore develop legal practices and institutions based almost exclusively on utility, rationality, common sense, and other practical considerations. This was one of many instances where Europe's backwardness proved an advantage, for the continent was to some extent like a cultural blank slate upon which ideas developed from both foreign borrowings and practical ingenuity could be inscribed.

Islam also developed on a cultural blank slate, which helps to account for its successful melding together of intellectual and technological achievements from all across Afro-Eurasia. Yet once the rules and institutions of Islamic life were set, following the revelation to Muhammed (the Qur'an) and the gathering of traditions associated with him (the hadith), further improvisation was difficult. For instance, Islamic inheritance law probably impeded the emergence of big Muslim companies.[49] The Qur'an requires that two-thirds of a deceased person's property be divided among numerous near and distant relations, thus ensuring the dispersal of most estates among many heirs. This rule impeded the accumulation of riches, the rise of powerful aristocracies, and the formation of large partnerships. After all, when a partner died, any one of his or her heirs could refuse to renew a given contract or could demand the sale of any asset of the deceased, a likelihood enhanced by the Muslim custom of polygamy. Out of prudence, therefore, Muslim entrepreneurs tended to keep their partnerships small. This in turn prevented them from creating economies of scale.

As early as the mid-1300s, European monarchs began to issue commercial charters to entrepreneurs. The heyday of the chartered company began during the Age of Discovery, following Columbus's voyage across the Atlantic Ocean in 1492. Such companies typically enjoyed monopoly rights over trade with a specific region, sometimes in exchange for granting a stake in the enterprise to the charter-granting monarch. The purchase of shares was usually open to anyone and conferred limited liability upon the purchaser. Whereas co-owners of a partnership risked losing all their assets should the firm go bankrupt, a shareholder's responsibility was restricted to the capital invested. The principle of limited liability, therefore, tended to embolden investors to take a chance on riskier ventures. It is significant that the principle of limited liability of business firms did not emerge in India, China, or the Islamic world until Europeans introduced it centuries later. The flexibility and expediency of European commercial law dramatically facilitated the success of European merchants, thanks, in the words of Timur Kuran, to "an organizational revolution that made Western economies increasingly efficient at pooling resources, monitoring their uses, and exploiting commercial opportunities."[50] Such commercial prowess facilitated the success and eventual dominance of European merchants, when they broke out of the geographical bounds of their region and entered the world stage, as discussed in Chapter 2.

CHAPTER 2
A PASSION FOR TRAVEL

Migration has been a feature of human existence since the emergence of Homo erectus some two million years ago. Our early ancestors migrated out of Africa and settled across Eurasia in a series of waves. Starting roughly 100,000 years ago, Homo sapiens also traveled from Africa to Eurasia, the South Pacific islands, and the Western hemisphere. As one evolutionary geneticist, Svante Pääbo, put it, "No other mammal moves around like we do.... There's a kind of madness to it."[1] It seems that mere survival or a desire for better living conditions drove most of this early seeking. After the domestication of plants and animals in Eurasia, beginning some 10,000 years ago, most cultures became sedentary. Henceforth, people migrated usually only when forced by unfavorable circumstances, such as drought, exhaustion of resources, attack, conquest, and the like. It is noteworthy that some of the earliest recorded stories of fiction involve extensive travel, such as *The Epic of Gilgamesh* and Homer's *Odyssey*.[2]

Early travelers

The first, and for a long time, only explorers to have systematically traveled, studied geography, and left written records of their discoveries were ancient and Hellenistic Greeks. The most detailed travel account was left by Herodotus (ca. 480–ca. 429 B.C.), who visited North Africa, the Middle East, Persia, the Black Sea region, the Caucasus, the Balkans, and perhaps India. His *Histories* ("Inquiries") gathered together social, political, and cultural observations; geographical descriptions; and investigations of natural phenomena.[3] Herodotus and other Greeks sketched out maps, composed geographical treatises, and may even have constructed terrestrial globes. The most sophisticated geographical study for many hundreds of years was Ptolemy's *Geographia* (ca. A.D. 150).[4] This work compiled all the known geographical information of the Greco-Roman world, articulated a cartographical methodology, included detailed general and particular maps (now lost), and calculated latitude and longitude for all the places described. Translations into Arabic in the ninth century and into Latin in the fifteenth strongly influenced the development of geographical knowledge in Golden Age Islamdom (late 700s to mid-1200s) and Renaissance Europe (1300s–1600s).

Several centuries after Herodotus, hundreds of Chinese Buddhist clergy traveled by land or sea to India for Buddhist pilgrimage and study.[5] Some left travel accounts, a few with rich detail about Indian society, culture, material life, and geography, though most were concerned principally with Buddhist doctrine and practice. With the mid-eleventh-century triumph of Islam and concomitant decline of Buddhism in India, such journeys from China dwindled. No other region attracted large numbers of Chinese travelers thereafter,[6] even after Chinese mariners devised a magnetic compass for use in navigation around 1090.[7]

Trade in luxury goods was robust between China and India and shifted toward bulk goods during the Tang era (600s–800s), drawing thousands of foreign traders from across Eurasia to Chinese cities. Yet few such voyagers recorded their experiences. Chinese scholars, civil-service examinees, officials, military personnel, clergy, merchants, artisans, and laborers traveled widely throughout the China, though rarely abroad.[8] Chinese, North African, Persian, and other non-European merchants remained actively involved in commerce throughout the Indian Ocean world, despite the conquest of northern China by Jurchen nomadic warriors in 1126 and of all of China by the Mongols, who established the Yuan Dynasty in 1279.[9]

Through violent conquest, Nomadic Mongol warriors forged history's largest contiguous land empire stretching from Eastern Europe and the Middle East to the Pacific Ocean. The Pax Mongolica they imposed established relatively secure commercial routes across all this territory, making possible the emergence of the first trading system reaching to the furthest corners of the Afro-Eurasian land continuum.[10] For nearly one hundred years, merchants safely plied their trade throughout much of the Eastern Hemisphere (see Map 2.1). The great commercial prizes were Asian commodities like spices, medicines, porcelain, sugar, and cotton and silk cloth. The decline of the Mongol Empire, beginning in the 1320s, and the Black Death, two decades later, disrupted international trade and weakened all the great powers of Asia.

In 1368, a rebellion brought to power the Ming Dynasty (1368–1644). The Yongle (1402–1424) and Xuande (1425–1435) Emperors expanded Chinese territory as far as Vietnam (1407) and authorized seven fleets of hundreds of enormous "treasure ships" to sail throughout the Indian Ocean

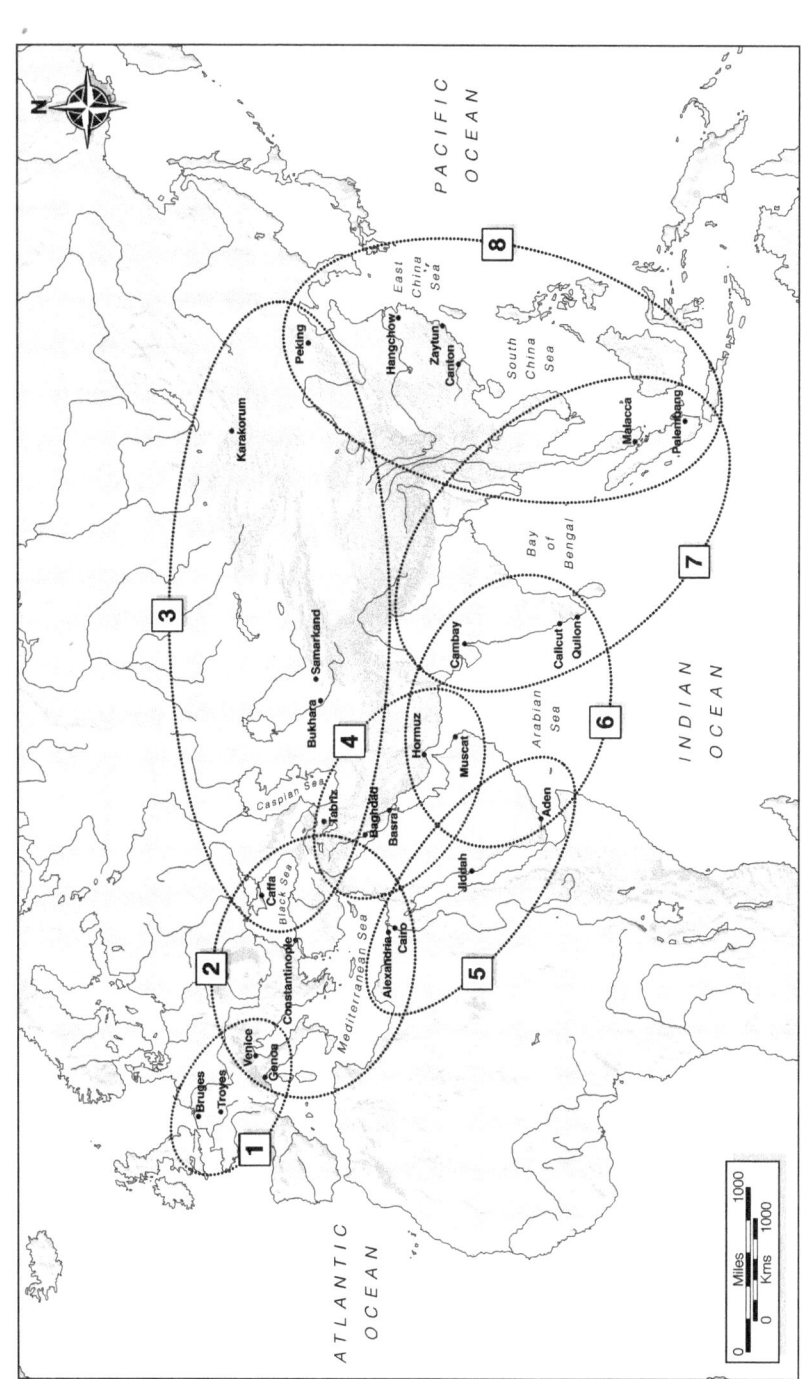

Map 2.1 The eight circuits of the thirteenth-century Asia-centered system of exchange. In the thirteenth century, the world's first globally interconnected polycentric system of economic and cultural exchange emerged. It was centered on Asia, and Europe played only a very minor role in it.

under the command of a Muslim eunuch, Zheng He (see Map 2.2). The vessels called at all major ports along the African and Asian coasts. Eunuchs ran the entire venture against the staunch opposition of the Confucian scholar-officials, who disliked adventurous exploits. The purpose of the voyages was to prove the greatness and might of China, to establish diplomatic contacts, to take control of foreign commerce from private traders and pirates, and to extend the emperor's tribute system. According to a recent study, the seven maritime expeditions "resulted in a tremendous increase in the circulation of people, goods and animals, … [and] also created unique platforms for cosmopolitan discourse."[11] It seems likely that eastern Eurasian trade and commerce reached a new high point thanks to the treasure fleets. They also constituted an impressive display of maritime technology, logistics, diplomatic influence, and expeditionary prowess. Though scholars still debate the ships' length—estimates range from 200[12] to 450[13] feet—they were at least three times longer than the ships Columbus's crew sailed across the Atlantic.

Yet size is not everything. The architecture and design of the treasure ships had been in use for over three hundred years.[14] Moreover, the fleets, which did not engage in discovery, plied well-known sailing routes. After Zheng's death in 1433, the expeditions ended, the records of his voyages were destroyed "in order to obliterate his memory,"[15] and imperial decrees forbade sailing beyond China's coastal waters.[16] High politics and fear of Mongol incursions turned China's rulers inward. In this way, China, a country that had dominated the Indian Ocean for decades thanks to the treasure fleets, now "lost control" of even its own southeastern coast.[17] Subsequent Ming emperors stressed the importance of China's ancient traditions, reinvigorated the civil service exam, set up military garrisons throughout the country to maintain political control, and weakened the social position of commercial elites.

From the Han (206 B.C.–220 A.D.) through the Yuan, or Mongol, era (1271–1368), Chinese mariners had gradually added to their store of navigational technology and skill and steadily expanded their geographical knowledge of overseas lands, throughout South East and South Asia, East Africa, and the Arabian and Red Seas—in brief, the entire Indian Ocean world. During Ming times, however, fewer discoveries and technological advances were made, and in general interest in exploration declined.[18] Though periodic prohibitions on foreign trade imposed by the Ming rulers only impeded but did not halt overseas commercial relations, China became more inward looking and less welcoming to visiting foreign merchants.[19]

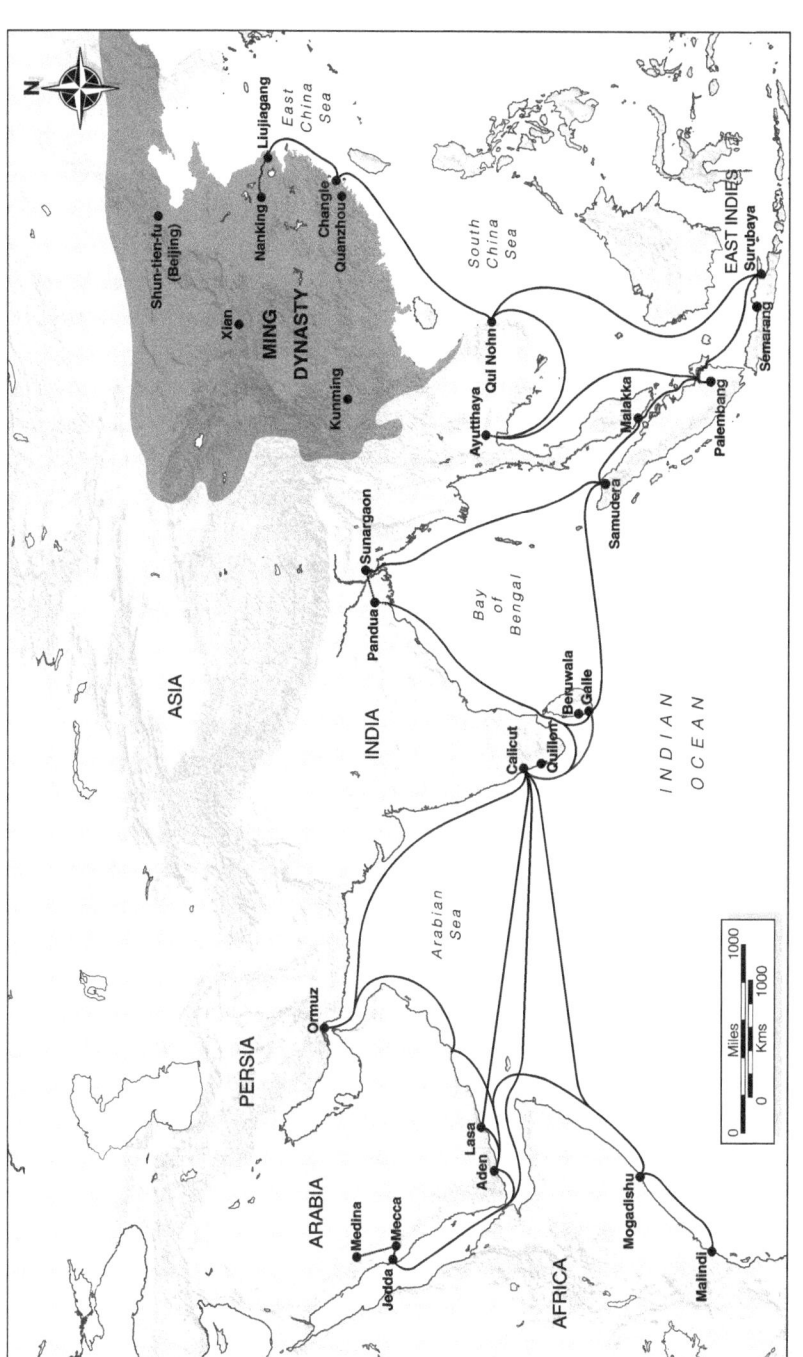

Map 2.2 Routes of the seven fleets of Ming treasure ships, 1405–1433. In the years 1405–1433, Chinese mariners sailed in seven fleets throughout the Indian Ocean region.

Felipe Fernández-Armesto is undoubtedly correct that "Chinese disengagement from the wider world was not the result of any deficiency of technology or curiosity. It would have been perfectly possible for Chinese ships to visit Europe or the Americas, had they so wished."[20] He argues further that commercial opportunities in the Indian Ocean were so abundant that breaking out into the Atlantic or Pacific was unnecessary. But the fact remains that the country turned inwards, and its rulers and governing officials focused on developing the resources and especially the land within China's territory.[21] Thus, the age of exploration, which to some extent can be taken as a metaphor for modern life, was initiated by Europeans and not by Chinese.

In the early modern era, India was, like China, a huge, prosperous, populous country with abundant natural resources, a vibrant economy, a wide range of exportable commodities and finished goods, and developed trade networks. Among objects of trade exported from India during the European Middle Ages were "textiles, spices, medicinal plants, jewels, ivory, horn, ebony, ... aloe wood, perfumes, sandalwood, and condiments"[22] (see Map 2.3). Indian craftsman and sailors had the basic technical know-how, necessary raw materials, wealth, and a seafaring tradition, at least in some regions and time periods, necessary for the development of sophisticated maritime technology and capabilities. In some instances, naval breakthroughs achieved by other peoples were readily adapted. Yet the societies throughout the Indian subcontinent were oriented toward the land, domestic trade, and development within existing territory. Foreign ships typically handled the overseas trade of Indian products. As a late seventeenth-century official remarked: "there is no deficiency of money or timber or other materials to form a navy, but there is lack of men to direct it," since, according to a recent study, "the nobility was fond of commanding a cavalry, whereas ship navigators were considered inferior."[23]

For centuries, the traders who dominated shipping and maritime trade in the Indian Ocean, especially with China and India, were Muslim. In fact, following the ancient and Hellenistic Greeks, the world's greatest premodern travelers hailed from Islamic lands. Muslims sojourned extensively, usually on Hajj (or pilgrimage to Mecca), and wrote many travel narratives. Thus, in the tenth century Ibn Fadlan journeyed up the Volga River and left a detailed account of the Islamic Bulgar people, resident Vikings, and possibly Slavs who traded with them, but he ventured no further west.[24] Abu Bakr Ibn al-'Arabī traveled in 1091 from Seville to the Middle East, where he abided and studied for nearly ten years in Jerusalem, Damascus, and Baghdad. The intellectual expertise and renown he gained opened many

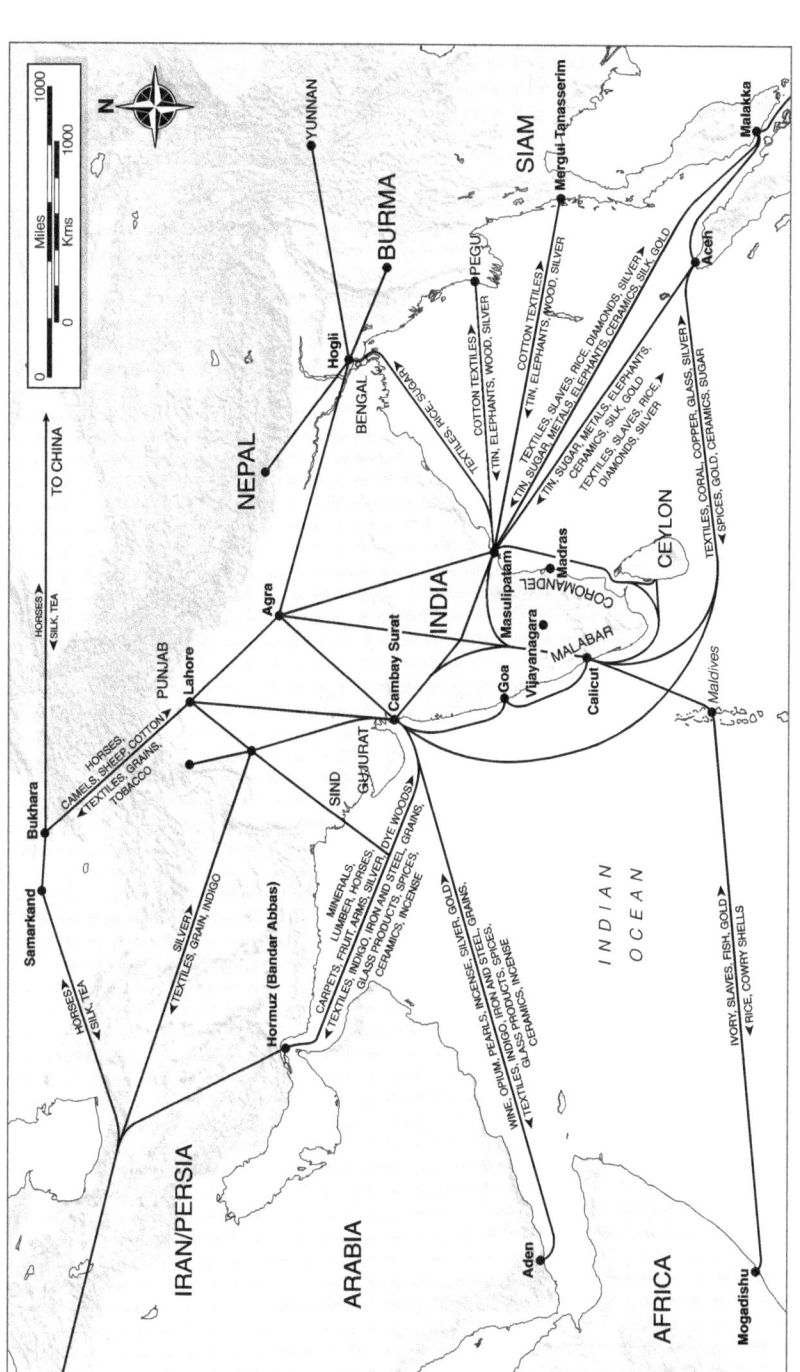

Map 2.3 Major trade routes of the early modern "Indian Ocean world." In the early modern world, the richest trade networks stretched across the Indian Ocean and adjacent lands.

doors upon his return to Iberia. He penned a travel account, which he deployed "like a curriculum vitae," yet the work fell into oblivion.[25] Probably the most well-traveled man before the modern age was Ibn Battuta, a Berber from Tangier. Between 1325 and 1345, he wandered throughout the Muslim world in Africa and Asia and wrote a lengthy account of his voyages. Of Christian lands, he visited (briefly) only Sardinia.[26] Another interesting case was al-Hasan al-Wazzan, a Moroccan who was kidnapped in 1518 and taken to Rome. He converted to Christianity, became known as Leo Africanus, and wrote a 900-page description in Italian of people, places, and things in Africa.[27] Published in 1550, it became a bestseller and was translated into several European languages. Yet after al-Wazzan returned to Africa he apparently did not write about his travels in Europe.

Although most Islamic voyagers steered clear of Latin Europe, many thousands, if not millions, of Muslims lived in Christian lands during the Middle Ages, in particular in the Near Eastern Crusader states and in reconquered Sicily and Iberia.[28] They lived as second-class citizens but alongside Christians, enjoying legal protections, and often able to settle disputes according to sharia law. Bilingualism and the socializing of Christians and Muslims were common. In all these regions, the skills of Muslim artisans were highly prized. Muslim professionals and scholars enjoyed high status especially in Sicily and southern Italy. Because of a changing political climate, by the mid-1300s, large communities of Muslims remained only in Christian Iberia. Discrimination against them also gradually increased, though Muslims, Christians, and Jews continued to socialize, until forced conversion and expulsion was imposed beginning in the 1400s. Some Muslims migrated to Hungary and Lithuania. Very few—mostly only slaves and a few diplomats—traveled to northern Europe before the late 1400s. Muslim slaves typically served in Christian households as "cooks, musicians, dancers, tailors, craftsmen, nursemaids, physicians, and tutors."[29]

Despite official, church-imposed restrictions on trading with Muslims, first declared in 1179, the volume of commercial relations with the Islamic world increased. Most of the commerce handled in the Islamic Middle East by Muslim traders went overland. As the Roman roads in the region deteriorated, camels proved an efficient means of transport. Yet conveyance by boat was gradually made more efficient through technological innovation. This is where the Europeans put their ingenuity and thus gradually bested their Muslim competitors.[30] Indeed, already in the 1100s, most trade in the Mediterranean Sea was controlled by Christians and through the Middle East to Asia by Muslims.[31] It is interesting that Muslims had no problem traveling on Christian-owned ships and trading freely with their Christian counterparts. Yet they seemed uninterested in Latin Christendom. Brian Catlos has recently studied Muslim communities in medieval Europe more thoroughly than anyone previously, and states: "It is remarkable how little Muslims living near Damascus around 1300 knew about Latin Europe and its inhabitants."[32] European rulers sent many more diplomatic envoys to Muslim lands than the other way around. In fact, Muslim rulers regularly sent envoys—mostly Christians or Jews[33]—to Europe only beginning in the 1600s.[34]

Why did so few Muslims travel by choice to Christian lands? Scholars have put forward many explanations. For one thing, Muslims viewed Europe as barbaric. As the tenth-century Muslim geographer al-Mas'udi opined of the Europeans, "their bodies are large, their natures gross, their manners harsh, their understanding dull, and their tongues heavy."[35] Also, the few Muslim travelers with experience of Europe devised negative stereotypes of Europeans as violently hostile to foreigners. This typecast recurred over and over in travel accounts.[36] Another reason was the poverty and backwardness of Europe. In the words of Brian Catlos, "Europe was a poor, inhospitable, and underdeveloped region with virtually nothing to offer the Muslim traveler or merchant."[37] Moreover, any desirable commodities produced in Europe were carried to market in Muslim lands by Christians and Jews. That remained true, even as Europeans were steadily producing more and more high-quality goods, such as glassware, paper, ceramics, silken textiles, and soap.

Fear of discomfort, the unfamiliar, and the alien also held Muslims back from traveling in Europe. Muslims would have risked persecution in medieval Europe, and the absence of mosques, bathhouses, *halal* butchers, and established Muslim communities would have impeded free travel within Christendom.[38] Muslims also felt a cultural and ideological aversion toward Europe. The Andalusian traveler Ibn Jubayr (1145–1217) declared: "There is no excuse in the eyes of God for a Muslim to stay in an infidel country."[39] The Muslim worldview was accepting of non-Muslim peoples of the book (Christians and Jews) within their societies, but intolerant of the idea of Muslims living under the authority of Latin Christian princes. This attitude conditioned the outlook of Muslim travelers. Such travelers sought not the exotic but the familiar, not the other but sameness. According to Houari Touati, Muslim travelers did not seek "to push back the known frontiers of the *oikomene*, but rather to define a geographically delimited space that some called the 'abode' (the 'house' or the 'territory') of Islam (*dar al-islam*) and others the 'empire' (*mamlaka*) of Islam."[40]

Most Muslims living under Christian rule gained some fluency in Latin or a Romance language, but it seems that few were interested in Latin Europe. Learned Muslims had avidly studied the scholarly works of Greeks, Persians, and Indians. Yet they were not interested in the broader ancient and Hellenistic Greek cultural heritage. They did not know its historical or literary works and had "no awareness of what classical Greek culture had been." Nor did even the Greek philosophical culture penetrate deeply into Islamic society the way it did in medieval Christian society.[41] Moreover, few Muslims carefully studied the growing output of scholarship in Latin. At the millennium, the Europeans may well have had precious few treasures of culture or learning to offer. Century by century, however, they acquired and produced a vast fund of them. Yet few non-Europeans seem to have noticed. One of the very few travelers from Asia to visit Europe, in 1287–1288, Rabban Sauma, was a member of the Nestorian Christian sect.[42] The first Indian ship to reach European waters arrived in 1788.[43]

Europeans explore the world

The story of Latin Christians was both similar to and different from that of Muslims of the Islamic Golden Age. Latin Christians of the Middle Ages were passionately interested in learning from and exploring other cultures. Like their Muslim predecessors, they traveled in greater number beyond their homeland than any other sedentary people since the time of the ancient and Hellenistic Greeks. Like the Greeks and the Muslims, the European Christians forged a precious synthesis of learning, knowledge, culture, ideas, stories, interpretations, and other breakthroughs in the life of the mind. Yet, the European age of exploration, which started slowly in medieval times, continued until Europeans had explored every region of the globe.

For centuries, even before the Crusades (1096–1291), hundreds of European pilgrims visited the Holy Land.[44] Meanwhile, beginning in the late 700s, Nordic warriors—the Vikings—began to explore and settle around the entire European coastline, across the North Atlantic to Iceland, Greenland, and Newfoundland, down the main rivers of European Russia, and into the Black Sea. Their age of exploration was an impressive, though lesser, counterpart to the sweep of Islamic warriors and settlers from the Atlantic to Central Asia.

As the Vikings were beginning to blend into Latin Christian culture and to cease marauding, the wave of European scholars seeking knowledge and enlightenment from the Islamic world began to rise. Gerbert of Aurillac (ca. 945–1003), a mathematician, inventor, scholar, teacher, and later pope (Sylvester II), spent several years in Spain studying Arabic works of mathematics and science translated into Latin. He was probably the first scholar to introduce Hindu-Arabic numbers, the astrolabe, and the abacus to Europe. Constantine the African (ca. 1020–1085), who was born and received medical training in Carthage in North Africa, settled in southern Italy, became a Benedictine monk, and prolifically translated scientific, especially medical, works from Arabic. A half-century later, Adelard of Bath (ca. 1080–ca. 1152) lived among Muslims in Sicily, the Near East, and Andalusia, apparently even pretending to be Muslim in order to gain access to texts and scholars. He translated philosophical, mathematical, and scientific works from Arabic, including Euclid's *Elements*, and published his own philosophical writings. The entire twelfth century witnessed dozens of Europeans traveling to the Muslim world, learning Arabic, and translating hundreds of scholarly and scientific works. Religious pilgrimages to the Holy Land had also become more and more popular.[45]

By the millennium, pilgrimages to the Christian holy places in Jerusalem had become common, but relations between Christendom and Islamdom were not strained. The reforming Pope Gregory VII in 1076 proclaimed to the Muslim ruler of what is now Algeria that they should work together and "ought to love each other … more than other races of men, because we believe and confess one God, albeit in different ways."[46] In 1096, when Pope Urban II called for a crusade to take back Jerusalem from the Muslim conquerors, however, a key justification he advanced was to protect and to keep open the pilgrim routes.[47]

Thousands of ordinary men, women, and children departed almost immediately under the guidance of a charismatic preacher, Peter the Hermit, and some knights without renown. Most died at the hands of superior Turkish forces. One is astonished that they marched idealistically across nearly two thousand miles of unknown and often hostile territory. In a world dominated by political hierarchy, warlords, clear lines of authority, and in a few places centralized government, masses of ordinary people simply never coalesced into relatively orderly legions with clear purposes and relatively strong cohesiveness. Thanks to local political strife, the proper army that followed the "People's Crusade" captured Antioch (June 1098) and Jerusalem (July 1099).

This was no "clash of civilizations," or at least it was not perceived to be, either by the Christian or the Muslim participants. The Crusaders felt little hostility toward Islam, sometimes made alliances with Muslims, and even fought alongside them. They had no interest in conquering Muslim territory, aside from the Holy Land and in particular Jerusalem. The capture of that city became "an iconic moment in the popular history of the relationship between both civilizations," but only because eventually both cultures viewed it that way.[48] The taking back of Jerusalem sparked jubilation throughout Latin Christendom, because Europe's Christians viewed it as the center of their universe, not because it was seen as a Christian advance *against* Islamic civilization.

Journeys to Muslim-dominated lands, both in the Near East and on the Iberian Peninsula, had a powerful impact on millions of European Christians as the crusading impulse slowly drove successful efforts to bring those lands back into the Christian fold over the next four centuries. Undoubtedly, contact with Islamic civilization, whose accomplishments far exceeded those of Latin Christendom at the time of the First Crusade, expanded many Europeans' mental horizons, challenged their preconceptions, and introduced them to novel cultural offerings and exotic social and economic patterns. The Europeans also extended control over Mediterranean trade routes, increased their logistical capabilities, and gained a stronger sense of their identity as Latin Christians but also as diverse peoples from across Europe.

Even after Saladin, the first sultan of Egypt and Syria, reconquered Jerusalem in 1187, European fascination for the Islamic world continued and indeed increased. Pilgrimages remained highly popular and were organized for profit by Venetian merchants and to the glory of God by Franciscan Friars in Palestine.[49] Likewise, in 1259, Dominican Friars instituted a center for Arabic studies in Barcelona and subsequently in other cities to train missionaries to preach directly to Muslims in their own lands.[50] Such efforts at conversion were rarely fruitful and often resulted in frustration. There was even a tradition within the Franciscan order of traveling to Muslim lands explicitly seeking martyrdom. In 1220, for example, five friars presented themselves in Morocco and purposely taunted the authorities with insults to the Prophet and other outrages. They were executed. In 1227, seven more friars sought and found martyrdom in a similar way in Morocco.[51] Nevertheless, Christian missionaries steadily founded churches and religious communities throughout the Islamic world.

The Pax Mongolia facilitated such mission work. Two Franciscan friars, Giovanni da Pian del Carpine and William of Rubruck, who journeyed to the court of the Great Khan in Mongolia in 1245–1247 and 1253–1255, respectively, left detailed and relatively objective travel accounts.[52] Most famously, in 1271 Marco Polo journeyed with his father and brother to the court of Kublai Khan as papal envoys. After he returned to Italy, Marco dictated an unusual memoir. Unlike those of Battuta or Rubruck, which presented other lands as foreign cultures, Polo "was quite proud of his ability to see the world from a Mongol perspective, not least because he could express himself in the language of his emperor."[53] In fact, he wrote his narrative according to the principles and genre of the Chinese narrative tradition, just like any other mid-level Chinese official preparing a detailed report of what he had seen and heard for the pleasure of the ruler.[54] Unlike Battuta and most other travel writers of the time, Polo was not recounting his own adventures and experiences. Instead, he provided wide-ranging information about political geography, social institutions and customs, trades and crafts, commerce and money, government revenue and spending, religious beliefs, mores, historical events, and, "above all, on the authority and court of Khubilai Khan."[55]

According to a foremost expert on Polo's book, he advanced geographical knowledge of the world for its European readership more than any other person "before or since."[56] The book was hugely popular in Europe and within a couple of decades was translated into several other vernacular languages, an unusual occurrence in those years.[57] The book seems to have been far more popular in Europe than Battuta's narrative was in the Islamic world, for the latter survives in only 30 manuscripts as compared to 150 of Polo's work.[58]

After the collapse of the Mongol Empire and thus the Pax Mongolica, journeying to Asia became much more difficult. Yet travel narratives encompassing stories of the East continued to excite European readers. The most popular travel book of the late Middle Ages was *The Travels of Sir John Mandeville*, a compilation of many travel accounts combined with some first-hand experience penned in the mid-1300s by a Flemish monk.[59] A distinguishing feature of his work, which survives in more than three hundred manuscripts, as well as in thirty-five editions in six languages printed before 1500, is his presentation of "Muslims in a surprisingly candid and positive light"[60] and his acceptance of "idolaters" in China and elsewhere.[61] (Not only travel writers, but also philosophers like St. Thomas Aquinas, poets like Dante, Christian missionaries like Ricoldo of Monte Croce, mystics like Julian of Norwich, and many other European Christians in the thirteenth and fourteenth centuries were well disposed toward Muslims and hated to imagine them condemned to hell for their lack of

Christian faith.)[62] The immense popularity of the book throughout Europe suggests enormous interest in—and great openness to—the wider world among late medieval Europeans.

It is interesting to note that Chinese maps of the world from this time placed China at the center, whereas Europeans cartographers centered their maps on Jerusalem, suggesting a European tendency toward looking outward.[63] Perhaps this helps explain why European Christians felt compelled to venture outside the bounds of their continent. Not only were travel narratives enormously popular in medieval Europe. Even some of the greatest imaginative literature of that time was composed in the form of journeys, including the greatest work in Italian, Dante's *The Divine Comedy* (1320), and the two masterpieces of Middle English, Langland's *Piers Plowman* (1367–1386) and Chaucer's *The Canterbury Tales* (1387–1400).

Meanwhile, a nautical revolution had begun in the 1200s in Europe. Gradually, seafarers plotted distances and directions between all the ports of the Mediterranean Sea into "port books," including one for the entire region. Drawing on all this information, in 1270 a Pisan craftsman drafted a marine chart, measuring about three feet across, with grid lines. Called a "portolan chart," it depicted to scale all the coasts and islands of the Mediterranean accurately.[64] Around the same time, European mariners improved on the magnetized compass, one of China's great inventions. As early as 1277, Genoese vessels sailed through the Strait of Gibraltar, into the rough and dangerous waters of the Atlantic, and up to Iberian and northern European ports. In spring 1291, the Genoans Vandino and Ugolino Vivaldi sailed out into the Atlantic Ocean, apparently seeking a passage to India. They were never seen again.

Ship design and naval architecture also dramatically improved, marking, in the words of an authoritative scholar, "the most important technological development of the late medieval era."[65] Around 1300, the addition to ships of a pintle-and-gudgeon rudder mechanism enhanced steering.[66] From the late 1300s, Iberian shipwrights fused elements of Mediterranean and Atlantic shipbuilding technology to produce ocean-going carracks outfitted with three (later four) masts rigged with square sails fore and triangular lateens aft. Caravels, with two or three masts and lateen sails aft and jib sails attached to a bowsprit, like schooners, were nimbler and better able to navigate shallow waters. European merchants, state officials, and entrepreneurs feverishly copied each other's ship-building technology. The fact that European shipwrights drew upon nautical technology from around the Mediterranean world, which itself was doubtless influenced by advancements further east, again shows the openness of Europeans to searching for and adopting best practices from other cultures.[67] The idea that medieval Europeans believed the Earth to be flat is a myth.[68] Ever since Pythagoras, most thinkers in the region had imagined the Earth as spherical. Yet they had disagreed whether insuperable obstacles divided its inhabitable parts. As early as 1267, an English Franciscan friar, Roger Bacon, claimed that only a narrow stretch of ocean separated Iberia from India. A French theologian and cardinal, Pierre d'Ailly, reiterated this theory in his geographical study, *Imago mundi* (1410).[69] A belief that the oceans could be used as highways to distant lands undergirded the ventures of the boldest European mariners.

The first global seafaring power was tiny Portugal, a country of only one million inhabitants. It was an unusual feature of Europe that so many peoples, even small and apparently "marginal" ones, contributed enormously to human development. Political fragmentation, and therefore general competition among states, can partially explain this phenomenon, but there also seems to have been a widespread ambition to innovate, to excel, and to embrace the new, which one scholar has called a "culture of improvement."[70]

The main goal of the Portuguese mariners was to find a passage to India in order to cut out the Arab and Turkish middlemen who controlled the existing east-west trade routes. A brother of the King of Portugal, Prince Henry the Navigator (1394–1460), was passionate about rising to that challenge. He hired skilled cartographers, sailors, shipwrights, and navigators, and outfitted scores of ships for exploration. The contrast was stark with the Chinese rulers who not only did not support Chinese overseas traders and voyagers, except during the brief era of the treasure fleets, but even considered them "deserters, traitors, rebels, and conspirators."[71]

The first Portuguese discovery, made by accident in 1419, was the Madeira archipelago, 450 miles off the coast of Morocco. In 1427, Henry's mariners discovered the Azores, 900 miles due west of Lisbon; in 1434, sailed past Cape Bojador; in 1444, landed on the coast of Senegal; and in 1456, reached the Cape Verde Islands, 200 miles due west of Senegal.[72] On Henry's orders, professional cartographers charted the progress of each expedition. Meanwhile, dozens of mercantile expeditions, mostly private, followed, bringing back gold and slaves. Slave trading in Lisbon and sugar plantations on the island of Madeira were yielding enormous profits by the 1450s. Muslims continued to dominate East African human trafficking, but henceforth Europeans monopolized that infernal commerce on the West

African coast. The wealth and glory to be had from maritime exploration drew thousands more explorers southward along the African coastline.

In the 1450s, vast regions of the globe remained unexplored by inhabitants of the Old World, including three continents and two oceans. At least four civilizations—Islamic, Chinese, Indian, and European—had the capacity to break open the oceanic frontiers. One seized the opportunity. For centuries, Islamic merchants had dominated the lucrative Indian Ocean trade. Minarets and prayers to Allah rose across much of Africa, the Balkans, and all of Asia. This was the most widely flung civilization the world had ever known. Yet the skilled Muslim sailors apparently never ventured into the Atlantic or Pacific Ocean. Nor did the Chinese, the most inventive people for many centuries.[73] Indian mariners were, if anything, even more reticent to explore the wider world. European ships, meanwhile, pushed further and further into the unknown.

Europeans seemed to have had a fascination for the unfamiliar in a way the Chinese did not. In 1414, the king of Bengal sent a giraffe as a good-will offering to the Chinese emperor. Having consulted learned scrolls, Confucian scholar-officials identified the beast as a unicorn, a creature with "the body of a deer, the tail of an ox, and the hooves of a horse." Its appearance was above all interpreted as a good omen attesting to the emperor's benevolence. The giraffe, situated within a known semiotic matrix, pointed to the central symbol of Chinese self-identification. It led nowhere outside China. By contrast, when the Mamluk Sultan of Egypt bestowed a giraffe on Lorenzo the Magnificent in 1486, poets sang its praises and a leading artist, Domenico Ghirlandaio, painted its portrait. For the Florentines, "the giraffe was a mere starting point for a journey of the imagination."[74]

Venturing into the unknown, even with eager anticipation, was risky. Seeking ultimately to break into environments dominated by powerful and highly developed states was downright perilous. The European seafaring entrepreneurs were far from naïve, however. From the early 1400s, ships plying European waters were outfitted with cannon.[75] By the mid-1400s, carracks and caravels sporting side-mounted guns could engage foes from a distance. Toward the end of the century, sliding carriages able to absorb recoil made it possible to install bigger guns. Thus equipped, Portuguese and other European explorers sailed intrepidly into unfamiliar waters.

A gradually improving understanding of world geography also increased the confidence of European seafarers. Most important in this regard was the recovery of Ptolemy's *Geographia*. Translated from Greek into Latin in 1406 and diffused widely from 1475, it described the Earth as mathematically proportional. An especially important innovation was Ptolemy's idea to overlay grid lines on his maps, enabling geographers to determine precisely any location and to conceptualize the world as homogeneous and continuous. Within two decades, European cartographers began to construct globes. In the final decades of the fifteenth century, the boldest mariners had begun to view the ocean less as an impediment than as a highway.[76]

The 1490s witnessed two of the greatest human achievements of all time. Both might have been credited to Portugal, had King João II not declined (twice) to fund the venture of the Genoese Christopher Columbus. Unlike in China, however, enterprising European mariners had many royal patrons to choose from, and none could forbid ocean-going voyages to all seafarers. Thus, the Spanish crown reaped the glory and riches resulting from Columbus's voyage in 1492 in three relatively small ships across four thousand miles of uncharted ocean. Soon dozens and then hundreds of European mariners crossed the Atlantic, seeking to explore, map out, exploit, and settle all the lands of the New World.

In midsummer 1497, Vasco da Gama set sail down the African coast with four ships. At Sierra Leone, they steered southwestward into the open sea to avoid adverse coastal winds and currents and to catch the South Atlantic westerlies. This was an extraordinarily daring but ultimately effective navigation strategy. After three months and six thousand miles sailing far from land, the ships arrived at the southern African coast. Da Gama and his crew then rounded the Cape of Good Hope and sailed up toward Zanzibar on the East African coast. Having hired an Indian pilot, they traversed the Arabian Sea and set anchor at Calicut on India's Malabar coast. Although he lost most of his ships and men, the cargoes with which da Gama returned to Lisbon made him a fortune and brought glory to King Manuel I. Numerous mariner-entrepreneurs followed in da Gama's wake, starting in 1500 with Pedro Álvares Cabral, who, on his way to India, claimed Brazil for Manuel. Cabral also lost most of his ships and crew, yet the voyage returned a one-hundred percent profit. A gold-rush mentality gripped Europe.

Portuguese and Spanish seafarers navigated the coastlines of North, South, and Central America; the Indonesian, Malaysian, and Philippine archipelagos; Africa; South, Southeast, and East Asia; and New Guinea—all before Ferdinand Magellan's expedition completed the first circumnavigation of the globe on behalf of Spain in 1519–1522 (see Map 2.4). In 1534, Jacques Cartier led the first of many French voyages of exploration to North America. In 1553, Hugh Willoughby sailed for England (and, in 1596, Willem Barentsz for Holland) into the Arctic region. In 1606, the Dutchman Willem Janszoon

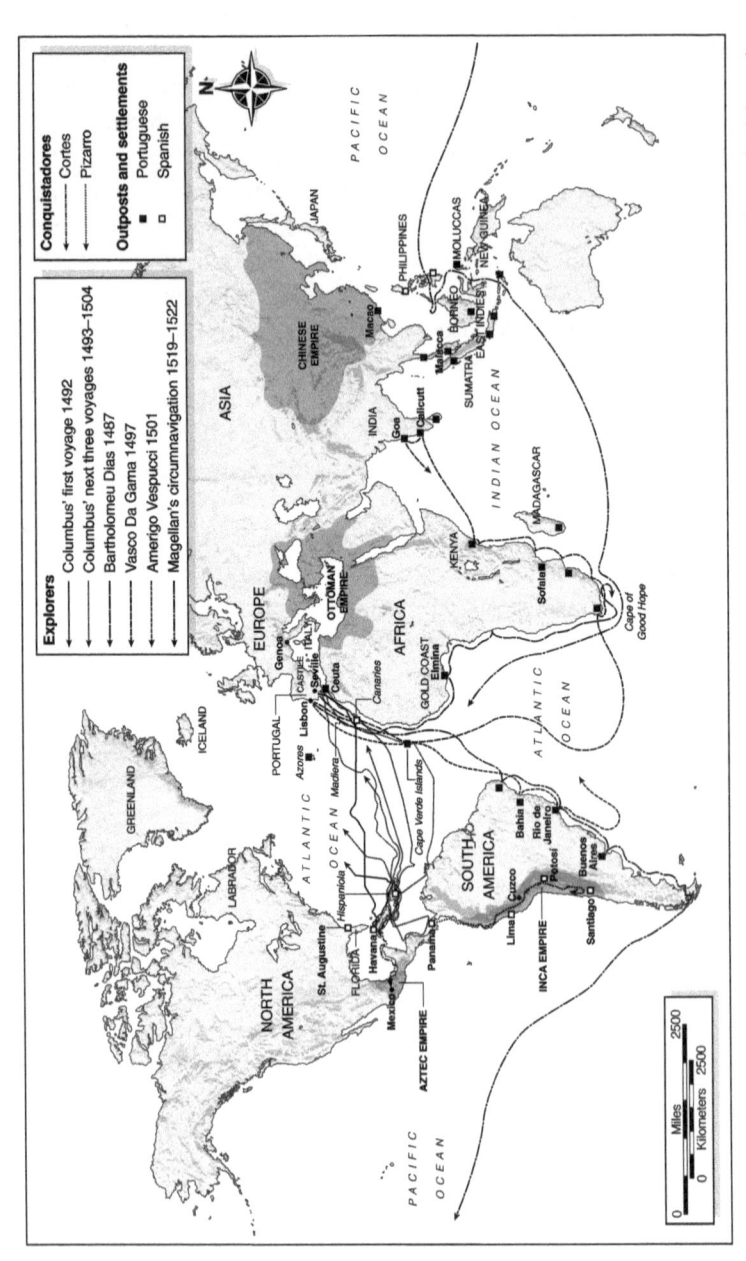

Map 2.4 European exploration and colonization, 15th–16th centuries. By the early 1500s, European explorers had knit the continents and oceans together into a vast and interconnected network of economic, cultural, technological, and intellectual exchange.

landed on the northern coast of Australia and, in 1642–1643, another Dutchman, Abel Tasman, sailed to New Zealand. Decade after decade, hundreds of expeditions from Europe charted the coasts and interiors of all these lands. Even the natural philosopher Isaac Newton, in 1669 at age 46, recommended to a colleague to travel widely and to make careful note of the "policys, wealth & state affairs of nations."[77] In the 1770s, James Cook crossed the Antarctic Circle, happened upon Hawaii and other Pacific islands, circumnavigated New Zealand, and sailed along the northern Alaskan coast. Cook himself claimed that he craved the "pleasure of being first" and to sail "not only farther than man has been before me but as far as I think it possible for man to go."[78]

In the 1600s, the greatest European shipping power was the Dutch Republic—yet another small country of fewer than two million people. Their share of the total European seagoing fleet rose steadily from sixteen percent in 1500 to perhaps forty percent in 1670, thanks to continuous improvements in shipbuilding design and logistical efficiency. As a result, the cost of Dutch shipping gradually declined and made their merchant marine more cost-effective than any other in the world.[79]

In Asia, Europeans explored and traded, often gaining commercial dominance, though rarely conquered. The Asian peoples were sufficiently numerous and developed to resist the comparatively small number of Europeans who made their way out East, even with their powerful gunpowder weaponry. The same was somewhat true of Africa, where the main impediment to European penetration into the interior of the continent were dangerous pathogens to which Europeans had no immunity. An inverse phenomenon helped them, though unwittingly, to conquer the Americas, whose peoples had been cut off from Eurasia for thousands of years. For them, common Eurasian diseases, like mumps and measles, were often fatal.[80] In the Americas especially, European conquerors plundered, maimed, enslaved, exploited, and killed.

Because of their encounters with peoples of whose existence they had previously had no idea, European philosophers and theologians began to articulate theories of human development. John Mair (1467–1550), a Scottish humanist teaching in Paris, described the native peoples in the Americas as incapable of mastering their passions and therefore psychologically unfit for a life of freedom. The Dominicans Francisco de Vitoria (1486–1546) and Bartolomé de Las Casas (1484–1566) argued by contrast that all mankind descended from a common human ancestor created and endowed with reason by God and that the very idea of "natural slavery" of such beings made no sense.[81] Europe's political fragmentation fostered competing ideas, which, in this case, laid the foundation for a philosophically grounded system of human rights for all persons (see Chapter 4). Other European intellectuals writing in the 1500s, like Michel de Montaigne, imagined the customs and institutions of other lands superior— less unfair or purer—to their own.[82] In the seventeenth and eighteenth centuries, many European intellectuals, like Gottfried Leibniz and Voltaire, respectively, admired the well-ordered and rationally minded Chinese monarchy. In other words, even as the Europeans gained wealth and power, the attraction of other cultures remained strong.

Because of the Europeans' feverish exploration, the globe was soon knit together for the first time into a network of economic, cultural, technological, and intellectual exchange. Chinese demand for silver was one important factor. So was the so-called Columbian Exchange of plants and animals between the New and Old Worlds: especially potatoes, corn, beans, peppers, peanuts, and tomatoes from the Americas and cattle, horses, swine, chickens, goats, sheep, wheat, rye oats, rice, apples, bananas, citrus fruits, coffee, tea, and many others from Afro-Eurasia.[83] European entrepreneurs and colonizers built an interconnected network of port cities—Quebec, New Orleans, Halifax, Boston, New York, Williamsburg, Savannah, Charleston, Kingston, Havana, Lima, Buenos Aires, Cape Town, Bombay, Madras, Calcutta, Batavia, and Manila, among many others—and brought all these products, peoples, countries, and continents together, binding them into one worldwide marketplace, all dominated by Europe.[84] As Greg Clark has argued, by bringing people of diverse cultures, experiences, skills, and outlooks together, what he calls global cities have for three millennia driven most of human advancement in technology, commerce, culture, politics, thought, science, and social justice.[85] All of the great heroes of human flourishing have involved interconnection and exchange. But never before had such synergies been achieved on a planetary scale.

European cartographers had also been systematically mapping all the lands European explorers had encountered. Other peoples had rendered visual accounts of their own lands and in some cases territories beyond. Sometimes these renderings had displayed relatively high levels of accuracy. But beginning in the 1300s, European maps grew progressively more accurate and detailed. Information from the travels of Polo, Battuta, and then the voyagers of the European Age of Exploration progressively influenced map-making in Europe.[86] In the 1500s, European maps became truly detailed, painstakingly accurate, and more and more precise—in a word, modern. They also grew vastly more numerous and therefore accessible, thanks to mechanical printing. According to one well-informed scholarly estimate, there was one map for every 720 persons in the heartland regions of Europe in 1500—and roughly one for every four persons in 1600—a 180-fold increase.[87] In 1569, the Flemish cartographer Gerard Mercator took an extraordinary leap of imagination to solve a conundrum: How to depict the three-dimensional and spherical globe on a flat and two-dimensional map?[88] Thanks to decades of study, calculation, consultation, travel, and collaboration, he produced history's first complete map of the surface of our planet. He then drafted and compiled a host of maps into a helpful book he dubbed an "atlas." (Jesuit missionaries imported European geographical and cartographical knowledge to the Chinese court in the late 1500s, with mixed results.)[89]

It is possible to conceive of the emergence of European mathematical cartography as representing a developmental loss. As one scholar has reflected: "This generalizing and abstracting power is one of the strengths of cartography, but it may come at the price of dehumanizing representation."[90] Abstracting topography from its human aspects may well represent an unfortunate tendency. But it is also a modern one, and in that sense European cartographers and intellectuals were steadily helping to bring to life the modern world with all of its abstractions. Or as one scholar has suggested,

> modern space—the space the modern world inhabits and "sees"—was created in Europe between 1475 and 1600. It was produced using a variety of means, including the use of the grid to plot the world; the use of the cosmographical sphere as the starting point for the mathematically derived practices of navigation and surveying; the increasing use of maps; and the creation of a cartographic language for new mappings of the world, states, and cities.[91]

It is interesting that seemingly no one in the Muslim world, which was so close to Europe, noticed any of the extraordinary happenings in that region beginning in the 1100s. The tallest buildings ever built were going up by the hundreds, often embellished with thousands of square feet of dazzling stained glass. Sophisticated philosophy was flourishing in great centers of learning, principally the universities, where scholars collaborated to investigate a wide variety of human, natural, and supernatural phenomena. Many of the greatest thinkers, like St. Thomas Aquinas, found much of value in Islamic philosophy, especially Averroes, the Latin name for Ibn Rushd, the eleventh century Andalusian polymath. Indeed, some European Christian thinkers, like Siger of Brabant (d. 1281), a professor at the University of Paris, became such passionate devotees that they were called "Averroists." Astonishingly, Ibn Rushd was more well-regarded among philosophers and even theologians in Latin Christendom than in the Islamic world (see Chapter 5).[92] In fact, some of his works have survived only in Hebrew and Latin but not in Arabic, and those that have come down to us in Arabic are available only in a few manuscripts, as compared to dozens in Hebrew and Latin.[93]

This divergence in attitude may shed some light on Muslim disinterest in Latin Europe. By the time when Averroism began to flourish in Paris and other European centers of learning, in the later 1200s,[94] the heyday of Muslim openness to the world had largely ended, as had its Golden Age. It is perhaps understandable that people from previously much more developed and advanced societies should fail to notice, or feel no attraction toward, the extraordinary ebullience in nearly every sphere of human endeavor in Europe's High Middle Ages—whatever the underlying reasons. Yet one cannot help but lament this disinterest, because of the missed opportunity, or ongoing series of missed opportunities. For, the Europeans were both developing their own resources at home and integrating into their projects and achievements everything they could learn from the peoples of Eurasia and soon from the peoples of the entire planet. The invention of mechanical movable-type printing in the mid-1400s by Johannes Gutenberg accelerated and amplified this process of development and integration, as discussed in Chapter 3.

CHAPTER 3
TSUNAMI OF THE PRINTED WORD

The use of complex language is a vital characteristic of being human. Between 100,000 and 50,000 years ago, our ancestors evolved the ability to communicate verbally with each other and therefore to work better together, to share insights, to interpret the universe, and to store up and to pass on knowledge and culture. Among such cultural artifacts, as noted in the Introduction, are thousands of scenes from nature painted on cave walls in many places throughout Afro-Eurasia. Viewers today often marvel at their fabulous beauty. Yet because those ancestors lacked writing, we can only guess at what they intended to express. Lost are the myriad other attendant cultural works, like poetry, music, mythological stories, and religious beliefs that must have accompanied the cave art. Prehistoric cave paintings are expressive, yet no more able to convey precise meaning than Mussorgsky's *Pictures at an Exhibition* (1874) could really suggest visiting an art gallery to a listener who knew nothing of the composer's intention.

The emergence of writing

Following the domestication of plants and animals in the prehistoric Near East beginning some ten thousand years ago, a sedentary lifestyle developed, permitting specialization and ongoing innovation. Cities emerged. Artisans developed clay firing, metal smelting, the wheel, and other technologies. Some five thousand years ago, systems of writing began to emerge in Mesopotamia, between the Tigris and Euphrates Rivers, and in the Upper Nile Valley in ancient Egypt. As these writing systems developed solely for governance and administrative purposes, they were cumbersome, complex, and difficult to learn. Only the narrowest elite, a tiny fraction of the elite, could master them. The same can be said of the Chinese pictographic script, which developed in the Shang period, after 1500 B.C.

A simpler form of writing began to develop nearly four thousand years ago by means of complex pathways and appeared in a practical form around 1000 B.C. in the Middle East.[1] The Phoenicians, a Semitic people who dominated trade and shipping in the eastern Mediterranean, devised this first workable alphabet. It comprised twenty-two letters, one per consonant, with no vowels. Unlike written language, which emerged independently in several places, including Central America (in the 200s B.C.), the alphabet appeared only this one time. All other alphabets stem from it. The Greek alphabet—named after its first two letters, alpha and beta—added vowels, an important element in Indo-European languages.

Alphabets made writing vastly easier.[2] The tiny ancient Greek civilization produced as much, if not more, scientific, philosophical, scholarly, and literary writing as ancient China but with a population ten times smaller. It also preserved and reinterpreted much of ancient Near Eastern literature, learning, wisdom, and lore that otherwise might have been lost, achieving the first "alchemical" cultural synthesis in world history—a vitally important contribution to human civilization. It seems likely that the relatively straightforward and uncomplicated Greek writing system facilitated this.

Early Egyptian craftsmen devised two portable writing materials: papyrus, made from a grass-like plant, and parchment, fashioned from dried animal skin. Sheets of these materials could be rolled into scrolls or bound into books. Libraries began to emerge in the ancient Eastern Mediterranean region. The library at Alexandria, founded around 300 B.C., held over 490,000 papyrus scrolls—the world's biggest repository for many centuries.[3] There librarians invented alphabetization and opened their massive collection to all scholars. Sometime around 100 A.D., Chinese artisans combined bark, rags, and plant fibers to fashion a coarse form of what we call paper.[4] Paper making diffused along the Silk Road, to the Middle East in the 900s, and on to Europe via Muslim communities in Spain and Sicily starting in the 1100s.[5] Paper production made it possible to build up huge libraries in the Islamic world, notably the 400,000-volume collection of the Umayyad Caliph of Córdoba, Al-Hakam II (r. 961–976).[6]

Printing also contributed to the proliferation of books and learning. The pioneers were again Chinese. Inked wood blocks carved with text and images were used to print on paper as early as the 500s. Such low-tech printing operations proliferated throughout the country to provide the classic texts on which hundreds of thousands of civil-service candidates were examined annually—China's "largest reading public."[7] Even so, books remained expensive. Movable type printing with ceramic and wooden typeface developed in the eleventh century and helped push down costs, yet the complexity of the non-alphabetic Chinese written language (one book could require 200,000 pieces of type) typically limited its use to big government projects.[8] Nevertheless, according to a leading scholar, "For the first time in Chinese history, book-collecting literati in the Sung, partly as a result of printing, probably realized the old cultural dream of ... becoming active collaborators in textual transmission."[9] Ironically, most literati continued to prefer manuscripts. Nor did commercial presses proliferate until the Ming Dynasty (1368–1644). As a result, printed books fully superseded "the manuscript permanently as the primary means for transmitting written culture in the lower Yangzi Delta only in the sixteenth century."[10] Even thereafter, published books were often printed to look like manuscripts, and readers and collectors frequently paid for handwritten manuscript copies to be made from printed books. As a result, "no sharp or absolute distinction can be drawn between manuscript and imprint in late imperial Chinese culture." Moreover, Chinese collectors also apparently never developed an ethic of collaboration, following the old adage "To loan a book is unfilial."[11] In other words, the invention of paper and printing had no revolutionary impact on Chinese society.

The printing revolution in Europe

At the other end of Eurasia, Islamic and Latin Christian societies devoted great efforts to copying secular and religious texts by hand. Medieval Europeans contributed two minor innovations. First, monks decorated thousands of ancient medieval texts with lovely illustrations and ornamentation, as they copied and recopied them for posterity and immediate use. Although manuscript illumination seems to have been invented in antiquity, it became a standard practice in the European Middle Ages. Second, during the Carolingian Renaissance (late 700s–800s), scribes developed a reader-friendly script—the Caroline miniscule—with capital letters used only for emphasis and words separated by spaces. These formalities made documents and literary works more accessible to people unable to devote a lifetime to mastering quirky ancient forms of writing.[12]

Lay schools became widespread in Europe beginning in the 1200s. As of 1338, in Florence, as many as ten thousand boys and girls were learning to read and write—in a city of ninety thousand. Likewise, at least one thousand more were studying business math and other practical subjects in six secondary schools, called *scuole d'abbaco*, while roughly half that number were receiving a rigorous classical education at four humanistic secondary schools.[13] Following the demographic catastrophe of the Black Death in the mid-1300s, labor costs dramatically increased, including for book copiers. With increasing literacy and universities still proliferating throughout Europe, there was a fortune to be made for an entrepreneur who could figure out a way to mechanize book production.[14]

By the mid-1400s, all the necessary elements were in place for a quantum transformation of printing in Europe.[15] Paper in Europe was relatively cheap, widespread, and of the perfect weight and texture. (Chinese paper was too fine to withstand the pressure of heavy printing equipment.) European languages are alphabetical. Fashioning movable type made practical sense for two dozen letters but not in those days for many thousands of complex Chinese characters. Lacking a taste for wine and olives, the East Asians had not devised screw-based presses.

Johannes Gutenberg (ca. 1400–1468) was an ambitious, but unprosperous goldsmith.[16] He conceived the idea of moveable-type printing and worked secretly for several years to achieve a series of technical breakthroughs: a letter punch, a special alloy for the type, a mechanical press that applied uniform pressure, a distinctive oil-based ink, and painstakingly developed methods of operation. It is worth noting that Gutenberg's invention depended on innovations and breakthroughs from around the world, including a mechanical screw press from ancient Rome, paper from China, and the metallurgical craft painstakingly developed for millennia all around Afro-Eurasia. Like an alchemist, Gutenberg combined these and other achievements, using his own genius to effect a world-changing breakthrough.

With a business partner and a half-dozen assistants, Gutenberg printed a Latin grammar book in 1450, followed by other small printing jobs. A few years later, his team of twenty produced some 180 copies of the Holy Bible—nine times more than twenty scribes could have completed in the same amount of time. Of course, once the type was set, a second printing could be produced in even less time.

European political and economic fragmentation, as well as the absence of patent law, meant that competitors, including several from Gutenberg's own workshop, set up print shops throughout Germany and the rest of Europe. In the 1470s, presses appeared in Venice, Paris, Kraków, Aalst (Flanders), and London (see Map 3.1). By 1501, entrepreneurs in 260 towns across 17 European countries operated 1,120 print shops, employing well over 10,000 printers as far west as Lisbon and as far north as Stockholm—a pan-European phenomenon.[17] In less than 50 years, publishers had produced nearly 30,000 titles in some 20 million copies. Roughly one-half of these books were religious, mostly in Latin. St. Augustine's *City of God* came out in

Tsunami of the Printed Word

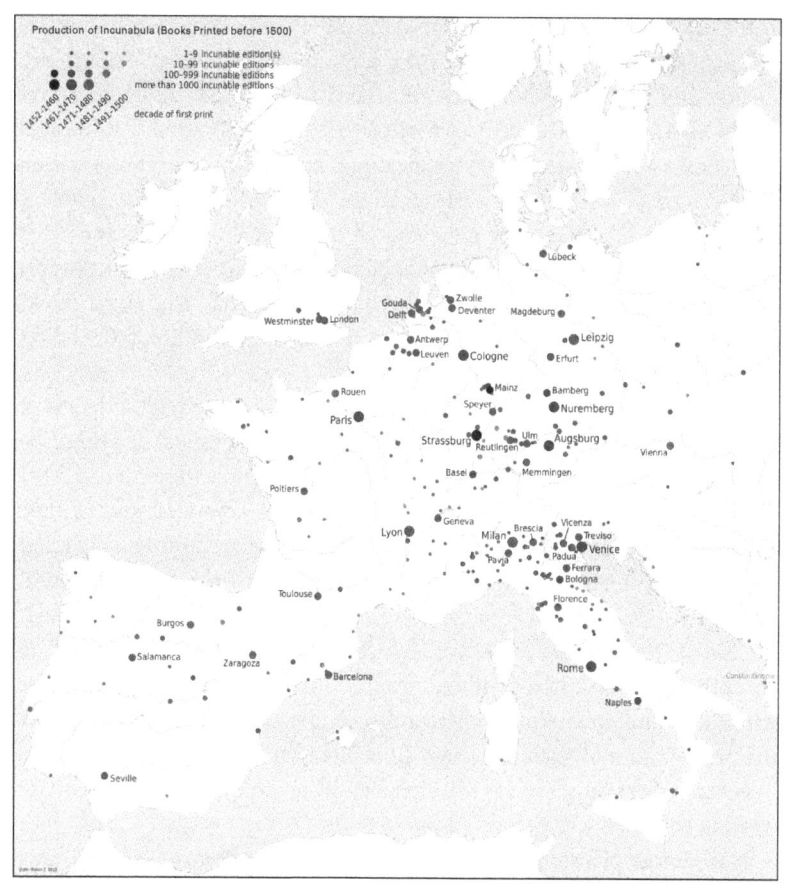

Map 3.1 The spread of printing presses in Europe. By 1501, entrepreneurs in 260 towns across 17 European countries were operating 1,120 print shops, employing well over 10,000 printers as far west as Lisbon and as far north as Stockholm—a pan-European phenomenon.

nineteen editions before 1500. The best-selling book was a popular religious devotional work by the mystic Thomas à Kempis (ca. 1380–1471) called *De imitatione Christi* ("The Imitation of Christ"). Between 1471 and 1500, it ran through 99 editions. Nearly all the great works of Latin and Greek antiquity also appeared. Hundreds of editions of the writings of Dante, Chaucer, and other "greats" came out in vernacular languages. Printing also made it possible to add technical and artistic illustrations. According to one reckoning, one-third of all books printed before 1500 were illustrated.[18]

Illustrations dramatically enhanced the usefulness of scientific books and technical manuals, in disciplines from accounting to zoology. In fact, art, science, and technology strongly influenced one another. Albrecht Dürer (1471–1528), one of the great artists of the age, authored and illustrated theoretical works on geometry, fortifications, and the artistic representation of the human body.[19] In early modern Europe, craftsmen, scholars, intellectuals, and dilettantes collaborated, conferred, and communicated more than in any other culture, then or before (see Chapter 6), thanks in part to the proliferation of books and other printed material. And these books began to accumulate: in the sixteenth century, up to 200 million more books came out.[20]

A law of legal deposit was promulgated first in France with a decree of 1537 requiring that one copy of all books newly published in France be furnished to the Royal Library at Blois. Similar ordinances were later adopted in many European countries.[21] European scholars compiled and printed huge collections of historical documents, often traveling thousands of miles and working in hundreds of archives, libraries, and other collections.[22] Scholars also subjected such materials to critical analysis. Étienne Pasquier (1529–1615), for example, rejected all legends about France and resolved "to say nothing of importance without proof."[23] Thanks to such efforts, and the printing revolution, the history of no other civilization is so well documented. The proliferation of such materials drove librarians to devise sophisticated classification systems, such as full alphabetization, to organize the massively growing collections.[24]

Mechanical printing soon spread to Europe's colonies—Mexico City (1539), Manila (1604), and Cambridge, Massachusetts (1638)—but not beyond. For some three hundred years throughout the Dar al-Islam, only one Muslim put mechanical printing briefly into use before it slowly began to spread across the Middle East from 1784.[25] Why did it take so long? Among the likely reasons were an inherent resistance to change, a mistrust of written texts, a love of calligraphy, a preference for oral learning and intellectual exchange, a horror of reproducing holy books mechanically, and a desire to control information flow. As proof of the latter point, one can mention that the Turkish Sultan Bayazid II made it illegal to possess printed matter in 1485. This prohibition was reaffirmed in 1515 by Selim I, whose dominions extended to Egypt, Syria, and Arabia.[26] The reason behind this prohibition may have been fear of "undermining the ability of religious authorities to confer legitimacy," which "would have raised the cost of collecting taxes and lowered the ruler's revenue."[27] Whatever the reasons,

Tsunami of the Printed Word

consumer demand could not have been great in the Ottoman Empire, since it proved easy for the authorities to suppress the circulation of printed matter,[28] something the European secular and ecclesiastical authorities lost the power to do as early as the 1200s.[29] Similar factors presumably contributed to the slow adoption of mechanical printing in the Mughal and Safavid Empires,[30] as well as in East Asia, where both Chinese and Korean artisans had invented methods of movable-type printing.

Why not China?

Yet did not China produce a huge number of books using the traditional woodblock printing methods? In reality, that output was relatively limited. Scholars have recently estimated the number of new titles printed in China from the early 1500s to 1644 at between 27 and 47 each year. The comparable statistic for Western Europe was 3,750 annually, or some 80 to 140 times more.[31] Given the great efficiency of the Chinese printing industry (producing books in early modern China seems not to have cost more than in Europe),[32] demand for books was presumably far weaker in China than in Western Europe.[33] Unfortunately, no data are available to indicate how many copies of each new title was produced in China, but it seems likely that here the lag behind European output was greater still, because movable type, given the larger initial capital inputs required, lent itself more typically to large print runs than did woodblock printing.[34] Even the massive government-funded Chinese encyclopedia projects did not enjoy much consumer interest. The largest ever such project, compiled in 1408, filled some 11,000 volumes. Once completed, however, the project was abandoned for want of funding, and subsequently the manuscript almost fully perished.[35]

The development of printing in China was evolutionary rather than revolutionary, because it "stretched out over a millennium."[36] Printing made invaluable contributions to the expansion of knowledge, the development of scholarship, the popularization of education, the increase of literacy, and the overall enrichment of Chinese culture. Yet it also strengthened traditional attitudes about culture and learning, "enforcing cultural and social coherence and asserting government control over canonical texts used in the civil service examinations."[37] As a result, according to another scholar, intellectual life even in the Ming era was highly fragmented, scholars were more isolated, and literati were less knowledgeable and less well informed than their counterparts in Europe. Thus, in China "collaborative scholarship, based on widely shared access to private collections, would have to wait ... until the eighteenth century."[38] Likewise, Ming era reference books for Chinese elites were focused mostly on such traditional subjects and pursuits as the civil examination, the Confucian classics, and family rituals. Only for ordinary people were practical manuals available on a much wider variety of subjects.[39] The reason for this bifurcation seems to have been that intellectuals and the practitioners of trades rarely worked together in China.

Intellectual and practical collaboration, by contrast, had been flourishing in Europe since the Middle Ages. The Benedictine and Cistercian monastic orders promoted the development of the mechanical arts and the invention of mechanical devices. This type of monk, as Lynn White noted, "was the first intellectual to get dirt under his fingernails."[40] Even a few leading medieval philosophers, like John Scotus Eriugena (ca. 810–ca. 877) and Hugh of Saint Victor in the twelfth century, "celebrated machine technology."[41] Similarly, the theologian, philosopher, mathematician, and jurist Cardinal Nicholas of Cusa (d. 1464) wrote authoritatively about eyeglasses, optics, and visual perspective.[42] As the commercial economy accelerated, men skilled in mathematics and logic enjoyed high demand as experts and collaborators in many fields of practical endeavor.[43]

This culture of cooperation and competition infused nearly every sphere of European society. Scholars and sailors, merchants and mercenaries, travelers and tradesmen journeyed from state to state, pursuing monetary gain, searching for masters to teach them the mysteries of their craft, or fleeing religious persecution. Political fragmentation was one factor fostering the emergence of the concept of rights in Europe. The weakness of central authorities, itself a function of political fragmentation, was another, as discussed in the following chapter.

CHAPTER 4
RIGHTS AND LIBERTIES

An important attribute of modern societies are liberties and protections for both individuals and collectives. Most people in developed societies take these social goods for granted, but they are a recent political achievement and primarily European in origin. In other major Eurasian cultures, states and rulers managed to concentrate more power in fewer hands than in Europe where diverse institutions, trends, customs, and practices tended to diffuse political power. Among the factors fostering such diffusion were power-sharing arrangements, charters of liberty, urban self-government, representative assemblies, the conciliar movement, the conceptualization of Christian believers as inherently worthy of rights, and philosophical theories of resistance to political authority.

Delegation of authority in premodern Eurasian societies

In the centuries before the turn of the first millennium (A.D. 1000), there seem to have been three main approaches to the delegation of authority by rulers for local governance across the Afro-Eurasian continuum. Two evolved from strength and one from weakness. Over two thousand years ago, Chinese rulers established a hierarchy of officials under direct governmental control.[1] Within several centuries, a formal and systematic mechanism for the recruitment of officials had been instituted. The famed Chinese civil service examination continued to function for nearly 1500 years—until the beginning of the twentieth century. It was open to any adult male, and, since the vast majority of the population were peasants, a very sizable proportion of civil servants hailed from that background. Such scholar-officials were entirely beholden to the ruler, so no landed or other aristocracy could or did emerge. The administrative corps was a powerful but dependent tool of governance.

In the Islamic world, a dependent governing class also emerged but in a different manner. Early Muslim rulers conquered vast swaths of land and with them multitudes—hundreds of thousands—of captives. Even as the conquests slowed, huge contingents of slaves were garnered as tribute or by purchase. In the early 800s, many thousands of mostly Central Asian slaves were acquired, apparently to establish a military slave system.[2] Why exactly early caliphs instituted this system remains open to debate, but the result was to undercut the development of a native Muslim aristocracy and to place a powerful instrument of military and government control in the hands of the rulers and their closest supporters. In fact, some slave-soldiers rose to those exalted ranks. In this way, power was devolved to aliens entirely dependent on the rulers "to the more or less complete exclusion of the free males of the community."[3] Indeed, ordinary people "became accustomed to think that they were ruled by foreign military aristocracies."[4] Moreover, such an administrative pattern characterized societies throughout the Islamic world but was almost never encountered in other cultures.

The approach to governance from a position of weakness is well exemplified in early medieval European politics. After the Roman Empire slowly declined from the 300s, power devolved in Europe to more and more petty warlords. In the late 700s, Charlemagne, King of the Franks, consolidated power over a territory encompassing much of today's France, Germany, and northern Italy. Yet he lacked the resources to build up an administrative apparatus on the Chinese model or even to purchase an army of slaves on the Islamic model. Instead, he ensured the support of warriors throughout his formal jurisdiction by entrusting them with populated landholdings. In time, these fiefs became hereditary. The great landed magnates in turn devolved land and authority to lesser lords, and so on, down the social hierarchy, as noted in Chapter 1. This was feudal society.[5] Not primarily an economic system, as Marx imagined, but a political, social, economic, and cultural world.

Feudal law and institutions enabled the medieval European aristocracies to extract more authority and autonomous power than could their Muslim counterparts.[6] As a result, political power fragmented in Europe (see Map 4.1), while it remained more concentrated in the Islamic world, albeit to a lesser extent than in China. Likewise, no landed aristocracy emerged either in the Islamic world or China, because in neither culture was it necessary for rulers to exchange semi-permanent and ultimately fully permanent landholdings for political and military support. Finally, impersonal institutions designed to diffuse political power, represent social interests, and work out political compromise in the context of relatively feeble central political authority emerged throughout Western and even much of Eastern Europe but not in the Islamic world or China.

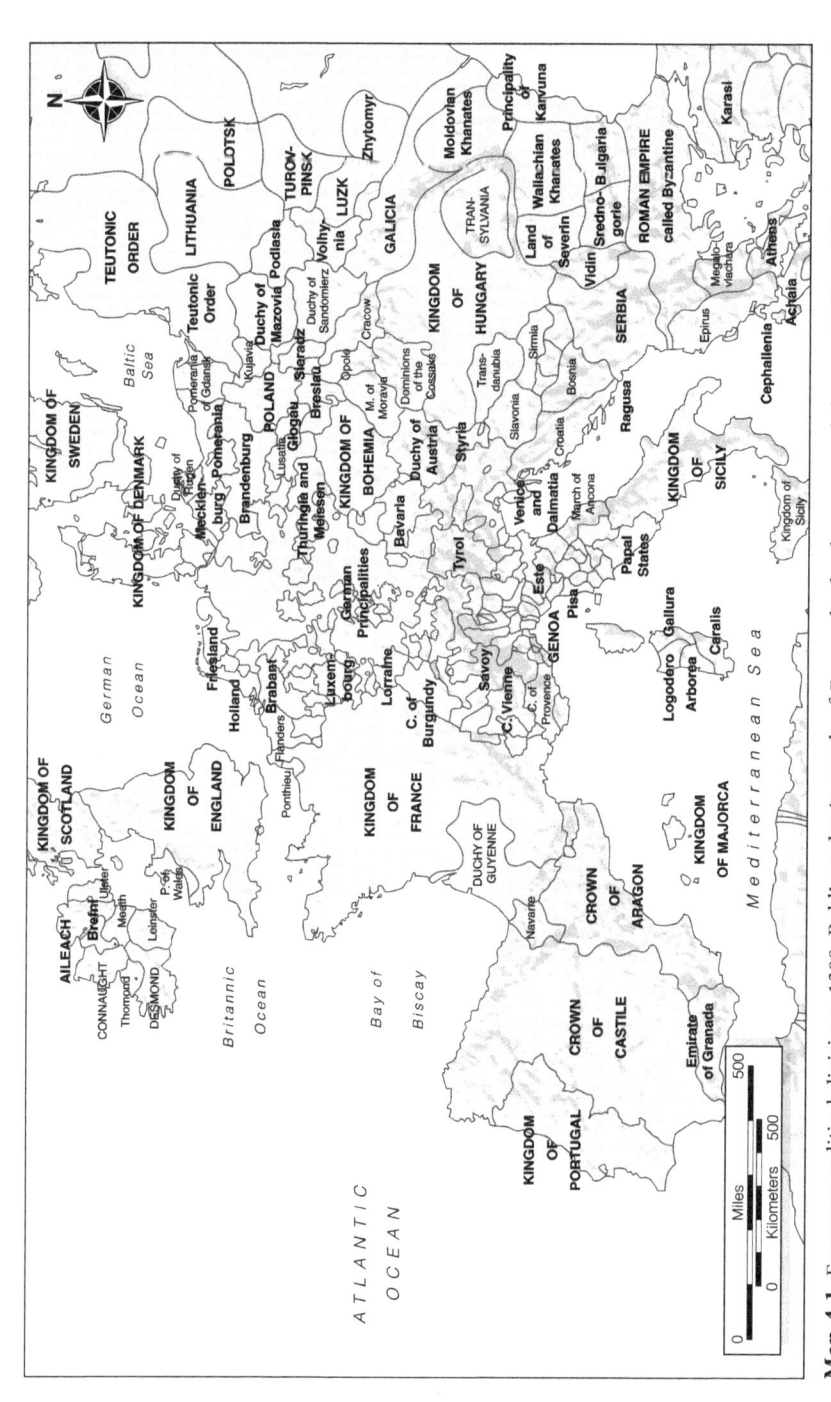

Map 4.1 European political divisions, 1300. Public order in much of Europe broke down around the year 1000 and for the next several centuries hundreds of polities (only a fraction of them indicated here) vied with one another, competing for resources and human talent, creating a check on concentrations of power, and stimulating a struggle for economic, technological, and military success.

The emergence of liberties and immunities in Europe

Just as European military leaders in the early Middle Ages enjoyed authority, jurisdiction, power, and prestige because of their indispensability in matters of war and governance, so, too, did church leaders at the highest levels of the ecclesiastical hierarchy. As early as the 600s, bishoprics and important monasteries acquired grants of royal immunity in England and elsewhere. In turn, bishops and other lords granted "liberties," privileges, and immunities to lesser monasteries and other church leaders. In such manner, medieval European lords were freed "from all labors, services, charges, or burdens," not counting help with defense and the maintenance of infrastructure, which typically were still required.[7] Again, European rulers lacked the institutional resources to govern the full extent of their realms and therefore had to devolve administrative duties to semi-autonomous agents who derived much of their power and standing in society from their control of landed estates. By the 900s, both the land and the power of European aristocracies had become strongly entrenched and all but immune even from royal interference.[8]

Liberties and immunities were granted both to territories and institutions, on the one hand, and to persons exercising authority within them, on the other hand. In general, such concessions amounted to governmental authority. This authority was distributive: the protection against harassment of secular and religious lords typically covered their dependents, who thus enjoyed freedom from harassment in their lord's name. Merchants and traveling administrative agents associated with such lords throughout the Carolingian Empire could expect freedom of movement and of buying and selling on their behalf, beginning in the first half of the ninth century.[9]

Towns in Italy acquired early privileges and liberties. From the early 900s, kings occasionally ascribed to Italian urban dwellers a status similar—or even equal—to that of the highest ecclesiastical lords. By mid-century, the inhabitants of Genoa gained full executive and legislative power at the local level, and a century later, the right to exercise judicial power, as well.[10]

Urban communities began to assert themselves in what is called the "communal movement," first in Spain and then France, Italy, and elsewhere in Europe, seeking to fill the power vacuum that opened up after the decline and collapse of the Carolingian Empire.[11] Sometimes the movement turned violent, but far from always. This grassroots development gave birth to, or merged with, the Peace and Truce of God movements, first in northern Spain and then throughout France and elsewhere, starting in the late 900s.

Here again, ordinary people and clergy banded together, in this case to use moral suasion to compel marauding knights to stop attacking defenseless people.¹² Rapacious lords did not always heed such demands, but they complied often enough to make the efforts worthwhile and to demonstrate the ability of Europeans to organize themselves for political purposes. These local initiatives spread widely and grew in sophistication and rhetorical power.

Oftentimes medieval European rulers facing difficult military or political circumstances granted charters of liberty to urban communities in exchange for military or even moral support.¹³ Thus, for example, during the investiture contest in the late 1100s, which pitted temporal rulers against the papacy, some German and Italian bishoprics and towns gained a wide variety of administrative and economic privileges, including authority over markets, mints, and tolls. Similar concessions were made on the Spanish March (in northeastern Iberia) as Christian armies slowly began to reconquer the Iberian Peninsula. But the process unfolded all across Europe.¹⁴ The recovery of Roman law, discussed in Chapter 1, played an important role in these developments, as urban leaders acquired intellectual tools to assert claims at princely courts.¹⁵ Immunities and liberties granted by high lords and rulers to urban communities could include freedom from trial and debt collection outside one's city, the right to collect taxes for a prince or king, protection within urban territory from seizure by military forces without due process, a prohibition on local nobles building strongholds within the vicinity of a given town, and security of property.¹⁶ The distributive effect of charter-granting culminated in England with Magna Carta, which conceded, according to Alan Harding, a variety of liberties "to the laity of the kingdom— not just to 'my barons and other tenants' as in Henry I's charter, or to 'my barons and vassals' as in Stephen's and Henry II's, but to 'all free men of our realm.'"¹⁷ It is worth noting that only around twelve percent of adult males were free men (including barons, knights, and a small portion of the peasantry). Even so, although the categories of persons with rights started out narrow, they steadily expanded over the centuries, based on this narrowly generalized assertion of rights.¹⁸

Indeed, drawing on foundations in the Bible, Roman law, and teachings of philosophers and theologians, legal experts in medieval Europe conceptualized and asserted in practice abundant rights, liberties, capacities, protections, privileges, powers, and immunities of individuals, guilds, corporations, officials, universities, monasteries, and urban councils, among many other legal entities. For medieval religious reformers, the freedom of the church from political control of secular lords was paramount. This included freedom from taxes, confiscation, military service, administrative interference, and compulsory testimony. Canon law also established detailed rules on internal church governance, the functioning of ecclesiastical courts, the roles and status of clergy and laypersons, church authority over believers, the status of nonbelievers, and kindred matters.[19] For urban political leaders, slipping from under the control of local and regional lords and asserting administrative autonomy were the main goals.

Urban self-government

As political order was gradually restored throughout Europe, following its breakdown around the millennium, domestic and overseas commerce expanded.[20] Royal and princely mints began to issue more coins. From the mid-1100s, new silver mines opened. Merchants learned business practices, like issuing promissory notes, from their Muslim counterparts. European producers and sellers increased their exchanges—grain from Picardy, the Baltic region, and southern England; sheep and wool from northern England and Scotland; finished cloth from the low countries; wine from southern France; fur and timber from Scandinavia and Eastern Europe. European merchants traded with Muslim intermediaries for Asian luxuries, like spices and silk. Mediterranean seaports grew busier. Trade fairs sprang up in strategic locations, like Champagne, roughly halfway between the Italian shipping centers and Flemish textile producers.

Gradually, from the later eleventh century, urban elites developed into an aristocracy of wealth. They bought up land surrounding their towns; some became lords of fiefs and were thus freed from taxes. Some lent money to lords and even kings. Urban dwellers, called "bourgeois" or "burghers," more and more often banded together to request or demand charters of liberty for their cities from kings or other great lords. The first known charter north of the Alps was secured by the Walloon city of Huy, which received free urban status in 1066 from the Prince-Bishopric of Liège.[21] Urban charters, which conferred on urban communities the right to self-government, were legally binding documents, which lawyers were required to draft, execute, and help enforce.

Granting urban charters was in a prince's or a king's interest for two main reasons. First, it weakened the nobility by eliminating an important source of noblemen's income: preying on towns. Second, it increased the wealth of the most important royal and princely creditors—the burghers. Free cities enjoyed great prestige and attracted more migrants from the countryside, further enriching them. Urban charters protected not the powerful—they needed no law to seize, exploit, plunder, and dominate—but rather the weak and the vulnerable. This was a key element in the emerging rule of law. While sensible from the prince's point of view, granting liberties to subject populations was extremely unusual and, on the scale at which European rulers practiced it, utterly novel in world history. Rulers everywhere had preferred to keep their subjects fully subordinate.

The emergence of self-governing urban communities in Europe illustrates well the conclusion reached by a prominent historian of the Islamic world, Marshall Hodgson. Europeans, he wrote, could "act far more effectively, as members of a group," than could other peoples of the world.[22] Ironically, social mobility was greater in China and the Islamic world, where the lowliest members of society could rise to the highest stations.[23] In Europe, professional advancement was open to talent, but rising in urban communities and the higher reaches of administrative and political power generally required adhering to detailed rules of seniority or legitimacy. There thus emerged a unique balance between ambition, on the one hand, and strict procedures, on the other. This result, it seems, enabled European communities to harness to a very great degree their human capital, while also developing a rule-respecting culture. In fact, chartered towns were legal associations, whose leaders were usually required to swear to uphold municipal law. As suggested in Chapter 1, the concept of leaders as standing under the law was an important European contribution to modern political theory.

The highly detailed Islamic law did not account for urban communities at all. In fact one scholar has asserted that "true urban autonomies would have been unthinkable in [the Islamic] world."[24] Thus, for example, although cities in the Ottoman Empire enjoyed some administrative decentralization, the head official was always appointed by the central government.[25] Despite the importance of commerce among the founders of Islam (the Prophet Mohammed was a merchant), slave-soldiers and religious scholars (*ulama*) stood higher in the social hierarchy than merchants by the 900s. Commercial enterprise continued to prosper, but merchants do not seem ever to have played an important political role collectively. (Nor did their status improve in the Ottoman Empire, from the time of its rise in the 1300s.)[26] By contrast, from the mid-1200s, commercial interests dominated nearly all towns throughout Western Europe, aside from Germany and Italy, where they nevertheless exercised great influence.[27]

Likewise, China boasted many vibrant cities. Each one contained a dense network of guilds. Chinese guilds were often wealthy, many maintaining temples, gardens, theaters, and schools.[28] Yet neither city nor guild exercised political authority, enjoyed autonomy, or possessed legal charters of any kind. The urban dwellers themselves felt strong allegiance to their families and ancestral villages and therefore never identified fully with the cities in which they lived. The government officials who administered the towns and regulated the guilds strenuously impeded any efforts to form the kinds of associations that distinguished European urban life. The Chinese social structure was so rigid that merchants had little hope of achieving independence from close government supervision. The dominant Confucian philosophy, moreover, disparaged business, even if government officials often accepted bribes in exchange for leaving merchants to their affairs. In other terms, Chinese cities did not shelter people from the oppressive weight of governmental power.

Although Indian merchants in some regions and periods—for example, in early modern Gujarat—wielded significant political power, enjoyed high status, engaged in sophisticated and large-scale commercial operations, and also formed big commercial associations, they felt no compulsion to establish political organizations or to unite with other segments of society, and indeed lacked social cohesiveness.[29]

To be sure, lords in Western Europe still interfered in urban affairs, depending on the region, local circumstances, political climate, and other factors. For example, rulers managed to impose their will more in France and England than the German lands, the Low Countries, or Italy. Towns sometimes banded together, as in the Lombard League in the 1100s and 1200s, to resist royal encroachments. In the early 1300s, however, urban government shifted toward one-man rule in northern Italy and became less "democratic" in many other regions.[30] In parallel with the strengthening of national monarchies, especially in France and England beginning in the 1200s, ordinary people, especially urban dwellers, brought suits against rapacious government officials—even the kings' own men—to the royal courts where they often received satisfaction of their claims. Such legal decisions resulted gradually in limiting the power of magnates, because their "willful lordship" was now seen as "incompatible with the customary rights of the community at large."[31] Moreover, a tradition of self-government remained embedded in urban culture throughout much of Europe and provided a foundation for the emergence of national self-government in the early modern era.

Rights and Liberties

By the 1300s, thanks in part to strong economic growth, the balance of power began shifting back toward the more successful monarchies, especially France and England. As secular rulers increasingly developed institutional power, they issued legislation weakening the authority of the Roman church in their territory. A notable case was the promulgation in England of Statutes of Provisors and of Praemunire from the mid-1300s.[32] Late medieval European rulers also sought to reassert their authority by relying on legal experts who gradually rose to form the nobility of the robe. This powerful new element of the aristocracy naturally reinforced the idea of *rex infra legem*, or "the king under the law."

Thus, first church leaders used the law to enhance their position at the expense of secular powers, and then those very powers used the law to reassert their authority. The modern Western legal order, with its procedural guarantees, checks and balances, constitutional restraints, deference to the law, and respect for individual and group rights emerged from the steady assertion and affirmation of such rights during the Middle Ages.

Representative assemblies

Meanwhile, a second foundational element of European political liberty had begun to develop in conjunction with urban self-government: representative assemblies. In the early Middle Ages, as noted above, monarchs convened assemblies of secular and ecclesiastical lords to demand counsel and support. Even the greatest lords could not make war without seeking the consent of their followers, retainers, and great men. The *Curia regis*, or royal council, was the key political institution in much of Europe beginning with the Carolingian era. The ongoing need of rulers to convoke such assemblies suggests that "political power was, to some extent, broken up and divided by the king and great dignitaries."[33] In the words of one scholar, the king's council should be "seen as a regular and sanctioned event, a social conjuncture, a set of interactions, the centre of a field of centripetal force, in short, as an institution."[34]

A key transition occurred when European rulers began to call up representatives of urban communities to attend the assemblies. The first such summons was given out in 1188 in León, in northwestern Spain.[35] Until that time, the kings of León had summoned only various grandees. At the assembly of 1188, called Cortes (or royal court), King Alfonso IX, who had just come to power in circumstances of political instability, pledged "to administer justice impartially and not to act arbitrarily" and not to make "war or peace or treaty except with the counsel of the bishops, nobles, and good men by whose counsel I ought to be guided." Among the attendees at this meeting, in addition to bishops, princes, and noblemen, were "elected citizens of each city," which apparently referred to cities dependent on the king and not on bishops.[36] Although royal councils continued to meet regularly, representatives of the towns were invited to take part much less often—only three times in the following twenty years, and always in times of political stress. Even so, it was obvious that Alfonso felt compelled to concede authority to urban communities in his realm and "to inquire into the administration of the municipalities, to adjudicate their lawsuits, to seek their counsel in military affairs, and to obtain their financial assistance."[37] Representatives of the towns took part in meetings of the Cortes more frequently after León was reunited with Castile in 1230, and especially in the second half of the thirteenth century. As the Castilian kings expanded Christian territory at the expense of Muslim rulers to the south, they felt compelled to guarantee the property, immunities, and privileges of merchants and other non-noble members of society, who previously had been living under Islamic rule in order to win their support.[38]

European rulers beyond León and Castile summoned representatives of towns for similar purposes, first in Barcelona (1192), then, over the following century, in other Spanish kingdoms (including Portugal), Sicily, Languedoc, the County of Toulouse, England, and France.[39] From the 1300s, representative assemblies spread to the rest of Europe and became a regular feature of political life in a variety of ways. In every case, a key result was restrictions on royal power.[40] Parliaments did not emerge in northern Italy, where the main city states were self-governing. In the Low Countries, the larger cities convened representative assemblies, which evolved into multi-estate convocations around 1400. It is interesting to note that such institutions did not emerge in Byzantium, the Ottoman Empire, or China, largely, it seems, because these societies had no independent cities with which rulers needed to negotiate for resources.[41]

Beginning in the mid-1400s, as absolutist monarchies rose to prominence in France, Spain, and elsewhere, many representative institutions fell into decline. Big states were unlikely sites for representative assemblies, since slow communications and travel made it difficult to gather in assembly and to monitor the workings of government.[42] Amid almost constant warfare in late medieval and early modern Europe, big agrarian countries with absolutist governments and urbanized countries with representative governments

Rights and Liberties

performed equally well at extracting revenue and therefore at projecting power on the battlefield.[43] By the late Middle Ages, European states were not only politically diverse, dozens of them managed in a variety of ways to hold their own and compete in a dangerous environment (see Map 4.1, p. 67).

The tradition of consensual tax increases throughout Europe fueled a series of rebellions against "taxation without representation," including the Dutch Revolt (the Eighty Years' War) beginning in 1568, the English Civil War (1642–1651), the English Glorious Revolution of 1688–1689, the American War of Independence, and the French Revolution of 1789. In the Dutch, English, and American cases, parliamentary institutions involving the participation of representatives of society in the political process became deeply and apparently irreversibly entrenched before the modern era. Constitutions, bills of rights, and similar documents affirmed limits on central government, popular sovereignty, and other modern political concepts. A push for rights, representative governance, and checks and balances also gained salience within the medieval European church.

The conciliar movement

Beginning in the late 1200s, a movement within the church aimed to endow leading ecclesiastical authorities with the right to take part in church governance on an equal standing with the papacy. Conciliarists, as its champions were called, advocated convening general church councils to bring about reform and to resolve pressing conflicts.[44] Some theologians and political theorists argued that representatives of such a duly constituted body, its authority ensured by the indwelling of the Holy Spirit, could more efficiently and more legitimately exercise leadership than the pope himself. It was further argued that pluralistic decision-making usually achieved superior results by encouraging rational argumentation and reconciling diverse points of view.

A pretext for convening such a council arose in 1378 when two separate popes, Urban V in Rome and Clement VII in Avignon, were elected and considered by various factions of supporters throughout Europe as legitimate. The standoff involved both political intrigue and military combat among partisans of the two pontiffs. In 1398, the French king convoked church leaders in France, including representatives of the mendicant friars (Dominicans and Franciscans) and the universities, some 300 participants in all, to gather in assembly. Despite their efforts, the schism persisted. Pierre

75

D'Ailly (1350-1420), a French theologian and church leader, argued persuasively that the ecclesiastical divisions required church leaders to assemble "not only on the authority of Christ but also by common right," because "any civil body or civil community or rightly ordered polity" will join together when danger threatens.[45] A general church council met in Pisa in 1409. Yet far from putting an end to the split, the participants elected a third pope, Alexander V. Intrigue and conflict continued. A council held in Rome in 1410 also failed to reconcile the opposing parties.

Finally, the Council of Constance (1414-1418), a vast gathering involving hundreds of delegates, deposed the three reigning popes and elected a new one recognized throughout Western Christendom, Martin V. The council's authority to remove pontiffs from office derived in part from the work of John of Paris (ca. 1255-1306), who defined papal and secular power as operating in separate spheres and concluded that a pope could be removed from office under some circumstances. The thought of the philosopher Marsilius of Padua (ca. 1280-ca. 1343) also influenced the conciliar movement. Marsilius denied the divine establishment of the papacy and argued that all legitimate government requires popular consent, because many members of the whole working together are far more likely to reach the truth than is a single person (e.g. the pope) or a small group of leaders. Some conciliarists, like Nicholas of Cusa, went so far as to argue that even kings should answer to the people as a whole and could be "banned or thrown out for maladministration or tyranny."[46] He even asserted that the legitimacy of any ruler or body derives first and foremost from the consent of its members and therefore all sovereignty and legitimacy are by their nature elective. Nevertheless, the papacy seemed stronger than conciliarism when the Fifth Lateran Council (1512-1517) successfully reasserted the supremacy of papal authority, for most conciliarists believed in clerical dominance. Popular sovereignty would require mobilizing the laity.

Yet the conciliarist doctrine and tradition persisted, justifying resistance to both ecclesiastical and secular authority for several centuries, both in Europe and abroad. One scholar has recently argued persuasively that American Catholics at the time of the Revolution and Founding rejected papal supremacy and advocated the separation of church and state. As he concludes, "American Catholics developed their church based on conciliarist ideas that rejected papal infallibility, affirmed national independence from the Holy See except in 'purely spiritual' matters, and insisted on clergy-elected bishops."[47] Such attitudes were part of a complex of movements dating back to the first centuries of the Christian era.

Christian liberties

Many early Christians had considered the institutional church an inadequate embodiment of Christ's teachings of selflessness and love for one's neighbor. A variety of reform movements thus emerged to purify the church and bring it back to apostolic traditions. The first was monasticism, which arose in the third century and flourished throughout the Near East and then Europe for many centuries. Calls for institutional reform and spiritual revival intensified at the millennium, when many believers expected an imminent return of Christ. Organized movements continued to appear in the following centuries. Peter Waldo in the mid-1100s in France, John Wyclif in the mid-1300s in England, and Jan Hus in the early 1400s in Bohemia attracted big followings, in part by denouncing priestly power and corruption, and seeking to bring vernacular translations of the Gospel to the faithful.[48] The ecclesiastical establishment brutally persecuted both leaders and movements. Hus was burned at the stake on orders of the Council of Constance. Yet far from disappearing or even fading, the urge to renew the church continued to swell. The invention of mechanical printing in the mid-1400s gave reformers a means to spread their visions of a truly spiritual Christian life that ecclesiastical and secular authorities could not easily suppress.[49]

The most influential vision was that of Martin Luther, a German monk. He came to prominence in 1517 when, as professor of biblical studies, he nailed ninety-five propositions on the door of Wittenberg University Chapel. In the text, by which he hoped to spark academic debate, he rejected the church's authority to remit sins by selling "indulgences." Although Luther was right that this practice was not grounded in biblical teaching and ultimately could be jettisoned without damage to Catholic doctrine, it was at the time seen as integral to papal authority. By contrast, as Toby Huff is surely right to claim:

> It is difficult to imagine a similar challenge and debate regarding the Confucian legacy, the "mandate of Heaven," or the mandarinate in China posted on the door of a great temple in Beijing in any previous era ... [or] a sixteenth or seventeenth century Islamic scholar posting such a challenge on the door of the Great Mosque in Damascus (or in Istanbul), inviting scholars and others to publicly debate the fundamentals of Islam, the meaning of the Koran, and what its sources might be.[50]

In this sense, intellectual culture in early modern Europe was undoubtedly freer than that of any other developed society.

Luther conceptualized the church as a community of the faithful and a priesthood of all believers. This was an extraordinary claim in an age when priests and especially monks and nuns were considered the worthiest members of society. Never before in human history had a set of doctrines so empowered ordinary people. And the message went out in torrents—primarily in the form of thousands of pamphlets printed on mechanical presses. By one calculation, Luther authored roughly twenty percent of the pamphlets printed in Germany from 1500 to 1530.[51] This was the world's first modern publicity campaign.

It was also the first time in history that a very ordinary person—in this case the son of a miner—stood up to all the powers that be on moral grounds—and prevailed. In January 1521, after the pope had excommunicated him, Luther appeared before the Imperial Assembly of the Holy Roman Empire. There, he asserted to dozens of noblemen and rulers, including the Holy Roman Emperor and King of Spain, Charles V, arguably the most powerful man in the world: "I am bound by the Scriptures I have quoted, and my conscience is captive to the Word of God. I cannot, and I will not retract anything, since it is neither safe nor right to go against conscience. I cannot do otherwise. Here I stand. May God help me. Amen."[52]

Soon a host of believers asserted rights based on the dictates of conscience. Anabaptists demanded exemption from military service (conscientious objection). Among the Anabaptists, and their offshoots like the Amish and Mennonites, arose the first pacifist movements and "peace churches." Established churches considered the Anabaptist doctrine of adult baptism heretical—and even a capital offense. Yet it fostered conceptualizing religious faith as a personal and voluntary decision (freedom of conscience).[53] The Peace of Augsburg in 1555 established the right of subjects to emigrate for reasons of conscience (the principle of religious pluralism). Thanks to its Calvinist leaders, the Dutch Republic became a haven of religious toleration welcoming persecuted minorities from around the continent, including Socinians, who rejected the doctrine of the Trinity, and Jews (the right of asylum). The leader of the Dutch Republic, William of Orange (1533–1584), formally granted exemptions from military service, a practice that gradually spread to other Protestant countries, though it became a movement only later in the American colonies. Also, in the Dutch Republic, advocates of "free prophecy, divinely sanctioned empowerment of the individual soul, and an invisible church" flourished, contributing to the emergence of the

Collegiant movement, which promoted absolute freedom of thought and expression and spread throughout the Netherlands from 1620 to 1650.[54] Its adherents were not required to believe anything in particular, and its "churches" had no clergy and no set institutional arrangements.

Perhaps inevitably the Calvinist minorities' assertion of freedom of conscience and civil rights encouraged others to demand toleration for their beliefs, since rights by their very nature have "a tendency to cascade," in the words of Lynn Hunt.[55] Political principles are either universal or not principles at all. There is no fundamental logic to excluding specific categories of people from rights once they are asserted as deserved by one particular category. Indeed, limited religious toleration was soon enshrined in law, in Rhode Island (1639), Maryland (1639), and England (1689). All these legislative acts excluded some believers—Catholics, atheists, or nontrinitarians—yet gradually legal protections were extended to all (for example, in France and the United States in 1789).

The religious fragmentation of Europe enabled dissenters to find safe havens.[56] Already in the early 1400s, English followers of Wyclif (Lollards) had sought refuge in Scotland. In the mid-1500s, Geneva and England offered asylum to Protestants. A century later, during the English Revolution and Civil Wars, thousands of English Protestants fled to the Low Countries, including the royalist Thomas Hobbes and the theorist of limited government John Locke. The Dutch jurist Hugo Grotius put forward a legal justification of the policy of asylum in *De jure belli ac pacis* (1625), the seminal book on international law. Friedrich Wilhelm, the Elector of Brandenburg, institutionalized this practice in 1685 by granting safe haven to French Huguenots (Protestants). Similar laws followed in other countries, including England (1708) and the English colonies of North America. This was the foundation of the contemporary policy of political and religious asylum now practiced throughout the world.

Rulers also enhanced their power and rights with appeals to conscience. Henry VIII sought to break with the church as a matter of conscience (though the proximate reason was to divorce his wife). To bring about this momentous change, the king needed the support of Parliament, which he convened repeatedly from 1529 to 1536. In 1531, the assembly made the king the "only and supreme lord and, as far as the law of Christ allows, even supreme head" of the church.[57] This concession to the monarch required a reciprocal act from the king, namely, the political idea of sovereignty residing in Crown-in-Parliament. As Henry himself asserted: "we at no time stand so highly in our estate royal as in the time of Parliament; wherein we as Head, and you as Members, are conjoin'd and knit together into one Body Politick."[58] Europe had been politically fragmented for centuries. The Reformation intensified the fragmentation by adding a third pole of authority: church, state, and now individual conscience.

Theories of political resistance

Theories of resistance to political authority, which gained strength in the Reformation era, had roots in the Middle Ages. John of Salisbury (ca. 1120–1180), a prominent bishop, argued that members of society who fail to remove a tyrant should be considered accessories to his crimes. All members of society, he claimed, must work harmoniously together toward the common good. A ruler who shirks this responsibility offends against justice itself and against God's will.[59] In the late 1200s, Thomas Aquinas justified both the murder of a tyrannical usurper and even insurrection against tyranny, for unjust laws are "acts of violence" against the community.[60]

Protestant theorists built on these justifications of resistance to unjust rule, drawing also on natural law theory, Roman and canon law, Roman republican ideals, and biblical teachings. An important work, *Vindiciae, contra tyrannos* ("A Protest against Tyrants"), which was published in 1579 and probably authored by the French Protestant, Philippe de Mornay, argues that every godly person, by virtue of his or her covenant with God, has the right to liberate the church from an unjust ruler—since all humans are brothers and children of God, and tyrants harm everyone and hinder the fulfillment of the divine plan. The book ran through dozens of Latin editions and translations into vernacular languages in the later sixteenth century.[61] Many other arguments justifying resistance to established authority were put forward by Protestant thinkers throughout Europe over the following decades.[62]

Among the first purely secular arguments for placing limits on political authority was that advanced by John Locke in the late 1600s. His *Two Treatises of Government*, published anonymously in December 1689 though written a decade before, propounded a contractual theory of government in which popular consent justifies the sovereign authority. He began with two principles. First, God created all people free and equal. Second, in the state of nature, which Locke posited as a theoretical construct, no individual could legitimately wield power or authority over another. Therefore, civil government could arise only with the consent of the governed. However, they would grant their consent only in exchange for some good or service. Trusting in the sociability of man, Locke argued that government emerged for the purpose of defending people's life, liberty, and property. Thus, absolute monarchy is inconsistent with civil society because government exists to prevent any individual—including rulers—from wielding the absolute power we all gave up when we left the state of nature.[63] Aligning the notion of contractual government with Christian worries about man's inherently selfish nature led logically to the idea of written constitutions aimed at placing limits on individuals, including rulers.

A plethora of written constitutions was adopted in the English-speaking world, starting with the Fundamental Orders of Connecticut (1639), the Instrument of Government of the Commonwealth of England, Scotland and Ireland (1653) following the deposition of King Charles I in 1649, and the Fundamental Constitution of the Carolinas (1669), to which Locke himself contributed. The most far-reaching and enduring was that of the United States (1789). Drawing on Locke and Montesquieu, the Framers aimed to separate the branches of government and to institute a system of checks and balances among them. The federal structure of self-governing states was intended to further decentralize political power. Preventing concentrations of power was meant to achieve the goal of securing the life, liberty, and property of individuals, as Locke had envisaged, and protecting political minorities, as James Madison emphasized. Thereafter, other European countries instituted written constitutions, beginning with France (1791), followed eventually by most countries of the world. No constitution is perfect. None has been flawlessly implemented. Yet modern conceptions of government as designed to serve the people, to safeguard popular sovereignty, to limit arbitrary political power, and to balance a variety of interests are all but inconceivable without one. The roots and early development of this quintessentially modern political achievement were European.

The idea and practice of political rights fostered a tendency to challenge authority, not only in politics and religion, but also in philosophy and interpretations of nature. Chapter 5 tells this story.

CHAPTER 5
AN ANXIETY FOR KNOWING

Careful investigations of nature—natural philosophy—occurred in all ancient and premodern societies. Starting in the Near East, then in Greece and China, and continuing through the Islamic Golden Age, brilliant early advances in the understanding of nature were made. Yet what we call modern science, based on systematic inquiry, empirical research, meticulous record-keeping, collaborative endeavor, mathematical analysis of data, extraordinary leaps of imagination, and the positing of "laws of nature" arose, just like modern conceptions and practices of political representation and rights, only in early modern Europe.

Early developments

Scholars in ancient Egypt and Mesopotamia, beginning some five thousand years ago, laid important foundations of natural philosophy. Successive peoples in Mesopotamia, above all the Babylonians, devised place-value notation, tables for squares and square roots, methods to solve linear and quadratic equations, the division of circles into 360 segments, and the development of celestial coordinates. Astronomers kept detailed records and calculations of the movements of the stars and other heavenly bodies, including quite accurate periodicity, and devised sophisticated calendars and horoscopes.[1] Much of Babylonian astronomical methods and achievements influenced the world's first comprehensive theoretical conceptualization of the cosmos: in ancient Greece.

In the sixth and fifth centuries B.C., pre-Socratic Greek thinkers wanted to know what things were made of, how they moved, and how they changed over time. Although they defined nature as made up of earth, water, air, and fire, several imagined that all material things are manifestations of these underlying substances, including water (Thales), air (Anaximenes), fire (Heraclitus), or combinations of the four elements (Empedocles).[2] Likewise, Anaximenes (ca. 585–525 B.C.) explained earthquakes as caused by avalanches of subterranean earth, and Anaxagoras (ca. 500–428 B.C.) as caused by water bursting into subterranean hollows.[3] Parmenides (ca. 515–450 B.C.) conceptualized the earth as spherical and grasped that the sun illuminates the moon. The Pythagoreans argued that one can understand reality in terms of mathematical relationships.[4]

Other Greeks, until the end of the Hellenistic era (323–31 B.C.), made an extraordinary panoply of discoveries and advances.[5] Democritus (ca. 460–370 B.C.) posited a theory of indivisible atoms. Eudoxus of Cnidus (ca. 408–ca. 355 B.C.) described the heavens as spherical and the planets as tracing spherical orbits. These ideas supplemented Babylonian arithmetical descriptions of the cosmos with geometrical ones.[6] Aristotle (384–322 B.C.) meticulously investigated and systematically presented detailed findings on a host of subjects, from anatomy to zoology. He also set out foundational principles of logic.[7] No earlier scholar anywhere had advanced such painstakingly organized and carefully articulated data and arguments about so wide a variety of natural, political, psychological, and social phenomena. In a treatise now lost, Aristarchus of Samos (310–230 B.C.) devised a Sun- (or helio-) centric model of the cosmos.[8] Aristotle's Earth- (or geo-) centric model, revised four hundred years later by Ptolemy (ca. A.D. 100–ca. 170), remained the world's dominant relatively scientific cosmological model for nearly 1,500 years. Euclid (fl. 300 B.C.) laid the foundations of geometry and applied geometric calculations to visual perspective. Archimedes (ca. 287–ca. 212 B.C.) formulated methods for calculating complex areas and approximating the number pi. Herophilus of Chalcedon (ca. 335–ca. 280 B.C.) and his students at the Alexandrian medical school developed the disciplines of anatomy and physiology thanks to systematic human dissection.[9] Galen of Pergamum (ca. A.D. 129–200) achieved an understanding of the nervous system, circulatory system, and general human anatomy that remained unsurpassed for over one thousand years.

Taken together, ancient and Hellenistic Greek thinkers advanced human understanding of nature more than any other people in history until the early modern era. They synthesized learning and knowledge from around the known world, but they approached it critically. One scholar has noted that "the extant remains of Egyptian and Babylonian medicine, mathematics, and astronomy can be combed in vain for a single example of a text where an individual author explicitly distances himself from, and criticizes, the received tradition in order to claim originality for himself, whereas our Greek sources repeatedly do that."[10] Roman scholars preserved and built upon these foundations, making advances in applied science and technology.[11] An important Roman achievement was the compilation of comprehensive encyclopedias.[12] When the world of classical antiquity gradually disintegrated, surviving encyclopedias preserved much of the Greek and Roman legacy.

Among the "Hundred Schools" that flourished during the Warring States era (475–221 B.C.) in China, followers of the philosopher Mozi (ca. 470–ca. 391 B.C.) made advances in logic, epistemology, ethics, mathematics, and geometrical optics, yet the movement was suppressed several centuries later, and most of their writings were lost.[13] Joseph Needham's massive study of Chinese advances in science and technology—twenty-seven volumes, many written by coauthors, so far[14]—show that ancient Chinese natural philosophers recorded observations of the stars, eclipses, comets, meteors, and sunspots; speculated about the effects of celestial bodies on the tides; devised mineral, herbal, and animal remedies; practiced inoculation against smallpox; described the hexagonal structure of snowflake crystals; dated the origin of the universe to tens of millions of years; applied urine analysis for the detection of diabetes; documented circadian rhythms; and understood key properties of magnetism, including declination.[15] State patronage contributed to many Chinese advances, including the world's first practical seismograph in A.D. 130, massive geographical surveys, and astronomical advances, thanks to an official astronomy bureau founded some two thousand years ago.[16]

Chinese artisans achieved greater early technological breakthroughs than any other people, including the "four great inventions" of premodern times: paper, the compass, gunpowder, and printing. Chinese technological advances were also abundant in agriculture, metallurgy, ship design, gunpowder weaponry, and a host of inventions in dozens of fields, including the iron plow, the fishing reel, lacquer, porcelain, the mechanical clock, the wheelbarrow, the umbrella, paper money, and relief maps. Chinese mathematicians made significant discoveries as well, conceptualizing the decimal system, place value, decimal fractions; calculating pi to seven decimal places; and making sophisticated use of algebra and geometry.[17] Nearly all of these breakthroughs, however, were made one, two, or even three thousand years ago; not one significant innovation in any of these areas was made after 1400, and few were made after 1200.[18]

Unlike the ancient and Hellenistic Greeks, the Chinese tended toward practical advances and eschewed seeking theoretical understanding or generalization about how nature functions.[19] For example, although Chinese scholars continuously studied and recorded the position of stars and other celestial phenomena, none constructed a cosmological system in the manner of Aristotle or Ptolemy. "Reality," they seem to have thought, was "essentially too subtle to be encoded in general principles."[20] Although the leading neo-Confucian philosopher Zhu Xi (1130–1200) advocated "the study of things," it seems not to have led to systematic study of nature. In fact, when the unorthodox neo-Confucian thinker Wang Yangming (1472–1529) strived for seven days and nights to understand the inner meaning of some bamboo shoots, he suffered a mental breakdown.[21]

Ancient Indians founded a sophisticated civilization, dating back several thousand years. Indian scholarship, medicine, astronomy, and especially mathematics achieved advances in parallel with the ancient Greeks—for example, the concept of zero and place value.[22] Around the same time, Siddhartha Gautama founded Buddhism. The first universal religion, it spread over the next several centuries to Afghanistan and throughout Southeast and East Asia. Two thousand years ago, ancient Greek and Chinese scholars traveled to the school in Taxila (in today's Pakistan). From the fifth century A.D., Persians, Chinese, Koreans, and others made the voyage to Nalanda, in northwest India, where for centuries thousands of students enrolled at a monastic complex that was "the largest residential teaching institution in the world at this time." As a result, India was the "the motor of higher learning for the whole of East Asia."[23] Here one studied, in addition to religious thought, grammar, logic, medicine, and various other arts and sciences, possibly including astronomy and mathematics. Many other monastic institutions of higher learning emerged throughout the Indian subcontinent in the premodern era.

Indian scientific and mathematical achievements reached their peak during the country's Golden Age, when the enlightened Gupta Dynasty ruled northern India from 280 to 550.[24] Aside, perhaps, from the Greeks, who learned from and influenced them, no people advanced mathematical knowledge as much, until the modern European age. According to one authority, between the third and ninth centuries, "Indian computational activity had few parallels anywhere in the world," and "there was no Western mathematician alive in 1400 capable of handling power series for trigonometric functions" like Madhava of Sangamagrama.[25] At the same time, however, Indian mathematicians and scholars did not seek to systematize their understanding of the natural world, perhaps because "all the Indian philosophical schools start from the assumption that worldly life is radically unsatisfactory and that liberation from suffering is both desired and possible."[26] The country remained rich, populous, and relatively developed. Indians continued to produce the world's most beautiful cotton prints, using secret methods evolved millennia before. By the mid-1600s, these commodities had become enormously popular in Europe, resulting in what some scholars have called a "calico craze."[27] Likewise, commercial culture more generally remained vibrant.[28] Yet, following a centuries-long series of invasions from Central Asia and Europe, Indian scholars made few great advancements in mathematical or scientific knowledge.

The second Afro-Eurasian intellectual synthesis was accomplished by Muslim scholars and thinkers during the Islamic Golden Age (700s–1200s). They blended learning from all the great known cultures of the time and prior centuries and made notable contributions to mathematics, commerce, medicine, astronomy, optics, and chemistry. Mathematicians developed the use of symbols for unknown quantities, a technique that is still called by its Arabic name, algebra (*al-jabr*).[29] In the late 900s, they adopted the Indian numbering system, which we call "Arabic numerals." Merchants developed credit mechanisms, bills of exchange, and commercial trading companies.

Pursuing alchemical experimentation, Muslim scholars methodically conducted chemical operations like calcination, reduction, sublimation, purification, distillation, and crystallization and discovered thousands of chemical substances and derivatives.[30] Artisans also applied such operations to industrial processes like metallurgy, dye making, and glass production.[31] Drawing on such advances, craftsmen invented the fountain pen, metallic-glazed ceramics, stained glass, and the oil lamp. Physicians advanced medical knowledge in anatomy, the treatment of diseases, physiology, pathology, obstetrics, pharmacology, ophthalmology, and surgery and were esteemed for centuries in the Christian courts of southern Europe.[32]

The Andalusian philosopher Ibn Rushd, or Averroes (1126–1198), produced a vast corpus of brilliant and detailed commentaries on the major works by Aristotle, in addition to dozens of works on law, natural philosophy, and theology.[33] Far more influential were the ideas of the theologian and jurist al-Ghazali (1058–1111), who denounced philosophy and mathematics as threatening to religious faith and argued against necessary causal relations and against secondary natural causes (because God can cause any effect He wants).[34] A few Muslim scholars continued to make significant advances, especially in astronomy, given the great importance of calculating celestial motions to the Islamic faith. The work of Ibn al-Shatir (1304–1375), Ali Qushji (1403–1474), and other astronomers seems almost certain to have influenced Copernicus—even made his breakthroughs possible.[35] Yet this fact is crucial as well: such Muslim thinkers contributed to a series of extraordinary scientific advancements in early modern Europe but not in the Islamic world.[36]

Medieval and early modern European natural philosophy

The starting point of European advancements was, as it had been for the ancient and Hellenistic Greeks and the Muslims of the Islamic Golden Age, a passionate assimilation of learning and knowledge from across the known world.[37] The late-eleventh century saw increased interest in translating texts, fueled in part by exposure to the Greek and Islamic worlds during the First Crusade. By the end of the 1100s, nearly all of Aristotle's works dealing with logic, grammar, metaphysics, natural philosophy, and cosmology had been translated—a vast and mighty corpus; a hundred years later, they were well known. Aristotle's treasures of natural philosophy and epistemological speculation—*Physics, On the Heavens, On Generation and Corruption, On the Soul, Meteorology, The History of Animals, The Parts of Animals,* and *The Generation of Animals*—were placed at the center of the university curriculum.[38]

European scholars also translated commentaries and original works by Muslim writers—especially those of Ibn Rushd (Averroes to the Latins). In the high Middle Ages, as noted in Chapter 2, Ibn Rushd was more revered—and had a much bigger impact—in Europe than in the Islamic world. In fact, it has been argued that the work of such rationalist philosophers as Ibn Rushd "led to the transformation of almost all philosophical disciplines in the medieval Latin world."[39] (Averroism remained influential in Europe into the early modern period.)[40] Some of his ideas were unacceptable to Christians, for example, his skepticism regarding the immortality of the soul. Nevertheless, philosophers like Thomas Aquinas wrestled with and assimilated his thought. The result was complex syntheses of reason and faith, philosophy and theology, demonstrating a staunch conviction that human reason can pierce the secrets of the universe.

University scholars pursued knowledge in nearly every direction, systematically interrogating nature and reality. For example, Albert of Saxony (ca. 1316–1390), posed scores of questions about Aristotle's physics, such as:

> Whether scientific understanding ... of what has been caused depends on the knowledge of its causes. ... whether every natural being has within itself active and passive principles of natural motion and rest. ... whether nature is properly divided into matter and form. ... whether every effecting thing is the cause of that which it is effecting. ... whether anything can happen by chance (*fortuna*) and accident

(*casu*).... whether of all the things that exist, some are permanent and others are successive.... whether there could be an infinite dimension.... whether the existence of a vacuum is possible.... whether some motion could be eternal.... whether time is eternal.... whether inanimate heavy and light bodies could be self-moved....[41]

Some scholars took this rationalistic optimism to such lengths as to question God's power. In 1277, the Bishop of Paris condemned 219 "propositions" then being discussed at the University of Paris, including, for example, "That God cannot be the cause of a newly-made thing and cannot produce anything new"[42]—an extraordinarily radical proposition for the Christian Middle Ages. Moreover, the condemnation was soon lifted. Speculation, questioning, skepticism, and pushing the bounds of knowledge continued, thanks to thousands of scholars at dozens of relatively autonomous universities throughout Europe.

For example, a team of logicians and mathematicians at Merton College, Oxford University, in the second quarter of the fourteenth century, defined velocity as intensity of motion. Just as a color can be more or less bright, they reasoned, motion can be more or less swift. They went on to formulate several theorems, such as: an object will travel the same distance in the same time whether accelerating uniformly or moving steadily.[43] Other scholars verified these results or built on their foundation. Thus, Nicolas Oresme (ca. 1323–1382) of the University of Paris devised geometrical proofs for the Mertonian principles.[44] Oresme also hypothesized that the Earth moves (and not the Sun). To those who objected that things would fly off the Earth as it spun, he contended that since everything spins together nothing falls off. His older colleague at Paris, Jean Buridan (ca. 1300–ca. 1360), revised the Aristotelian theory of projectile motion. Drawing on an idea passed down from the Hellenistic Near East through Islamic natural philosophers, he argued that projectiles move not because of a continuous external force but because a force, at the time of launching, becomes internal to the object. He called this force "impetus" and concluded that only resistance could diminish its effect. This idea was strikingly close to the modern conceptualization of inertia.[45]

Building on Greek and Islamic investigations, European alchemists made important discoveries. In the early 1300s, Geber—probably Paul of Taranto, a late-thirteenth-century Italian Franciscan friar, who named himself after the Muslim polymath Jabir ibn Hayyan (ca. 721–ca. 815)—described and classified chemical substances according to their physical properties, extensively theorized about his findings, and produced a systematic alchemical textbook. Most important, it presented uniquely detailed and methodical laboratory procedures. Among the operations Geber described were the purification of chemical substances, the preparation of acids, chemical testing by means of fire and corrosive substances, and the construction of laboratory equipment. His discovery of sulfuric acid, the first strong acid described scientifically, proved itself a powerful tool for chemical analysis.[46]

Medical knowledge expanded dramatically in medieval Europe also thanks to translations from Arabic, most of them based on earlier Greek advances. In particular, the so-called translation school of Toledo in central Spain brought together many scholars in the 1100s and 1200s who systematically translated works in many branches of learning. Gerard of Cremona (1114–1187), for example, translated some eighty-seven books, including twenty-four relating to medicine, the most important of which was Ibn Sina's *Canon*, a million-word systematic compendium of medical knowledge, which "became the blueprint for academic medicine of the Christian scholars."[47]

Hellenistic Greek physicians like Galen systematically practiced human and animal dissection. For centuries thereafter, the technique was abandoned in the West (and rarely practiced in China).[48] It was taken up again by Muslim physicians like Ibn Zuhr (1094–1162),[49] and then legalized in several European countries in the years 1283–1365.[50] Given the extensive borrowing of medical techniques and knowledge from Muslim practitioners, it seems likely that European physicians were following in their footsteps. Certainly, Gerard's translation of Ibn Sina's *Canon* inspired Mondino de Liuzzi, a professor of medicine at the University of Bologna, who laid out principles of dissection in a textbook of 1315 and incorporated dissection classes into his curriculum.[51] The accuracy of European anatomical studies steadily increased. By the late 1400s, north Italian universities began to set up temporary spaces in which to teach anatomy. Over the next century, all the major universities of Europe established permanent anatomy theaters within their medical schools.[52] From this point, the advancement of medical knowledge in Europe expanded faster and more fully than anywhere else.

Breakthroughs toward modern science

Across Europe, knowledge of plants and animals increased exponentially. Chairs in botany were created in several universities, beginning at Padua in

1533.[53] Herbaria were instituted from the 1540s.[54] In these decades, many cities established botanical gardens.[55] Botanists published encyclopedic surveys of known plants, including their habitats and medicinal properties, based on both ancient and Muslim authors and extensive field research and accompanied by thousands of extraordinarily accurate illustrations.[56] As one scholar explained, "a revolution took place as authors, in despair at the inadequacies of purely verbal description, sought the aid of skilled draftsmen and artists trained to observe carefully and well."[57] The printing revolution enabled Andreas Vesalius, a professor at the University of Padua, to incorporate nearly one hundred detailed illustrations into his *On the Structure of the Human Body* (1543). The work was revolutionary in its uniting of art, science, and the latest technological innovations.[58] Other scholars produced zoological compendia, like Conrad Gesner's *Historiae animalium* (1551–1558), which ran to 4,500 pages, with large illustrations on nearly every other page.[59] Others still, including Georg Bauer, called Agricola (1494–1555), undertook a systematic study of "fossils," meaning anything dug from the ground, as well as of mineralogy and geology.

European scholars collected and studied plant specimens from around the vast web of European colonial possessions, as well. For example, the Dutch naturalist Hendrik Adrian van Rheede carefully examined the botanical diversity of India's Malabar Coast. After seven years of work, he published *Hortus Malabaricus* (1678) in twelve large volumes and graced with 793 illustrations.[60] Such detailed and systematically compiled information about plants, animals, and other natural phenomena flooded into early modern Europe from around the world, contributing immensely to the rise of modern science. Altogether, scholars and natural philosophers published immense numbers of treatises, dictionaries, encyclopedias, atlases, star charts, compendia, bibliographical aids, and other scholarly works, many with alphabetical indexes.

European scholars developed new methods and instruments of analysis. Some were conceptual. In 1623, the Swiss botanist Gaspard Bauhin published a classification of some six thousand plant species.[61] Over the next two centuries, European naturalists would refine this concept, culminating in the Linnaean division (into kingdoms, classes, orders, genera, and species) still used worldwide today. The systematic collection and study of plant specimens from around the world contributed directly and intentionally to the emergence of the Linnaean classification system. As he wrote in 1753, "the world is the Almighty's theater . . . we must research these creations by the Creator, which the Highest has linked to our well-being in such a way that we shall not need to miss anything of all the good things we need."[62] To this end, he trained numerous students and sent them overseas to collect plant specimens. Another important conceptual tool was mathematics, which artisans, engineers, scholars, and painters all applied to their crafts. Fra Luca Bartolomeo de Pacioli (1445–1517), a professor of mathematics, for example, helped Leonardo with spatial calculations.[63] Natural philosophers drew upon mathematical tools, such as logarithms (first described by the Scot, John Napier, in 1614), which the printing revolution made widely accessible.[64] Physical instruments also boosted the development of modern science. Microscopes, devised in the late 1500s or early 1600s in Holland, enabled researchers to examine fine details of nature. Beginning at the University of Leiden, in 1669 a freestanding chemical laboratory was established for the first time outside a medical school. Other universities followed suit.[65]

Access to masses of newly published astronomical data—drawn from both ancient and Near Eastern compendia and recent observations— enabled European natural philosophers to reconceptualize the heavens. A brilliant mathematician steeped in ancient Greek and Golden Age Islamic theories, Nicolaus Copernicus (1473–1543) spent decades trying to demonstrate that the planets revolve around the Sun, the Earth rotates on an axis, and the stars stand at an extremely far distance from the solar system.[66] The model was vastly simpler and thus more elegant than Ptolemy's. His *On the Revolutions of the Heavenly Spheres* (1543) had no immediate earth-shattering effect, however, largely because what he was trying to demonstrate was "contrary to the impression of the senses," as Copernicus himself admitted. It seems that before 1600 fewer than a dozen Europeans accepted his heliocentric theory.[67]

Yet challenges to Aristotelian-Ptolemaic Earth-centered cosmology were now coming fast. Tycho Brahe (1546–1601), a Danish court astrologer, was in charge of sophisticated and well-equipped observatories, first in Denmark and then in Bohemia. Thanks to refined instruments, his researchers could measure celestial angles (which are necessary for calculating the relative position of stars and other celestial bodies) five times more accurately than had previously been possible.[68] Tycho formulated a partial heliocentric model with the Sun and the Moon revolving around the Earth and the remaining planets revolving around the Sun.[69] Aristotle's interpretation, which deemed the heavens immutable, began to lose credibility when a nova burst into the sky in 1572 and a comet tore across the heavens in 1577. The invention of a simple telescope, apparently in Holland in the late 1500s, enabled stargazers to perceive even more "irregularities" in the Aristotelian cosmos. In *A Message from the Stars* (1610), Galileo Galilei catalogued what he believed were four new planets (actually moons orbiting Jupiter) and a host of new stars in the firmament.[70] Although Galileo was forced by the Inquisition to repudiate the Copernican system in 1633,[71] he continued to conduct experiments and to publish his results in the fields of dynamics, mechanics, and kinematics. Working as "an entrepreneurial scientist," Galileo developed a "new philosophy of nature" that became the model for scientific research, applying mathematics and experimentation to common physical materials, objects, and processes.[72]

A brilliant mathematician, Johannes Kepler (1571–1630) held that "numbers and magnitudes" could enable him to attain to a comprehension that is "the same as God's, at least insofar as we are able to understand it in this mortal life."[73] In 1600, Brahe invited Kepler to join his team. The resultant synergy—Brahe's data and Kepler's mathematics—enabled Kepler, in *New Astronomy* (1609), to posit unseen forces simultaneously pulling each planet away from and toward the Sun and to formulate two laws of planetary motion. The first states that planets can orbit only elliptically. The second describes any planetary orbit as regular despite fluctuating velocity.[74] Kepler's third law, set out in *The Harmony of the World* (1619), portrays a proportional relationship between the mean distance from, and the period of orbit around, the Sun of any two planets.[75] Describing natural regularities as "laws" was a foundational achievement of modern science. It emerged in early modern Europe and nowhere else.

Rapid and dramatic advances were also made in physiology. For centuries, no one in the world correctly understood how the circulatory system works. Drawing on results from human and animal dissection,[76] Ibn al-Nafis (1213–1288), an Arab Muslim, accurately described pulmonary circulation, whereby blood is enriched with oxygen and returns to the heart, yet few European scholars paid attention.[77] Finally, thanks to years of meticulous empirical study and possibly knowledge of al-Nafis's work, William Harvey demonstrated in 1628 that blood circulates in two closed systems. First, the heart pumps blood through the lungs, which enrich it with oxygen; then, it pumps the enriched blood throughout the body via the arteries. The depleted blood returns to the heart through the veins, and the process starts over.[78] Simple and elegant, Harvey's theory both described reality and radically altered the whole of physiology, since a proper understanding of the circulatory system led to a more accurate comprehension of the respiratory, digestive, and other bodily systems. Within decades the microscope had revealed capillaries, blood cells, and microorganisms to European researchers. Antoni van Leeuwenhoek (1632–1723) described one bug as "more than a thousand times smaller than the eye of a full-grown louse" and estimated its number in a drop of water at tens of millions.[79] Of course, such numbers seemed absurd, yet van Leeuwenhoek was vastly closer to the truth than anyone had ever been.

Scholars in Europe began to theorize in new ways about how to approach nature. Francis Bacon's *New Organon* (1620), for example, advocated combining Aristotle's observation and classification with Plato's theorizing.[80] Bacon entreated scholars to view nature with fresh eyes, to plan their observations and experiments in advance, "to pay attention to known things," to maintain detailed laboratory notebooks, and above all to formulate searching questions about natural phenomena, such as "what is lost and disappears; what remains and what accrues; what expands and what contracts; what is combined, what is separated; what is continuous, what interrupted; what impels, what obstructs; what prevails, what submits ..."[81] More radically, René Descartes (1596–1650) used his "methodical doubt" to question all received knowledge, everything we know from our senses, even the functioning of our rational mind. He concluded in *Discourse on the Method* (1637) that he could know only one thing for certain: Cogito, ergo sum, or "I am thinking; therefore I exist."[82] This proposition permitted Descartes to divide reality into two sharply distinct phenomena—*res cogitans*, or thinking things, and *res extensa*, or extended things.[83] The length, breadth, depth, shape, position, and motion of material objects (extended things) could all be measured, he recognized, opening the door to a mathematical physics. Combined with Descartes's work in linking algebra and geometry, this development made it possible to view nature philosophically as a pure object of experimentation.[84]

Isaac Newton (1642–1727) used powerful mathematics—calculus, which he and the German, Gottfried Leibniz (1646–1716), independently invented—and an extraordinarily creative imagination to systematize accumulated advancements in physics. Above all, he formulated the law of universal gravitation. The idea that the Sun could transmit sufficient force to hold the Earth in its orbit across ninety-three million miles space "without the mediation of something else, which is not material," was to Newton himself "inconceivable."[85] Yet he mathematically demonstrated precisely this conclusion, as well as three universal laws of motion (relating to inertia, acceleration, and action and reaction), in his *Philosophiae Naturalis Principia Mathematica* (1687).[86] By applying all four principles, one can account for the behavior of all physical objects larger than an atom and moving more slowly than the speed of light.

The number of practitioners of natural philosophy was multiplying fast all over Europe and soon Russia and the United States. Many were joining together to form learned societies and other science-oriented institutions (see Chapter 6).[87] Experimenters and artisans with whom they collaborated were designing more and more sophisticated instruments, including barometers, electrostatic generators, prisms, lenses, vacuum pumps, and air pumps, achieving greater and greater accuracy of measurement.[88]

Using an air pump, Robert Boyle recorded and published in 1660 the results of forty-three experiments, setting out in detail the properties of air[89] and conceptualizing his approach as the "mechanical philosophy." This conception departed radically from the medieval European (or traditional Chinese) organic interpretation of nature, for the "mechanical philosophers saw living beings as mechanical devices, the heart as the motor, the veins as canals, the bones as levers, the muscles as forces."[90] In 1676, the Danish astronomer Ole Rømer estimated the speed of light at 214,000 km/s, only twenty-nine percent below the correct velocity.[91] In 1672, two European scholars observed the parallax of Mars simultaneously in Paris and in Cayenne, making possible for the first time an accurate measurement of the distance of the Earth from the Sun.[92] In 1676–1678, Edmond Halley led a scientific expedition to the South Atlantic and set up an astronomical and meteorological observatory on the island of Saint Helena. Deploying all the latest astronomical instruments (including a twenty-five-foot refracting telescope, a sextant with telescopic sights, and an eyepiece micrometer), and applying Kepler's laws of planetary motion, Halley observed, described, and catalogued some three hundred stars in the southern hemisphere, a lunar eclipse, and the transit of Mercury across the Sun. All these data permitted comparisons with available northern hemisphere observations, some of which contributed significantly to subsequent scientific achievements, including Newton's *Principia*.[93]

Newtonian experimental method permitted a dramatic increase in scientific understanding. In the early 1700s, lecture courses in "experimental philosophy" and experimental displays in coffeehouses were all the rage in London (see Chapter 6).[94] A half-century later, Newtonian method enabled Benjamin Franklin, far across the Atlantic Ocean, to elucidate the nature of electricity, formulate the law of conservation of charge, and hypothesize that lightning is a form of electricity.[95] Applying Newton's methods of experimental physics to chemistry, Antoine-Laurent Lavoisier (1743–1794) demonstrated the role of oxygen in combustion, in rusting metal, and in animal respiration. He also articulated the law of conservation of mass.[96] Researchers discovered and isolated dozens of elements in localities around the world, from barium, chlorine, and manganese in Sweden (1774) to uranium and zirconium in Prussia (1789), to name only some.[97] In fact, European and American researchers, inventors, and scholars were making significant advances in science and technology every year or several times a year. This trend, moreover, was accelerating and has continued to accelerate ever since.

Why Europe?

Why did modern science develop first in Europe? Why, in other words, did Europeans first devise a rigorously scientific method of studying nature, involving a faith in the rationality of the universe, an inveterate optimism that its secrets can be unlocked and understood, an extravagant openness to new knowledge and ideas, careful observation, systematic classification of data, the application of mathematics to natural phenomena, the invention of sophisticated instruments of measurement, the formulation and testing of hypotheses, and the articulation of scientific laws?

One argument emphasizes a European obsession with the study of nature.[98] This attitude, it is argued, followed from the idea that God created a rational, lawful, stable universe inviting investigation. European natural philosophers from Oresme to Newton sought to discover regularity in the universe as evidence of God's majesty and to study the "book of nature" in order to know God's handiwork. It seems that already by the late 1500s in Europe, "the idea of a 'law' of (universal) nature as inviolable and ordained by God was … fairly commonplace among Protestant authors."[99] Likewise, the belief that God became incarnate as a human and "dwelt among us" suggested not only the intrinsic worth of the material world but also its authenticity.

Numerous other explanations have been advanced. One underscores the legal and juridical heritage of Europe. The ancient Greeks, it is noted, conceptualized objective, blind legality, and the Romans developed and codified a highly sophisticated system of law. Medieval European jurists recovered Roman law, which in turn influenced the development of natural philosophical methods.[100] Another scholar has argued that scientific advances require a rigorous separation of fact from value and moral life from physical reality, something Europeans managed to achieve during the medieval period, if not earlier, but which their major East Asian counterparts did not.[101] Alternatively, experimentation, tinkering, and other dabbling in the mechanical arts carried a social stigma in many human societies, even the most dynamic and creative ones. In medieval Europe, by contrast, craftsmen and intellectuals began gradually to appreciate and learn from each other, as noted in Chapter 3.

Europe's historical evolution may also have contributed to its scientific development. Just as Europe was geographically fortunate—close enough to the great civilizations to learn from them but far enough away not to fall prey to conquest—so Europe may have similarly been culturally well-off. Europe received its scientific heritage from the great Mesopotamian and Egyptian civilizations, but only through the intermediary of Greek and Roman culture. The Europe that emerged during the Middle Ages was an underdeveloped *tabula rasa* on which any number of cultural achievements from other societies could be inscribed without doing violence to an uninterrupted ancient tradition. The same was undoubtedly true of the Islamic world during its Golden Age, which probably explains its relatively uninhibited assimilation of ideas, concepts, institutions, stories, inventions, methods of inquiry, and other precious cultural and social goods. In the long run, the Islamic tradition seemed incompatible with such continued freewheeling importations, whereas they did not cease in Europe from the eleventh century until the present time. Moreover, algebra from the Islamic world and paper, the compass, printing, and gunpowder from China all had a revolutionary impact in Europe but not in their cultures of origin.

Why did they have a revolutionary impact in Europe? According to one interpretation, incompatible ideas and contradictions among the borrowings Europeans assimilated from every corner of the globe both propelled scientific, intellectual, and technological advancement and produced anxiety in thinkers who tried to reconcile all of them.[102] Aristotle's law of non-contradiction, for example, made it impossible to square Aristotle's teaching on the eternity of the universe and the Christian doctrine of divine creation *ex nihilo*. Nor could one harmonize Democritus's elegant atomic theory with the traditional Greek theory of the four elements. Likewise, the Pythagorean-Platonic vision of the world as informed by mathematics did not conform to Aristotle's numberless qualitative approach. In each of these instances, the Aristotelian teaching conformed to common sense experience and thinking. That is why the geocentric model proved irresistible and why the alternatives seemed ridiculous. Only extremely powerful abstract mathematical tools, like calculus, enabled Newton to demonstrate once and for all geocentrism's falsity. Each of the great early civilizations made potentially world-changing breakthroughs of abstract thinking: the sun-centered model of Greece, irrational numbers of China, and India's concept of zero. Yet each of them, taken in isolation, could be compartmentalized, ignored, or integrated into traditional worldviews. They could not challenge, much less drive the dismantling of, such worldviews. "Euclidean geometry had no numbers; premodern algebra had no dimensions"—only in combination could they yield powerful tools of scientific analysis.[103]

Because Aristotle's multitude of teachings in physics, biology, cosmology, botany, and other spheres of learning involved countless factual assertions, many of which ultimately proved false, his writings necessarily opened a rich field for empirical verification and intellectual challenge. Premodern Chinese and Indian natural philosophers, by contrast, formulated far fewer concrete assertions about the functioning and makeup of the natural world. Islamic scholars during the Golden Age verified and built upon Aristotelian and other Greek bodies of knowledge but rarely questioned them probingly and then gradually curtailed such investigations, apparently in part because of the challenges they posed to key elements of Islam. Many European authorities also wished to shut down such investigations, but the political fragmentation of the continent—and the invention of moveable type printing—made this all but impossible. Thus, to take only one example out of many, even after Galileo was placed under house arrest in Italy, he published in Holland the results of studies that continued to undermine the Aristotelian worldview.

Of course, Aristotelianism was only one of a wide variety of ancient, Hellenistic, and post-Hellenistic Greek doctrines and theories, including Platonism, Sophism, Neoplatonism, Stoicism, Epicureanism, Gnosticism, Euclidean geometry, and Archimedean statics and mathematics. All such systems of thought, moreover, had to be harmonized with such "maximally counterintuitive" Christian doctrines as the triune nature of God, transubstantiation (or the transformation of the bread and wine in the Eucharist into the body and blood of Jesus Christ), the virgin birth of Jesus, and the divinity of Jesus. Not surprisingly, the dedicated assimilation by European scholars of Aristotle's rules of logical thinking and exposition "caused great cognitive agonies for sensitive European intellectuals."[104]

Likewise, the geographical discovery of new lands, especially the Americas, undermined the credibility of even the most brilliant Greek geographers (as well as the authors of the Bible), who had had no idea such lands existed. New peoples and previously unknown plant and animal species also enhanced this tendency. The discovery of sunspots, new moons, and hitherto invisible stars simply increased the cognitive dissonance and threw further doubts on accepted theories and doctrines. No wonder many seventeenth-century natural philosophers were drawn to thoroughgoing skepticism and methodical doubt. Dengjian Jin notes that philosophical skepticism had been fairly common in premodern cultures. Yet the available tools and methods made it difficult to attain certainty of knowledge. Al-Ghazali's skepticism led him toward mysticism rather than seeking to build a new edifice of science upon perceived intellectual foundations of certainty and reason.[105] It was the obsessive desire of leading European thinkers to resolve profound contradictions in their culture that drove them to seek absolute certainty by means of mathematical analysis, controlled experimentation, powerful scientific instruments, and conceptual and mathematical tools.

Why did modern science not develop first in China?[106] After all, for centuries, Chinese artisans and natural philosophers achieved more advances in science and especially technology than any other premodern people. Culturally, historians have pointed to the Chinese attachment to traditional ways, disdain for innovation, capacity to integrate novel developments and breakthroughs into existing patterns, resistance to foreign ideas, strict separation of intellectual and mechanical arts, widespread disinterest in exploration, and a tendency to restore the cultural status quo after every major perturbation. Mark Elvin concluded that even the best early modern Chinese minds pursued techniques of divination, especially those developed in the nearly three-thousand-year-old *I-Ching* (*Book of Changes*), in order "to bring one's subconscious into a suitably responsive state."[107] This outlook, according to Elvin, made it possible to view any anomaly in nature as something intuitively comprehensible and therefore not requiring a new conceptual framework. Socially, nearly all ambitious Chinese devoted their youth to preparing for the civil service examinations and their adulthood to the civil service. Intellectually, the traditional Chinese organistic understanding of nature probably impeded a breakthrough to mechanistic conceptions—the first key advance of European natural philosophers. As the historian of Chinese science, Joseph Needham, articulated this idea, "The Taoist thinkers were groping for a universal Einsteinian world picture without having first laid the foundations for a Newtonian one."[108] Most other Chinese intellectuals shunned the study of nature and especially the pursuit of wide-ranging interpretations of natural phenomena, preferred the study of human society, resisted applying quantitative methods to natural phenomena, avoided formulating positive law, did not showcase debate in dialogic treatises, and organized scholarly disciplines holistically rather than as separate spheres of inquiry. Indeed, China produced no systematic philosophers like Aristotle who were interested in critically organizing available knowledge of humanity and nature.

Likewise, brilliant Chinese artists seem never to have collaborated with technical experts or to have acquired detailed technical knowledge, the way Leonardo da Vinci, Albrecht Dürer, and Michelangelo did. A tradition of striving to represent technological devices, or even to accurately depict ordinary objects, through a painstaking development of such tools of illustration as perspective, drafting standards, and drawing to scale never emerged in China. The artists who prepared illustrations for technical manuals generally did not understand the functioning of what they were drawing. The value of visual depictions was held above all to reside in showing the underlying unity of things rather than in illustrating concrete reality. This lack of interest in technical illustration stemmed in large part, according to an authoritative scholar, from the "complete absence of professionalization, not to speak of academization, of technical knowledge in traditional China."[109] The rigid bifurcation between theoretical science and applied technical expertise may help account for China's extraordinary technological advances and comparative paucity of theoretical achievements.

When Jesuit scholars introduced European mathematical scientific breakthroughs (but not the Copernican revolution) to China beginning around 1630, some Chinese thinkers integrated the new knowledge into Chinese interpretations, others tentatively broke new ground, and still others strived to prove that the European advances had ancient Chinese roots. Yet no transformation of Chinese intellectual life, much less of society, occurred.[110] Of course, Chinese society was complex, sophisticated, and extraordinarily successful. It was also highly populous, wealthy, and powerful throughout East Asia. Its influence on Europe was immense. Yet it developed slowly and steadily, its leaders striving to maintain political and cultural stability and to avoid the sort of radical change that rocked early modern Europe. Perhaps such changes in Europe were fostered in part by the Republic of Letters that brought together in continuous communication thousands of intellectuals, as discussed in the following chapter.

CHAPTER 6
THE REPUBLIC OF LETTERS

Joel Mokyr, a leading intellectual historian and interpreter of the rise of the West, has recently deemed the Republic of Letters the key factor in triggering "the generation and continuous improvement of new 'useful knowledge,' both scientific and technological," which he considers the main engine of economic history.[1] Mokyr defines the European Republic of Letters as a "transnational network of individuals connected by letters, books, and pamphlets" and as "a competitive market for ideas."[2] In this virtual commonwealth, "National boundaries and lineage mattered but little; observations, experiments, and formal (often mathematical) logic ruled supreme."[3] Its elite, intellectual citizens cooperated in the pursuit of truth and the common good but also competed for honors, esteem, patronage, research funding, and high reputation. With thousands of brilliant minds coming together, they advanced our understanding of nature, founded institutions for sharing knowledge, joined forces to impose limits on rulers, supercharged commercial development, brought learning and information to ever-wider population circles, gave birth to a public sphere, and inspired millions to explore the life of the mind. In other words, the Republic of Letters began with intellectual elites and gradually encompassed a broadening sphere of educated people.

Intellectuals

Correspondence

The first denizens of the Republic of Letters were Renaissance humanists of deep and extensive learning, like Pico della Mirandola. At twenty-three, in 1486, he challenged any scholar in Europe to debate him on 900 propositions concerning religion, philosophy, nature, and magic.[4] Inhabitants of the Republic studied Greek, often Hebrew, and sometimes Arabic, along with all branches of humanistic and naturalistic learning. They flocked to such intellectual centers as Louvain, Strasbourg, and Basel; Leiden and Prague; and Amsterdam and London.[5] The Republic of Letters was highly cosmopolitan, its members scattered across the Continent, including in such peripheral areas as Croatia, Transylvania, and Bohemia.[6] Members were skeptical and critically minded but highly trustful of members of good reputation from any corner of Europe and eventually the world. They also believed that "ideology, religion, political philosophy, scientific strategy, or any other intellectual or philosophical framework were not as important as their own identity as a community."[7]

Among the citizens of the Republic were many women. In fact, already in the 1680s a leading French dictionary included the word *académicienne*.[8] Royal and aristocratic women sponsored scholarship, research, and art, serving "as intellectual powerbrokers at a time when natural knowledge was organized through highly personalized patronage systems."[9] Others worked in private research laboratories alongside their husbands or sons. Some, like Mary Sidney Herbert, Countess of Pembroke (1561–1621), built personal laboratories in their own homes and hired tradesmen as assistants.[10] Still others organized and took part in naturalist expeditions.[11] Some women scholars were famous, such as Émilie du Châtelet who translated *Newton's Principia* (1745–1749) and Laura Bassi, the first woman in the world to win a university chair in a scientific field of studies (in physics at the University of Bologna in 1776).[12] Finally, "women novelists during the second half of the eighteenth century enjoyed an unprecedented degree of literary and financial success," according to James Melton. It helped the success of intellectual women that intellectual men in early modern Europe often idealized companionate marriage.[13]

At first, interconnected diplomats, merchants, and missionaries fostered a "truly global network of epistolary exchange."[14] To take just one example, the Italian Jesuit Matteo Ricci mastered Classical Chinese and sent back to Europe detailed observations about Chinese culture and society from 1580 to 1609.[15] The gradual development of both private courier and state-sponsored mail services also promoted the emergence of correspondence networks. By the early 1600s, mail circulated among all the towns of the Dutch Republic. A century and a half later, all larger English towns had daily mail delivery to and from London.[16] Thanks to such conveniences, leading intellectuals often wrote tens of thousands of letters. Yet not only intellectuals: the Republic was far broader. Some 12,000 letters from the pen of George Washington are extant.[17] In fact, people of nearly every social station in Europe, even the illiterate who had others write or read letters for them, were using correspondence for both personal reasons and professionally.[18]

Scholars and intellectuals wrote to each other in Latin until the 1600s, thereafter usually in French,[19] and had high standards of politeness. Erasmus

(1466–1536), who seems to have written dozens of letters daily,[20] compiled hundreds of ways to express the sentiment "as long as I live, I shall remember you."[21] Letters of introduction from a leading scholar would open many doors. Polite requests were usually requited. "Excuse me, Monsieur, the liberty I am taking," wrote one scholar in 1721, "but I am availing myself of the privileges accorded in the Republic of Letters, which authorize one to seek out the help one needs."[22] Such ideals of intellectual solidarity within the Republic of Letters were upheld very broadly among scholars, writers, thinkers, and other educated elites.[23]

Members of the wider Republic of Letters also created smaller networks of like-minded intellectuals, such as what one scholar has called a Republic of Arabic Letters. It coalesced in the later 1600s among scholars and collectors who enthusiastically studied Arabic, Persian, and Turkish, and sought out manuscripts in these languages from repositories in both Europe and the Middle East. Such intellectuals translated and published many such works for European readers. Some aimed to polemicize with and discredit Islamic culture, but others found much to admire, giving "Islamic historical, religious, and literary achievements due attention without needing to relate them to the study of Christianity."[24] From around 1750, the enthusiasm began to diminish as such intellectuals as Voltaire and Montesquieu tended to perceive Islamic culture as backward. Yet this negative turn emerged only after vast stores of information, ideas, insights, and motifs had been assimilated by European intellectuals. Just to take one example, Daniel Defoe's iconic story of a shipwrecked *Robinson Crusoe* (1719) apparently derived inspiration from the medieval Iberian Muslim polymath Ibn Tufayl.[25]

It seems to have been a natural impulse of many early modern European intellectuals to seek knowledge not only in libraries, "places where authorities were revered, not criticized," according to Francis Bacon (1561–1626), but in travel, direct experience of nature, and laboratories.[26] Thus, as noted in Chapter 2, Isaac Newton urged a younger colleague in 1669 to travel with an eye to carefully studying every detail of foreign countries. Indeed, large numbers of early modern students, political refugees, pilgrims, professionals, soldiers, clerics, mendicants, and craftsmen, as well as wealthy young men (and some young women) on the "grand European tour," ventured far beyond their hometowns, entering into contact with each other and with the wider European world.[27] Such encounters undoubtedly broadened their intellectual horizons, fostered synergies of innovative thinking, and led to advancements of all kinds.

Learned societies

Institutionally, much scholarly and natural philosophical investigation began to move away from universities already in the Renaissance era toward princely and royal courts.[28] Aristocrats and royals—including many women, such as Margaret Cavendish, Duchess of Newcastle (1623–1673); Christina of Sweden (1626–1689); and Sophia Charlotte of Hanover (1668–1705)—eagerly promoted advancements in natural philosophy, mathematics, astrology, medicine, and letters.[29] Galileo, Copernicus, Tycho, Kepler, and Descartes spent part of their careers at princely and other courts.[30] Many rulers kept "cabinets of curiosities" and retinues of artisans and artists who interacted among themselves and with court scholars. Some supported the founding of learned societies.[31]

The crucial early modern European institution for formally assembling, critiquing, reconciling, and integrating steadily accumulating information and knowledge was the learned society. Here, intellectuals "staged formal discussions over everything from proper Latin usage to the upcoming reformation of the world."[32] The first such association was the Academy of the Mysteries of Nature, founded in Naples in 1560. Many others followed, including the Academia dei Lincei in Rome (1603), which published reports of its proceedings.[33] An embodiment of the interconnectedness in Europe of all branches of knowledge, learning, and even commercial endeavor was Sir Thomas Gresham (ca. 1519–1579), who founded the Royal Exchange in London in 1571, in imitation of the New Bourse at Antwerp. When he died, his will provided for the creation of seven professorships. By 1597, his mansion had been transformed into Gresham College.[34] In *New Atlantis* (1627), Francis Bacon advocated establishing institutes staffed by dozens of specialized researchers. In the 1640s, leading scholars, like Robert Boyle, were meeting regularly in an "invisible college." In 1660, a dozen of them gathered at Gresham College and founded the Royal Society of London.[35] Its members were expected to present inventions, experiments, or reports for consideration, registration, and occasionally general discussion. Registration was important, not only as a means to share the fruits of one's research and scholarship, but also to establish authorship and precedence, an invaluable marker for the status- and reputation-conscious members of the Republic of Letters.[36]

Similar scholarly institutions emerged in other major cities—in Paris in 1666 and in Berlin in 1700. By 1789, cities from Trondheim in Norway in the north to Naples in the south, and from Saint Petersburg in the east to Lisbon (and Philadelphia) in the west were home to some seventy chartered scientific societies, as well as dozens of smaller, unofficial associations for the study of subjects from architecture to zoology. In regular communication with one another by correspondence, members thought of them as "diverse colonies of the Republic of Letters."[37] Although more cutting-edge work was carried out under the auspices of learned societies and academies, in some cities, such as Bologna, Saint Petersburg, Göttingen, and Montpellier, the work of universities complemented them.[38] Together and separately they functioned as clearinghouses for knowledge about the natural and human worlds.

The webs of learning and knowledge gradually expanded to include the wider world. An interesting example is presented by Hermann Busschoff, a physician and Dutch Calvinist minister posted in Batavia (now Jakarta). For years, he had suffered from gout. Having found relief from a traditional Chinese remedy by means of moxibustion, or the burning of dried mugwort on the affected area, he described the procedure in great detail in a letter to his son. The latter in turn published a treatise on the subject in Dutch in 1674. Constantijn Huygens, Secretary to the Prince of Orange, read the treatise and described it in a letter, along with a copy of the treatise itself, to Henry Oldenburg, the secretary of the Royal Society. Oldenburg arranged for its translation and publication in English in 1676. Likewise, via another intermediary, the amateur microscopist Antoni van Leeuwenhoek was introduced to Oldenburg. After requesting further letters of recommendation, for example from Huygens, Oldenburg invited van Leeuwenhoek to send regular updates on his work. Among his most significant reports was an account of his observation of blood flowing through microscopic capillaries.[39] Thus, the networks of the Republic of Letters expanded through personal contacts, recommendations, the sharing of valuable knowledge, and demonstrations of practical and theoretical advances. Also important was the institution and practice of peer review, instituted by Oldenburg at the Royal Society, which soon spread throughout the Republic.

Many other means of sharing knowledge developed. Scholarly journals began to appear in 1665 with *Journal des sçavans* in Paris and *Philosophical Transactions of the Royal Society* in London, followed by many imitators across Europe.[40] Scholarly proceedings of learned societies were translated and gathered into compendia, such as the 13-volume *Collection Académique* (1755-1779).[41] Most learned societies maintained standing committees, such as the Committee of Papers of the Royal Society. Many also organized scholarly collaboration. Thus, the secretary of the Royal Society in 1721–1727, James Jurin, issued open invitations throughout Europe and the British North American colonies to work together on the standardized collection, analysis, and pooling of meteorological data.[42]

The critical mass of brilliant minds sharing and advancing knowledge dramatically accelerated the pace of development. To take but one example, a few decades' worth of controlled experiments permitted Josiah Wedgwood (1730–1795), in the ceramic industry, to match and surpass a "thousand years of trial and error experimentation" in China.[43] Learned amateurs in China studied and shared knowledge but formed few independent corporate bodies. Private academies developed in the Ming era for the purpose of philosophical contemplation and political discourse. By the late 1660s, however, government repression had all but overpowered the public voice of the academies. Under the Qianlong Emperor, in the late 1700s, scholars faced "extensive literary inquisitions and growing intellectual conformity as the empire's literati were awed into a submissive clienthood before their grand dynastic patron, the longest-ruling monarch in all of Chinese history."[44] The early 1800s witnessed an informal and subdued revival of literati networks and public-mindedness, which grew stronger throughout the century, but did not lead to a European-style public sphere.[45] The main impediment to its development in China seems to have been the absence of limits on executive power and the related weakness of society and independent social institutions. As one scholar has argued, "strong arbitrary powers and weak infrastructural ones ... tend to go together."[46] European societies exhibited dynamic information networks, social organization, and other infrastructural attributes among the best educated, but also a growing vibrancy throughout all social layers.

Ordinary people

Literacy

As discussed in Chapter 3, the printing revolution fueled a monumental increase in the output of books. The appetite for reading material surged, with a per capita (every man, woman, and child) consumption of books *each year* in the first half of the 1700s reaching seventeen in Great Britain and thirty-nine in the Netherlands.[47] People bought such big quantities of books in northwestern Europe not because they were significantly cheaper than, for example, in China; as noted in Chapter 3, they were not. Nor did printing technology dramatically improve from the 1480s until 1800 in Europe.[48] The main driving force seems to have been strong demand across socioeconomic levels, thanks to rising literacy.

Accurate early modern literacy statistics are notoriously difficult to come by, yet eyewitness evidence indicates that literacy was extremely high in the Netherlands. One Spanish visitor noted in 1549 that "almost everyone," even women, could read and write.[49] The typical marker historians have used to establish literacy rates more scientifically is the ability to sign one's name, typically on legal documents, including marriage registers. On this basis, it seems that the male literacy rates were highest in the world in the early 1600s in New England and the Netherlands at roughly sixty percent, followed by forty percent in England. The numbers for urban dwellers were even better. Progress continued to be made decade after decade. Women began to catch up in the 1700s across Western Europe, as well.[50] By 1800, roughly sixty-eight percent of the entire Dutch population could sign their name, as could fifty-three percent of the English, thirty-seven percent of the French, and thirty-five percent in the German lands.[51]

Since most people learned to read before they learned to write in the early modern era,[52] and since a higher percentage of women learned to read than to write,[53] the criterion of being able to sign one's name probably underestimates people's ability to read. Indeed, a unique data set for the Swedish diocese of Skanör establishes that ninety-one percent of males and ninety-three percent of females could read already in the 1740s, almost entirely without formal schooling.[54] By contrast, it has been estimated that only about six percent of northern Indian adult men, and many fewer women, could read or sign their names in 1800 (figures rising for the whole of India only to 9.8 and 0.6 percent, respectively, in 1901),[55] and that 30–45 percent of males and 2–10 percent of females, or 18–27.5 percent of the whole population, were literate in China in the mid- to late 1800s.[56] Likewise, in 1901 the literacy rate for Egypt was only seven percent. (By this point, the literacy rate in France was 83.5 percent and in the United States, 91 percent.)[57]

What can explain Europe's advance in this area? Some scholars have credited Christian reform movements, like the Brethren of the Common Life (founded in 1374 in the Netherlands), which strongly promoted learning, reading, and publishing religious texts as a means to deepen people's Christian faith.[58] Others have pointed to the expansion of practical education starting in roughly the same era. For example, an English statute of 1406 provided for both boys and girls to learn reading and writing in "petty schools." From the 1580s, such youngsters also learned arithmetic and elementary accounting.[59] Likewise, tuition-free secular municipal schools open to boys and girls multiplied rapidly across Europe after 1500.[60] Such schools often taught both letters and numbers. Previously, reading and counting had been seen as distinct subjects of study, largely because doing sums had involved manipulating objects. From the 1500s, Hindu, or Arabic, numerals gained currency throughout Europe, beginning in Italy in the Renaissance era at the growing number of business schools.[61] Arabic numerals were not adopted right away in England, according to one scholar, "in part because interpreting and calculating with them required the same skills as interpreting and reproducing alphabetic symbols—that is, a form of literacy."[62]

Not surprisingly, the first European region to experience a numeracy breakout was the Netherlands, where by 1600 Flemish and Dutch women "were able to count and reckon just as well as men."[63] Drawing on extensive data sets from 130 localities in 16 European countries, one recent study shows that Western Europe had already begun to break away from Eastern Europe, reaching numeracy rates of seventy percent or higher in the Netherlands, Britain, northern Italy, and probably even France by 1600.[64] Thanks to practical learning, often on the job, even in places of relatively low literacy, such as the Austrian Netherlands, where less than forty-eight percent of Antwerp witnesses could sign their name in court, eighty-four percent of people were numerate in 1750. In fact, from northern Italy to Norway and from the German lands to England, numeracy rates ranged from eighty-six to ninety-six percent in that year.[65] In other words, what scholars call "human capital" was abundant, doubtless more abundant than anywhere else in the world, excepting Colonial North America.[66] Scanty historical records from other regions of the world make it next to impossible to undertake comparative analysis. Nevertheless, a clever examination of court records from the Cape Colony indicates that ninety percent of European defendants demonstrated numeracy in the century from 1650 to 1750, while only twenty-five percent of Southeast Asians, thirty percent of Indians, and fifty-three percent of Chinese did.[67] Of course, the small and probably unrepresentative samples from these four regions undermines the value of such a comparison. Still it seems likely, given other evidence of the weak development of human capital in those non-European areas, for example comparatively low book production, that these statistics are faithfully indicative of broad historical trends.

Newspapers

Given the relatively high literacy rates in early modern Europe, it is not surprising that periodical publications first emerged there. Beginning with irregular news reports in the 1500s, newspapers developed from the early 1600s in the German lands, England, and Holland as a medium that gradually placed the European reader's "own society within the context of the Continent and the world."[68] Amsterdam was the world's earliest major center of news reporting with more than 140 different newspapers drawing on a host of special correspondents sending reports from around the world in 1626.[69] By the 1630s, regular news bulletins were appearing in more than twenty German towns in a semi-official form with strong censorship.[70] News was nevertheless a business in which many entrepreneurs made a good living. The medium quickly spread to France with similar government controls and commercial drive. In this way, information about the wider world became systematically available to European readers.

The strife of the English Civil War, beginning in 1640, virtually put an end to censorship for two decades, resulting in the freest and most tumultuous expression of political views in history. Suddenly, domestic events held greater fascination for most English readers that anything going on in the outside world.[71] Pamphlets fostered "provocative and imaginative engagements with the world of news, politics, ideas, and words." The number of titles soared from some five hundred in 1639 to four thousand in 1641.[72] The traditional and highly formulaic practice of humbly petitioning Parliament about perceived injustices was also transformed radically by the Civil War. In 1640, petitions, many with thousands or even tens of thousands of signatures, began to appear as pamphlets or, from 1641, were reported on in newspapers. Printers made a good living, as opposing political factions responded to each other's petitions in print and thereby "'invented' public opinion in politics in a distinctively modern form."[73] The Restoration of the Stuart monarchy in 1660 led to the reimposition of censorship controls, yet news reporting continued to develop all across the Continent. By the late 1600s, in England and the Dutch Republic the only press restrictions stemmed from laws on "sedition, libel, and blasphemy."[74]

A political public sphere came into its own in the early 1700s in England, when the massive costs of the war of Spanish succession (1701–1714) obliged the crown to summon Parliament annually, driving "incessant electioneering." In this "overheated political climate," the two main political parties competed for allegiance by means of the periodical press. Such frequent political campaigns, according to an authoritative scholar, "generated a regular and sustained flow of political information between rulers and ruled," resulting in "a measure of public exposure and transparency" entirely modern, yet for the time being unavailable in the major Continental countries.[75]

Indeed, in the mid-1700s London boasted six weeklies, six thrice weeklies, six dailies, and a few decades later fourteen morning papers. The press also developed steadily in France, but more slowly: the first French daily newspaper was founded in 1777.[76] Toward the end of the 1700s, journalism had become a viable career and "newspapers found a strong editorial voice" in the major Western European countries.[77]

One of the most important forms of information available in the European periodical press was commercial. In commerce, the more accurate, reliable, and consistent information one possesses, the more successful one's investments and operations are likely to be. The range and accuracy of such information available to the business interests of Holland and Great Britain in this era, along with much greater access to capital, effected what scholars have called a financial revolution.[78] Already in the 1580s, the city brokers of Amsterdam began to publish commodity price lists on a weekly basis, and in the same century all English customs records entered the public domain.[79] Such developments made it difficult for financiers and entrepreneurs in the rest of Europe—and next to impossible for those elsewhere—to compete with the major banks and trading companies of Amsterdam and London.

Also important for the emergence of a modern outlook were knowledge and data about the natural world, which poured into Amsterdam in the 1600s and into London in the 1700s. European explorers, missionaries, merchants, naturalists, ship captains, private "intelligencers," commercial representatives, and others sent observations, organic specimens, natural medicines, minerals, curiosities, and kindred novelties to the major European centers of natural philosophy, where they were catalogued, examined, discussed, and studied to the benefit of what eventually would be called science.[80] Such knowledge, made widely available thanks to the periodical press, gained material value, became "commodified," and therefore spread more rapidly.[81]

Newspapers, as a private, commercial, independent, and wide-ranging medium, developed only quite slowly outside Europe. Officially controlled newspapers first emerged in the British North American colonies in the early 1700s; by mid-century they had gained significant independence. Latin American countries exhibited the same pattern, but with a 50-year lag. Only in the later 1800s did newspaper industries emerge elsewhere.[82]

The Republic of Letters

In China, official bulletins had been produced for hundreds of years, but only reached a narrow segment of scholar-officials. The Beijing *Gazette* circulated more broadly beginning in 1638, but the range of news it provided was narrow. Commodity price information was available in both China and Japan, but "one had to gather it with great labor."[83] Permitting the free circulation of financial and commercial information would doubtless have stimulated economic development and empowered entrepreneurs. It might have also undermined the ability of traditional authorities to collect taxes and maintain order locally—a likely reason for the Ottoman sultans' prohibition of press freedom for over three centuries, as noted in Chapter 3.

Both China and the Ottoman Empire had a long-standing tradition of petitioning the ruler to seek redress for perceived injustices. Petitions tended to be formulaic, like English petitions to Parliament, with vehement expressions of humility. The Ottoman Imperial Council typically responded to the petitioner by ordering local authorities to look into the issue and "to deal with the matter according to the sharīʿa."[84] In Ming China, the highest scholar-officials occasionally "petitioned the palace" in collective actions in order "to dispute right and wrong with the emperor," sometimes at risk to life and limb.[85] Such practices, in both societies, show that neither was entirely despotic. Yet in the absence of a free press, political petitioning remained private and therefore did not contribute to the immergence of a public sphere, did not help shape and mobilize a broader public opinion, did not awaken a shared public understanding of social, political, and economic issues, and thus did not help nudge those societies toward modern life.

Coffeehouses, libraries, and salons

This disparity is even more apparent with that public venue par excellence, the coffee shop. The first known coffee shops appeared in Mecca and Cairo in the 1510s.[86] By the reign of Selim II (1566–1574), Istanbul—the world's coffee capital for at least a century—boasted some six hundred coffeehouses.[87] One could find them throughout the Middle East, often with beautiful gardens. In the Ottoman Empire, men (though not women) of all social stations frequented coffee shops to relax, listen to poetry and music, play games, watch performances, share gossip and news, participate in the illicit pleasures of sexuality and drugs, and occasionally engage in subversive and political communication, typically in the form of satire.[88] The coffee-drinking public managed to resist repeated official efforts to shut down the emporia, revealing "that joint resistances of consumers and coffeehouse owners were effective," thanks in large part to a pro-coffee Sufist discourse.[89] The result was the "diffusion of leisure consumption,"[90] the beginning of sociability in the Ottoman Empire, and a "public culture of fun,"[91] but not a public sphere.

The contrast with European coffeehouses was stark. Here one found leisure, entertainment, literary exchange, and some artistic performances, but rarely drugs, sex, or other frivolity. On the contrary, European coffeehouses were usually serious places of business, intellectual pursuits, and scientific exchange, as well as clearinghouses of information essential to all such endeavors.

The first coffeehouse in Europe opened in Venice in 1645. Five years later, one opened in Oxford.[92] Within a few decades, the major cities of Europe were home to dozens and then hundreds of such emporia. As in the Ottoman Empire, there were official efforts to prohibit coffee shops, which failed thanks to strong popular resistance. Nor, for the most part, did women (aside from employees) feel welcome.[93] Coffee was often marketed with Turkish images.[94] Beyond that, the similarity to Middle Eastern practice was limited.

By 1708, there were five or six hundred coffeehouses in central London alone. A French Huguenot visitor wrote in 1699 that coffeehouses in London served as a place where "all Comers intermix together, with mutual freedom."[95] Specific topics of conversation—such as politics, painting, the new philosophy of nature—often became associated with particular tables within the shops.[96] Some clienteles went to specific shops: members of the Royal Society to the Grecian Coffee-House; entrepreneurs to Garraway's, Jonathan's, and Lloyd's in or near Exchange Alley; writers and actors to Button's, the Bedford, and Slaughter's in Covent Garden; or politicians to the St James's and White's in St James's, to mention some.[97] At various London coffeehouses, patrons founded political clubs, a fire insurance company, the London Stock Exchange, and the Royal Society of London for Improving Natural Knowledge.[98] One scholar has catalogued a set of twelve unwritten rules he believes the English patrons followed, including that "debate should be rational, critical, skeptical, polite, calm, and reasoned ... gossip and chit-chat ... and irrelevant or inconsequential topics are not tolerated."[99]

The Huguenot visitor mentioned above praised English coffeehouses as places where one could read "all foreign and domestic News."[100] (The same was also true in a few Viennese coffeehouses by the early 1700s.)[101] Beginning in 1735, many London coffeehouses served as libraries, sometimes even lending libraries, typically housing collections of pamphlets, newspapers, and other ephemera. Such collections, the biggest of which seem to have run to a couple thousand titles, were often numbered according to date of receipt. It was therefore possible for patrons, in some cases paying subscription fees, to request specific back issues at need. In this way texts that accumulated in London coffeehouses "acquired an archival quality: ordered, retrievable, and historical."[102]

As noted in Chapter 5, English coffeehouses hosted a growing number of public lectures popularizing the latest advances in experimental philosophy.[103] Beginning in 1704, James Hodgson, a mathematician and Fellow of the Royal Society, taught classes in natural philosophy and astronomy in various coffeehouses in London to "lay the best and surest Foundation for all useful knowledge." Deploying the latest scientific instruments and apparatuses, he aimed to demonstrate to the educated public the veracity of experiments conducted by Boyle and Newton.[104] Many other entrepreneurial popularizers followed with paid lectures in coffeehouses and even in taverns. Among them was Reeve Williams (fl. 1682–1703), an engraver and mathematics teacher, who ran a "school" at the Virginia Coffee-House. In this way, philosophical lecturers "rubbed shoulders with mariners and merchants," as a result of which "links between the popular science of the Newtonians and the mercantile community were far more extensive than has been generally assumed."[105]

Most Europeans until this time had read "intensively": that is, they read a few books—typically devotional literature—over and over. The transition to *extensive* reading unfolded most rapidly in England, where popular journals regularly featured book reviews beginning in the 1730s and 1740s.[106] In the second half of the 1700s, reading clubs, private subscription libraries, and commercial circulating libraries began to proliferate all across northern Europe with at least a few thousand operating in the major European countries.[107] Most subscription libraries avoided political controversy and exercised moral censorship, such as suppressing Lord Byron's popular but risqué long poem *Don Juan*.[108] In this cautious way, hundreds of libraries remained open for business, avoiding state interference, at least in England, and feeding the public appetite for books. Even professionals and tradesmen thirsted for self-improvement. For example, many late-eighteenth-century farmers' associations maintained libraries to disseminate useful information.[109] On the Continent, interest in radical books was greater and state control was tighter, but there, too, official watchfulness over libraries gradually eased during the following decades.[110]

Another important venue of the Republic of Letters was the salon, which emerged in Paris in the 1740s under the guidance of a number of remarkable women. The most famous was Madame Marie Geoffrin (1699–1777), who "invented the Enlightenment salon."[111] She did so by inviting a wide range of intellectuals, cultural figures, and professionals to her home for regular meals and conversation. On Mondays, she received artists and on Wednesdays, men of letters. She insisted on politeness, patience, decorum, egalitarianism, and the right of each interlocutor to complete his or her train of thought without interruption. Of course, her role required not only a forceful personality but also a lot of hard work. It was necessary for her to read relevant texts and plan out each gathering, like a "student or teacher preparing for class."[112] These *salonières* "regarded themselves as better arbiters of grace and style in writing than the men they supported and specifically favored language they thought more refined, delicate, and 'feminine.'"[113] In the late 1700s, salons gained prominence in the German lands, particularly in Vienna and Berlin, but they never played much of a role in England, where women enjoyed many more opportunities to participate in literary, intellectual, and other forms of public life.[114]

Voluntary associations

Voluntary associations began to emerge in France in the late 1700s for the discussion of literary, political, artistic, philosophical, or natural-philosophical topics.[115] Masonic lodges—social clubs often intended as rationalistic alternatives to church-attendance[116]—proliferated first in Britain (London boasted 184 in 1770).[117] As they diffused to continental Europe, they instilled British constitutional principles and ideals. The British passion for team sports also spread to the Continent (and later to the wider world) and also, it can be argued persuasively, contributed to the development of modern political and social institutions, because they fostered cooperative action among disparate people.[118]

Voluntary associations established schools, hospitals, and seminaries; combated slavery, cruelty to animals, and prostitution; and promoted Christianity, Bible-reading, temperance, self-help, and many other pursuits. They proliferated across Europe but perhaps most abundantly in the early American Republic.[119] Why? There were fewer grandees than in Europe (or other societies), so joining forces was often the only way to accomplish big projects.[120] (The early modern Gujarati elites, for example, wielded such great power that they felt "no need of forming a united front" to secure formal political rights and representation.)[121] Americans rose to that challenge by creating a society with the greatest grassroots social, political, and economic activism in history. This was a striking attribute of a modern society.

At the other end of the scale of social organization were the major non-Western countries. Şevket Pamuk holds the Ottoman Empire's leaders to have been "very flexible and pragmatic, willing and able to adapt, utilize talent, adopt new technology, and accept allegiance from many sources." At the same time, continuous central control by the bureaucracy over society and politics were such that "landowners, merchants, manufacturers, and moneychangers exerted little influence on economic matters and, more generally, on policies of the central government."[122] In fact, most wealthy people found they could earn more from tax farming than from trade, agriculture, or manufacturing. Thus, autonomous social organization was difficult to achieve and not very profitable, even for entrepreneurs. It was doubtless even less so for men and women of letters.

In a later study, Pamuk ascribed Europe's divergence from the other major Eurasian cultures to higher urbanization rates and labor costs after the demographic catastrophe of the mid-thirteenth-century Black Death. Labor scarcity, he notes, led to labor mobility, looser apprenticeship rules, laborsaving innovations, the relaxing of guild regulations, and moving industry into suburban districts where state control was weaker. High labor costs also drove maritime innovations and the development of firearms, making it possible to sail with smaller crews and fight with smaller units. Similar advances were made in many industries.[123] Greater concentrations of people in the most advanced European urban areas likewise promoted innovation, by creating critical masses of potential innovators. Looking at comparative urbanization rates reinforces this insight. The urbanization level in China hovered around four percent from the 1500s to 1890, while that of England and Wales jumped from three to sixty-two percent and that of Europe as a whole from six percent to thirty percent. In the same years, Japan's urbanization rose from three percent to sixteen percent, suggesting why it was able to develop so much more successfully than China beginning in the late 1800s.[124]

People in neither China nor the Ottoman Empire seemed able to mobilize social capital without state direction, except in exceptional circumstances. For example, Kaifeng merchants, Muslims, and gentry, responded to the disastrous flood of 1841 with advocacy and a vigorous rebuilding campaign. This activity led one scholar to conclude that "the ability of Kaifeng urban communities to act coherently in the face of disaster bespeaks potent organizational capacities awaiting only opportunity or necessity to become manifest."[125] Chinese civil society had, in other words, capacities, but not institutionalized actualities. Society only weakly distinguished itself from politics: "Both were subsumed under a common umbrella of Confucian cultural hegemony," in the words of R. Bin Wong.[126] Civic initiative in the Ottoman Empire was also weak. A recent study reveals that benevolent aid societies like the Ottoman Red Crescent Society, which emerged during the Second Constitutional Period (1908–1918), resulted only in the "'nationalization' and 'militarization' of philanthropic activity."[127] The contrast with robust European civic activism could not have been plainer.

Synergies of practical and theoretical knowledge

People of different walks of life, professions, trades, expertise, and experiences coming together and sharing knowledge are hallmarks of modern life. Such exchanges came to England before other lands.

Robert Hooke personifies such professional synergy. A maker of scientific instruments, a civil engineer, an urban planner, and an architect, he also served as curator of experiments of the Royal Society in the late 1600s. "Often," according to Robert Iliffe, "he would work on his instruments or drafts of buildings in the morning, run from a meeting at the Guildhall to an inspection of one of various surveying and architectural projects, and then—if on Thursdays—to the Royal Society to end in coffee houses."[128]

Practical difficulties in everyday life drove artisans and scholars to seek and propose a wide variety of solutions. The inability to calculate longitude at sea, and therefore to determine a ship's position, was one such problem.[129] Already in 1598, King Philip III of Spain offered a monetary prize for solving the longitude puzzle. A century later, the French regent, Philip, Duke of Orleans, followed suit.[130] The first breakthroughs, however, were made in England. In 1706, James Hodgson, a mathematics instructor at the Royal School of Mathematics at Christ's Hospital in London, proposed that recording the interval between the flash and report of a cannon shot could help determine "the distance of Ships at Sea and Places at land," an important first step in calculating longitude.[131] In 1714, William Whiston, a theologian, mathematician, and popular lecturer on natural philosophy, helped found a Board of Longitude to offer monetary prizes for contributions to determining longitude at sea. John Harrison (1693-1776), a carpenter-turned-clockmaker with no formal education, devised a number of marine chronometers, contributed massively to solving the problem of calculating longitude, and pocketed more prize money than any other entrant.[132]

Individual scholar-entrepreneurs undertook to compile information about the widest variety of natural and cultural phenomena. One can mention the systematic geological survey of England, Wales, and part of Scotland carried out by William Smith (1769–1839), which one writer has called "the map that changed the world."[133] Even more spectacular was the *Encyclopédie* of Denis Diderot, which came out between 1751 and 1772 in 35 volumes with 71,818 articles—all alphabetized—and 3,129 illustrations. No work as comprehensive and widely available (it circulated in thousands of copies) had ever appeared anywhere in the world.[134] Among the masses of information presented were detailed expositions of Chinese "techniques of handcraft manufacturing" and "engineering feats in irrigation, fortification, and bridgebuilding."[135] Although many European intellectuals had gradually come to view China as falling behind Europe, there remained a widespread admiration for Chinese achievements.

The era's extraordinary profusion of information drove intellectuals and practitioners to learn from one another in more and more organized ways. Benjamin Franklin formed one of the world's first formal cross-discipline discussion groups in 1727 in Philadelphia.[136] More famous, and important, was Birmingham's Lunar Society, which brought together prominent scientists, businessmen, and intellectuals beginning in the 1770s. Among those who attended were Erasmus Darwin, a leading naturalist; Joseph Priestley, a theologian who first isolated oxygen; James Watt, who designed the first mechanically efficient and economically viable coal-fired steam engine; and Matthew Boulton, Watt's business partner.[137] Most members of the Lunar Society were also elected fellows of the Royal Society.[138] Since few fellows wished to appear involved with "private trade and profit," the Society of Arts was founded in 1754 to promote commercial success "in all arts, trades, and manufactures."[139] Many other similar associations appeared across Europe and early America.

It seems that barriers separating educated elites and craftsmen were narrower in England, the Low Countries, and early America than anywhere else in the world or at any previous time. Robert Boyle, one of the greatest early scientists, expected to gain valuable insights from around the world, including from ordinary people, such as "Midwives, Barbers, Old Women."[140] It was in northwestern Europe, according to Deirdre McCloskey, that commerce, finance, entrepreneurship, and in general profitable innovation began to be viewed in a more favorable light than ever before.[141] The landed aristocrats, intellectuals, great magnates, priests, and other elites, who since time immemorial had dominated human societies, had always looked down upon such activities and stifled them through both contempt and detailed rules and regulations. Once entrepreneurship began to enjoy wide social esteem, she argues, the creative abilities of vast numbers of people throughout society were unleashed.

Europeans of all walks of life applied rationalism, skepticism, constructive criticism, systematic thinking, and methodical problem solving to challenge tradition, authority, prejudice, intolerance, and custom. Feeling a great sense of urgency to seek "improvement" through the application of natural philosophy to practical endeavors,[142] they developed such powerful new concepts and ideals as the political separation of powers, the economic division of labor, human rights, the emancipation of women, limited government, and making punishment fit the crime, to name only a few. It has been argued that Adam Smith may have formulated his concept of the economic division of labor under the influence of medieval Persian Muslim scholars.[143] Given the openness of European thinkers to ideas from around the world, it seems likely that other social, economic, political, and technological advances of Europe's eighteenth century owed much to non-European antecedents. This was the apotheosis of the Enlightenment and of the Republic of Letters: intensively borrowing and sharing ideas, best practices, and methods of improvement.

Nothing like it emerged in China or any other non-Western society of the age. This is perhaps especially astonishing of China where artisans—and to a much lesser extent scholar-officials—had assembled a wide variety of technical knowledge in numberless treatises as early as the eleventh century, many with abundant images and diagrams beginning in the fourteenth century—thus, far earlier than in Europe. The Dutch scholar Karel Davids advances a detailed explanation for why this pursuit of "useful knowledge" did not lead to an era of "enlightenment."[144]

First, the centralization of knowledge production probably restricted its diffusion. Major Chinese technical works typically appeared in very limited, officially sanctioned print runs. The *Tiangong kaiwu* (1637), which Joseph Needham called "China's greatest technological classic," was apparently "preserved over a relatively short period of approximately forty years and then totally disappeared until the nineteenth century."[145] Already in the 1400s, by contrast, Europe experienced "a veritable explosion of technical treatises."[146] Second, the mobility of people was far less extensive in China

The Republic of Letters

than in Europe.[147] After 1350, apprentice craftsmen in Europe had to take part in tramping (*Wanderschaft*). Frequent travel among interconnected European monastic communities fostered the diffusion of technical knowledge. Military campaigns and the circulation of mercenary soldiers, as well as pilgrimages, were far more frequent than in China. Business competition drove entrepreneurs to seek out trade secrets across Europe, while patent laws introduced by many states from the 1400s attracted migrants with skills and drive.[148] Finally, travel guides flourished from the mid-seventeenth century in Europe with the express purpose of recommending the proper methods for "observing technological practices and artefacts," a genre with no equal in China.[149]

Third, Chinese scholars devoted far more effort to preparing and preserving technical works on agriculture than on the mechanical arts. There was nothing like the "machine-books" tradition, which reached a climax in the Dutch Republic in the 1730s—for example, two volumes written by millwrights on every type of windmill. Fourth, specialized journals in natural philosophy began to appear in Europe, such as *Chemisches Journal für die Freunde der Naturlehre, Arzneygelehrheit, Haushaltungskunst, und Manufakturen* (Chemical Journal for the Friends of Natural Science, Pharmacology, Domestic Art, and Manufactories) in 1780. Fifth, Chinese libraries rarely opened their doors to the public or even to scholars. Likewise, private Chinese individuals, as noted Chapter 3, usually refused to lend books, whereas most Europeans scholars felt morally obligated to do so. In general, according to Joseph McDermott, "The concept of a 'community of learners' described more an ideal than the reality of the world of learning in China between 1000 and 1700."[150]

The extraordinary vibrancy of European information networks and collaborative associations exceeded that of any other region beginning in the Renaissance, a trend that continued century by century. Europe, in this regard, was already strikingly modern. Similar developments in many other spheres of life—including the arts, war-making, the status of women, the use of laborsaving technology, and a steadily rising standard of living—contributed to this overall trend, as discussed in the following chapter.

CHAPTER 7
BREAKING WITH TRADITION

Modern societies and cultures break with tradition. They set out on new pathways. They seek efficiency. Such approaches foster competition, unleash human creativity, and increase output. Novelty and efficiency can transform any sphere of human endeavor. Holding to established ways and means does not need to be explained. It is how humans have always existed. Breaking away, trying new things, glorifying a culture of improvement is new under the sun and is the key hallmark of modernity. The results may be a matter of taste like oscillating trends in art, frightful like advances in military technology, or almost universally praised like rising female equality and unburdening ourselves of drudgery thanks to machines. In all these areas, a bold embrace of innovation has transformed life and made the world modern.

Inspired transformations

Our early ancestors soared artistically. At least 66,700 years ago, Neanderthals traced hand stencils on cave walls in northern Spain.[1] Homo sapiens depicted animals in caves on the Indonesian island of Sulawesi 35,400 years ago[2] and, with stunning realism, near the southern French town of Chauvet 2,500 years after that. At Chauvet, the German film director Warner Herzog saw "the modern human soul emerging vigorously, almost in an explosive event."[3] For the next 20,000 years, cave painters kept up this artistic tradition in northern Spain and southern France with few changes in style or subject matter. Such an adherence to established patterns is in evidence in the creative arts of most world cultures. An obvious example is Chinese landscape painting, which upheld a set of philosophical principles for hundreds of years and, one may argue, even to this day.[4] In Chinese civilization, "the defining criteria for value were inescapably governed by past models, not by present experience or by future ideal states of existence," according to an authoritative scholar.[5]

By contrast, Europe experienced a dramatic breakout from established artistic conventions in the early 1100s. This burst of creativity was inspired in part by the Neoplatonic philosophic writings of Pseudo-Dionysius the Areopagite (fl. ca. 500) and John Scotus Eriugena (ca. 800–ca. 877), his main Carolingian interpreter. Pseudo-Dionysius conceived of perceptions of light as returning "us back to the oneness and deifying simplicity of the Father who gathers us in."[6] This vision resonated in the monastic world of Abbot Suger (1081–1151), the founder of the Gothic architecture movement.[7] For Suger, God intervenes in the world such that "the material conjoins with the immaterial, the corporeal with the spiritual, the human with the Divine."[8]

Animated by such thinking, Suger oversaw the restoration and reconstruction of the Royal Abbey of Saint-Denis, just north of Paris (narthex completed in 1140). Replacing its thick-walled, narrow-windowed Romanesque predecessor, the new edifice celebrated soaring height, radiant color, and gloriously flooding light. The towering stained-glass windows presented sophisticated theological interpretations in the form of biblical exegesis—for the first time transposed from texts to images. Precisely in these decades a growing, though still narrow, segment of the European urban population was learning to read and desiring "to participate more actively in the acquisition of elite spiritual knowledge." The exegetical stained-glass of Saint-Denis was designed specifically for this emergent urban lay elite as "an essentially new form of visual art that would become a fundamental part of artistic culture in the West for centuries."[9]

Architects across Europe adapted the style, with interiors of many churches rising to 140 or 150 feet, for example, at Beauvais, Metz, and Notre Dame of Paris. Outside of Western Christendom, only the basilica of Hagia Sophia in Constantinople, constructed in the 500s A.D., could rival them. In no other culture had architects and engineers erected such soaring, open spaces. Like modern builders competing to raise up the "world's tallest building," designers and patrons of the new style strived to construct towers and spires to almost unimaginable heights. Two English churches, Old St. Paul's, London, and Lincoln Cathedral, both completed circa 1310, edged past the world's tallest structure, the Great Pyramid of Giza.[10] One can sense an almost "modern," forward-looking attitude in the "enthusiasm for the innovatory aspects" that Gervase of Canterbury (ca. 1141–ca. 1210) expressed in regard to the rebuilding of Christ Church, Canterbury.[11]

A dramatic break in painting was also under way, thanks to Giotto di Bondone (ca. 1267–1337), an artist recognized in his own lifetime for his charisma and creative originality.[12] Unlike the work of his predecessors, which appears flat, stilted, two-dimensional, and lacking in personality, Giotto's individualized figures recede in depth within a three-dimensional framework. They reveal distinctive personality traits, emotions, and purposes. He also painted ordinary people, like his *Girl Spinning Wool*, and people interacting with nature, as in his *Saint Francis Preaching to the Birds*.

Over the following centuries, European painters experimented continuously, and at an ever-accelerating rate, with innumerable genres, styles, techniques, symbols, media, and themes. Jan van Eyck (ca. 1390–1441) constantly experimented, "as one who took delight in alchemy."[13] Hitting upon a felicitous mixture of pigments and oils, he invented oil-based painting, which dramatically brightened his works and transformed European artistry. Filippo Brunelleschi (1377–1446), rejecting the medieval tendency to collapse and distort space, invented linear perspective, in which parallel lines converge toward a vanishing point, for this is how human vision functions.[14] As one scholar has argued, "Perspective was not only an artist's or architect's tool, it also was a way of examining and recording the natural world."[15] The result was ever-more accurate depictions of natural phenomena and built environments, a very modern conceptual development.

Seeking greater visual accuracy, many artists studied mathematics, anatomy, and nature. Leonardo and Michelangelo, who both flourished just after 1500, studied and personally conducted anatomical dissection—participating in a "culture of dissection"[16]—in order to more faithfully depict humans and other living creatures.[17] They also strived mightily with one another and other contemporaries for honor, reputation, prestige, and patronage.[18] Portraiture and self-portraiture took on great importance, as artists plumbed the depths of temperament, feeling, and character.[19] They also continued to experiment with symbols, allegory, and artistic skill. In *The Ambassadors* (1533), for example, Hans Holbein the Younger inserted an anamorphic depiction of a skull into the foreground of a double portrait of a nobleman and a senior cleric surrounded by a host of meticulously detailed objects, including globes, scientific apparatuses, musical instruments, and books. The skull can be perceived correctly only from one of two awkward angles. Why would a talented artist mar the beautiful ensemble with an unsightly smudge? The answer is probably the playfulness and showing off of an independently minded creative genius. It was a characteristic of European culture, as it is of the modern world, that gifted individuals felt freer to set out on roads not traveled in pursuit of bold visions.

Many other artistic movements succeeded one another, from the exuberance of the Baroque to the mystical in Romanticism. Within these broad movements, dozens of prodigies expressed an extraordinary range of artistic visions. A canon developed, but one that strived to break free of tradition, convention, established styles and techniques, and, in a word, sought uniqueness of self-expression. Moreover, each movement had counterparts in other realms of artistic endeavor.

The emergence of polyphonic music is an interesting case.[20] By the early 1200s, Pérotin, choirmaster at the Cathedral of Notre Dame in Paris, was composing sacred music for three and four distinct voices whose melodic lines were woven together like a rich tapestry. Often two secular songs in the vernacular were superimposed upon a sacred Latin text and melodic line, typically from Gregorian chant. In compositions of the next century, two or more of the voices would express opposing or contrasting thoughts.[21] This approach stemmed from the medieval European tendency to grasp disparate elements of reality into one whole. Guillaume de Machaut's four-part *Mass of Our Lady* (before 1365) is a notable example.

Meanwhile, musical notation grew more standardized, precise, and expressive.[22] Its development was a collaborative venture of many scholars and intellectuals over the course of centuries.[23] For example, innovations in rhythmic notation were carefully described in treatises by the mathematician and astronomer Jehan des Murs in the first half of the thirteenth century.[24] As scholars and practitioners gradually refined the methods of notation, they paved the way toward more and more intricate compositions. This was an extraordinary conceptual leap—a new technology, really—that was unique in world history. No other culture had developed such comprehensive means for transcribing musical performance.

Over the next few centuries, European composers added still more voices and then contrived new forms, including the sonata, concerto, and symphony, calling for complex instrumentation. The culmination of this trajectory probably occurred in 1844 when Hector Berlioz and an assistant, along with five choir directors, conducted a "mega-concert" in Paris with over 1,000 performers.[25] The entire Western musical tradition seemed to be moving toward a crescendo.

The Islamist, Bernard Lewis, interprets polyphonic music as an important achievement of Western culture, one that suggests a distinctive departure from traditional forms. In such compositions, he writes, "Different such performers play together, from different scores, producing a result that is greater than the sum of its parts."[26] Lewis believes this collaborative action was related to democratic politics and team sports, both of which involved the cooperation of individuals according to specific rules and competition within distinct structures. Polyphony also requires synchronization—as do so many other modern endeavors, such as scientific research. These features were central to Western development but did not easily take root in other cultures. This result, it seems, enabled early modern Europeans to "act far more effectively, as members of a group" than could other peoples of the world, in the words, quoted in Chapter 4, of the Islamist Marshall Hodgson.

War and military technology

An area where Europeans learned to pool their social power with ultimately devastating results for the rest of the world was warfare. It is hard to argue with the fact that military might helped European explorers and merchants fight their way to dominance in the Indian Ocean, to conquer the Americas, and to establish colonies along the coasts of Africa and Asia starting five hundred years ago. It seems obvious that European fighting capacity emerged gradually, as one of many parallel political, economic, social, and cultural developments.

Chinese Daoist alchemists invented gunpowder in the mid-800s and went on to devise fireworks and firearms. Yet, after the recipe diffused across Eurasia in the early 1200s, apparently thanks to the secure trade routes established across the Mongol Empire (1206–1368), it was European artisans who built more and more powerful, accurate, mobile, and inexpensive cannon.[27] In the Middle Ages, castle defenders could usually hold out against besiegers.[28] In the 1400s, however, an "artillery revolution" enabled the richest states, in particular France and Spain, to dominate European battlefields. Yet in the early 1500s, Italian engineers and architects discovered relatively inexpensive methods for building effective defensive fortifications able to withstand prolonged artillery sieges.[29] By the 1570s, even smaller states, with fewer resources, could hold their own against powerful armies. For example, the Dutch Republic "raised more resources per capita than any other seventeenth-century state and organized these resources into large permanent armed forces of high quality."[30] Also important, the Dutch Republic had access to cheaper credit, thanks to sophisticated financial institutions, which also tended to level the playing field with larger states.[31]

Likewise, competition drove military specialization, systematic training, the application of science and mathematics to military affairs, the standardization of weaponry, continuous experimentation, and the proliferation of war-relevant treatises. In the early 1600s, under Maurice of Nassau, Prince of Orange, soldiers learned to function with their fellows in unison and at command.[32] Such training tapped into a subconscious source of sociability, rendering the soldiers utterly dedicated to comrades and officers, irrespective of social origin. European governments found they could conscript destitute men and drill them into excellent soldiers.[33] In the late 1600s, European gunsmiths developed flintlock muskets, which were safer and far more efficient than matchlocks, and equipped them with socket bayonets. This simple device enabled marksmen to defend themselves in the face of a charging enemy.[34]

France, England, and Holland all funded large, well equipped navies. France's Royal Academy of Science was founded in 1666 in large part to promote naval progress through advances in cartography, chemistry, and engineering. By 1759, fourteen two-decker British ships carried seventy-four guns apiece, part of the biggest, most effective navy in the world. This ocean-going force contributed greatly to Britain's triumph in the Seven Years' War (1756–1763).[35] Following that conflict, Britain and China were the two greatest powers of the age—one outward reaching, the other inward focused. Whereas the Chinese Empire constituted a single realm, however, Britain was only one of a half-dozen dynamic and expansive European powers.

It is ironic and not a little surprising that gunpowder had such a powerful impact across most of Eurasia, but not in China, its birthplace—at least not until British gunboats fought their way up the Pearl and Yangzi Rivers in 1841–1842 in the First Opium War. It was doubly surprising in that warfare had been central to Chinese state-building. Firearms were incorporated into the Chinese army and navy from the fourteenth century, but, according to a leading expert, "without dramatically changing their fundamental structure or producing any noticeable effects outside the military sphere."[36] Why did gunpowder weaponry not result in a military revolution in China? One explanation emphasizes the Chinese devotion to the ideal of historical continuity. Another points to the Chinese rulers' fear of uncontrolled military power, which prompted them routinely to execute competent generals and to avoid building up large standing armies.[37] Instead, China's rulers preferred to "form expeditionary armies on an ad hoc basis when required."[38] Joel Mokyr argues further that the Chinese government had much less to lose from inhibiting military innovation than its European counterparts, where "there was a market for ideas."[39] Failing to compete, to foster and benefit from the development of ever-improving military techniques and technology was risky amid Europe's constant military competition.

Yet, as the economic historian Philip T. Hoffman argues, "competitive markets do not always stimulate innovation." India and Southeast Asia in the eighteenth century had both "markets and incessant warfare," but not significant military innovation.[40] Why? Hoffman proposes a "tournament" model involving frequent warfare, large military expenditures, emphasis on gunpowder technology, and constant innovation. As a result, the cost of pistols in England from the mid-1500s to the early 1700s plummeted by a factor of six.[41] Likewise, in the early 1600s muskets cost three to nine times less in England and France than in China relative to the price of food.[42]

None of the other major Eurasian powers innovated in military affairs at such an incessant rate as the Europeans and for all sorts of reasons. For example, China was too big to face constant military rivalry, the Japanese shogun established hegemony by the mid-1600s and thus halted military innovation, few Indian states were able to mobilize significant resources for war, and the nomadic foes of both the Ottoman and Russian Empires drove them to invest heavily in an antiquated military branch, the cavalry. The rulers of Mughal India imported European firearm technology, and some cultivated further innovation, though only fitfully and intermittently in the early modern era.[43] By contrast, many European rulers encouraged or at least did not discourage private entrepreneurship in warfare, exploration, conquest, and overseas trade. For example, private entrepreneurs were essential to the exceptionally efficient operations of the Dutch naval shipyards, given their "veritable obsession with calculating, comparing, and orderly management."[44] By contrast, the Chinese and Japanese monarchs hindered or even prohibited many such activities.

Another important factor driving increased military power in Europe was rising wages. According to Şevket Pamuk, as mentioned in Chapter 6, high labor costs in Europe after the Black Death contributed to maritime innovations, including bigger ships that could sail with smaller crews, and the steady development of firearms, since "soldiers had become much more expensive and those with firearms could fight much more effectively than those without."[45] At the same time, the high incidence of warfare in Europe drove many people to seek shelter in urban centers. Since innovation tended to be fostered better in cities,[46] Europe's rising urbanization rate in the early modern era fueled greater economic growth,[47] which inevitably funded more military spending. But since labor costs were high, there was "a European bias in favor of capital over labor."[48] Thus, technological innovation was more likely in Europe than in China. It also seems probable that continuous warfare in Europe kept wages high by causing incessant population losses, which two scholars, ironically, call "gifts of Mars."[49]

A higher status for women

Many commentators have also assumed that "gifts of Venus" contributed to the rise of Europe and marked Western societies as reaching modernity earlier than others. Marx and Engels asserted in 1845 that "the degree of female emancipation is the natural measure of general emancipation."[50] Around the same time, Alexis de Tocqueville concluded that the United States embodied Europe's future and that "the chief cause of the extraordinary prosperity and growing power of this nation ... is due to the superiority of their women."[51] Tocqueville does not seem to have meant intellectual or other forms of personal superiority, but rather the higher status and greater influence of women as a whole in the United States. As shown in Chapter 6, women in Europe on the eve of the Great Divergence were more literate, more numerate, and—among elites—more active in the life of the mind and in public life than women in any other major culture. How did this come about?

First, it is important to note that women's experiences differed widely in early modern Europe, depending on their social class, geographic location, degree of urbanization, marital status, occupation, spouse's livelihood, health, number of offspring, political context, economic trends, and family connections, among many other factors.[52] Women's opportunities and position in society were rarely static. Some facets of life may have been improving, while others were deteriorating at any given time.

With these caveats in mind, one can turn to demographic and economic historians for insights into why the status, influence, and authority of European women increased in the early modern era. One line of inquiry concerns the ability of European couples to decide when and whom to marry, which was a feature of what scholars call the northwestern European marriage pattern, the key element of which was delaying both marriage and thus childrearing by several years compared to families in other parts of the world.[53] The ability to earn wages, even at an unequal rate compared to men, conferred on women an autonomy unusual in other cultures. For example, in Ming China only some 1–2 percent of the female population participated in the labor market, compared to 25–60 percent in northwestern Europe in the early 1500s[54]—and 72 percent in 1700.[55] Likewise, whereas fathers controlled all household income in early modern China, young men and women in Holland enjoyed astonishingly high levels of autonomy and could for all practical purposes live on their own at will. Moreover, whereas young couples tended to devote more energy to caring for parents in early modern

China, in the Low Countries a greater share of efforts went toward the raising of children, thus endowing the next generation with more social capital.[56] Among the most important elements of social capital imparted to children in northwestern Europe and especially the Low Countries was literacy and numeracy, as discussed in Chapter 6.

The European marriage pattern may have played a key role in the divergence between European and Asian cultures for several reasons. Consensual marriage empowers women more than arranged marriage. Marrying outside one's kin group restricts the choice of marriage partner less than marrying within it. Delaying marriage until age 25.4 in early modern England ensured that women had greater agency and confidence than women who married at age 18.6 (late Ming China) or 16.0 (Qing China).[57] Female inheritance regimes favor women's socioeconomic opportunity. Setting up a new household away from the families of both partners tends to place the spouses on a more equal footing. Finally, monogamy more than polygamy fosters female agency.

Some non-European societies exhibited one or other of these tendencies, but no major non-European society exhibited all of them. The authors of a recent study call them "female friendly" and believe they correlate with strong European economic development.[58] The female-friendly institution of monogamous marriage is, in particular, an extremely rare occurrence in the anthropological record, extending, according to another recent study, to only fifteen percent of known societies throughout history. This study finds that monogamous marriage "shrinks the size of the pool of low-status, risk-oriented, unmarried men."[59] This factor alone seems in general to diminish criminality, spousal abuse, and conflict within the household, while increasing parental involvement, economic output, and female agency.

The trend in Chinese society into the early twentieth century was starkly different. For one thing, a high proportion of girls underwent the process of foot binding. The goal was to stunt the normal growth process to achieve the ideal of three-inch "lotus feet." According to tradition, women with bound feet were much more likely to enter formal marriage and to avoid being handed off or sold as a concubine, slave, or bondservant.[60] True, some elite men advocated schooling for elite women, and some women attained a high level of education and intellectual accomplishment. Even among such women, however, there was no question of joining scientific academies or participating in public intellectual exchange. After all, a woman was supposed "to stay within bounds of domesticity and keep her mouth shut," and it was considered a great virtue to commit suicide following one's husband's demise.[61] In fact, the Confucian authorities extolled domesticity to such an extent that "any participation in the outside community was conceived as treason against a woman's duties towards family and home."[62] Within this conception, such authorities, at least through the end of the nineteenth century, repeatedly forbade the participation of urban women in religious rituals and their attendance at temples. Although many urban women took part anyway, it is clear that their scope for action was drastically more limited in China than in Europe.

In the Islamic world, women generally enjoyed more secure property rights than women in Europe. In particular, they controlled some property within marriage and were guaranteed an inheritance (though much smaller than male inheritance). Free women (that is, not concubines) also enjoyed some reproductive rights. A newlywed free woman could refuse intercourse and, according to some legal schools, could request dissolution of her marriage before consummation. A wife could deny her husband coitus interruptus, refuse to breast-feed her child if the father had the means to hire a wet-nurse, and could demand wages if he declined to hire one.[63] Women could also work as dyers, weavers, spinners, and in other crafts and could also legally retain control over the resultant wages. Only seldom, however, could they take part in such activity when men were present.[64] Indeed, according to one authoritative scholar, because of "social pressure furthered by the preaching of moral values, particularly by market supervisors, or the result of pressure applied by the family itself, Muslim women were not encouraged and often forbidden to venture into the public sphere."[65] Muslim societies were not "female friendly" in other ways too. Female circumcision, while not supported by Islamic law, was widely imposed by custom, especially in Egypt. While Muslim women could be married to only one man at a time, Muslim men were allowed up to four wives and unlimited female slaves (concubines).[66] Likewise, men enjoyed the right to divorce their wives, but women were not allowed to divorce their husbands. Women sometimes played significant roles in Islamic religious life, in particular in the Sufi orders and in the transmission of prophetic sayings (hadith). Nevertheless, a leading scholar concludes that in the Islamic world "women possessed agency, but generally lacked authority."[67]

Of the major non-European cultures, early modern India provided the fewest opportunities for female agency. Although women's property rights were more secure in most regions of early modern India than in contemporaneous European countries, in practice this distinction often vanished. Lower-class women were routinely sold as slave girls, widows were typically prohibited to remarry, honor killings were not uncommon, wife-beating was widely accepted, and widow immolation and female infanticide were widespread within many social classes. Moreover, women performed much of the rural drudgery and strenuous construction work. Mughal miniatures of the 1500s depict "women breaking stones or bricks, sieving lime, and carrying mortar on their heads at building sites." It is not surprising, therefore, that early modern Indian women participated in the urban public space far less often than their northwest European counterparts.[68]

In sum, it seems that the talents and abilities of women gained freer rein in early modern Europe, thus adding significantly to the available human capital, than in the other advanced cultures of Eurasia. Progressively unleashing more human potential is, of course, an important hallmark of the modern world.

Breaking the power barrier

Another key feature of the modern age has involved harnessing new sources of energy—beyond muscle power—to save labor and produce more material goods. It is uncontested among scholars that European societies, beginning with England, were the first in world history to mechanize industrial production. The Industrial Revolution, which began in the late 1700s, is held by most historians to mark the turning point in the Great Divergence of Europe from the other leading cultures of the early modern era. Much recent research suggests that Europe's transition began at least a century earlier, though it seems clear that many preconditions of the Great Divergence were falling into place earlier still.

The first human society that began to break the power barrier was Northern Song China (960–1126). From the mid-1000s, owing to a growing shortage of wood, coal was resorted to more and more often for both heating purposes and producing iron. An early study by Robert Hartwell calculated the total annual output of pig iron around 1058 at between 75,000 and 150,000 tons.[69] Hartwell also estimated that the biggest metallurgical centers, in the Honan-Hopei border region, which may have produced half of the country's pig iron total, probably consumed as much as 140,000 tons of coal each year.[70] A recent study has questioned Hartwell's calculations of iron output and deems them unverifiable, given the present state of our knowledge.[71] Other scholars have reached much lower assessments of yearly pig iron production in the Northern Song era,[72] reckoning it to have ranged only from 35,000 to 70,000 tons.[73]

The debates surrounding Hartwell's half-century-old investigations are important because the outcome could shed light on whether China, nearly one thousand years ago, had to some extent become the first modern economy. As Hartwell argued:

> extensive coal mining enterprises require an organization that is essentially modern in nature. Heavy capital investment is required to dig deep shafts and construct drainage and ventilating equipment. Large numbers of workers must be concentrated at one establishment and they are dependent on the mine owner and the wholesale trade for their market. The existence of a large urban center employing coal in domestic heating and in manufacturing was an important stimulus to the expansion of this type of industry.[74]

In any event, scholars are in agreement that the impressive economic development achieved during the Northern Song era did not accelerate in a continuous chain of growth.

Indeed, that growth ended with the Jurchen invasion, destruction of the capital city Kaifeng, and dynastic overthrow in the 1120s. Nomadic conquests continued, culminating in the Mongol imposition of the Yuan Dynasty in the 1270s. Also inimical to economic growth were increased restrictions on free economic entrepreneurship, growing recourse to unfree labor, and what Hartwell called "structural limitations of traditional Chinese society."[75] As Jack A. Goldstone explains, growth occurred from time to time in premodern Eurasia "but in a pattern that was periodic and efflorescent, rather than self-sustaining and accelerating."[76] In an ironic twist, the Song-era economy may have declined because of its fiscal and financial sophistication. The excessive printing of paper money and the floating of government debt, as a means to finance war-making, drove monetary inflation, which undermined the Chinese currency. Song China seems to have been the world's first instance of a "tax state," which derives most of its revenues from indirect taxation, and even a credit-issuing "fiscal state"—centuries before the most advanced European countries.[77]

Prominent world historians like Kenneth Pomeranz and Bozhong Li attribute the lack of further industrialization—and modernization—in post-Song China to its failure to transition from muscle power to the systematic use of mineral fuel.[78] By contrast, England was already well on its way toward breaking through the power barrier in the 1550s, when the annual coal consumption in London alone was around 10,000 tons.[79] Given a population of roughly 80,000, Londoners were consuming some 250 pounds of coal per person—a figure that had soared to 1,587 pounds by the 1710s. From beer brewing to home heating, "England had been a fossil-fueled society almost two centuries before Watts' steam engine," according to William M. Cavert:

> and during the seventeenth century the only place in the world famous for burning prodigious supplies of mineral coal was London. London was by far the world's largest coal market, its largest energy consumer, and endured its most polluted air.[80]

This was certainly not the most pleasant or salubrious feature of modern life, but it was undoubtedly a quintessential feature. Yet since large coal deposits were available all over Europe and Asia, why did so few people develop advanced methods to mine and utilize coal?[81] The answer is surely to be found in the recurring pattern that is the subject of this book.

The story with iron production was similar. In the first half of the 1600s, between 21,000 and 26,400 tons of pig iron (or between 15,400 and 18,704 tons of more fully refined bar iron) were produced in England and Wales.[82] Since the population of those lands rose from 6.25 to 7.5 million in those years, the per capita output for the entire country ranged from 6.7 to 7.6 pounds of pig iron. That was at least ten times the output in China during the same period of time.[83] (It was also between two and ten times the Chinese output in 1058, depending on whose figure for that year one chooses.) The coal output in England and Wales held fairly steady before taking off from the 1750s, reaching over 121,000 tons in 1790, or nearly 27 pounds per capita. Production then more than doubled over the next two decades before doubling again within fifteen more years. Song-era industrialization aborted within a century. The one that began in the early 1600s in England and Wales continued to gather strength.

A rising standard of living

Coal to dramatically boost available energy, iron to forge radically more efficient tools, and one more advancement—mechanical power—together made the Industrial Revolution and the Great Divergence possible. Recent scholarship has discounted earlier claims of uniquely expansive industrial use of watermills in medieval Europe.[84] Rather, it seems, watermills were just as widespread in the medieval Islamic world,[85] and medieval

Europeans used them mostly for flour production.[86] Consequently, Adam Lucas concludes that there was in Europe no "industrial revolution of the Middle Ages."[87]

The story began to change, however, in the 1400s, when "industrial milling became relatively commonplace," particularly for the production of woolen cloth and iron.[88] (The same seems to have been true of another capital-intensive mechanical device, the building crane, whose use gradually declined in the Islamic lands but increased in Western Europe beginning in the 1300s.)[89] From the late 1500s, the Dutch took the lead in using windmills for sawing, crushing, beating, squeezing, and other processes.[90] In the second half of the 1600s, entrepreneurs of the Dutch East India Company (VOC) introduced both windmills and watermills in Asian lands, including those now called Indonesia, India, and Sri Lanka, in particular for sawing timber, refining sugar, and producing gunpowder.[91] Most of these ventures failed for want of sufficient local skilled labor and because of an abundance of animal-drawn mills (first introduced by Chinese artisans), which were, however, less efficient, productive, and laborsaving.

If this technology did not "take off" in Asia, the same cannot be said of Europe. Artisans and entrepreneurs traveled to Holland to observe the mills' functioning, to hire Dutch millwrights, to commission the construction of windmills in other lands, and to purchase operation manuals. One such manual, translated into English, appeared in 500 copies in 1760. English craftsmen went on to design and build even more efficient and powerful windmills requiring only periodic maintenance and no regular labor.[92] Many Europeans were clearly eager and willing to incorporate such advanced technology into their productive systems and to gradually improve upon them in ways that no other peoples were yet ready or able to do. "Response cannot be anticipated," Eric Jones helpfully argues; "it is merely a simplifying device on the part of economists to assume that every opportunity ... will be seized."[93]

In the historical record, many opportunities were in fact not seized. Watermills and windmills, building cranes, coal-burning and iron-smelting had all been introduced throughout Eurasia at various times. Here or there, entrepreneurs and artisans made intensive and fruitful use of them. Yet only beginning in early modern Europe did that intensity and fruitfulness reach a continuous, rising development right through to the present day. Many explanations have been put forward for this divergence, including differences in religion, culture, the law, institutions, labor costs, and interest rates. All of these factors probably contributed, though a recent study suggests that the cost of borrowing and therefore the cost of investing in expensive capital equipment may have been the decisive one, when all these factors are carefully correlated with historical developments.[94] Of course, lower interest rates depended on a sophisticated financial infrastructure, which in turn required the development of highly favorable economic, political, cultural, and social conditions.

Achieving industrialization required "the adoption and implementation of innovations on a broad front involving energy, materials, transportation, the organization of production, the organization of governance, and industrial processes."[95] Figuring out how to extract and deploy coal was insufficient by itself. Basic technological expertise was also indispensable. According to Chinese historian Benjamin Elman, "by 1600 Europe was ahead of Asia in producing basic machines like clocks, screws, levers, pulleys."[96] No less important was the development of science, literacy, numeracy, infrastructure, political stability, and sophisticated financial institutions. Thanks to a network of interconnections across Europe "that was almost ecological in its intricacy," especially in Britain, modern economic growth spread to many other European countries before reaching most other shores.[97]

Taken together, these developments began to make a big difference in the standard of living of ordinary people—and fairly early. Recent comparative study undertaken by Bruce Campbell indicates that the per capita economic output (GDP) of Italy in 1400 was significantly higher than that of China ($1,601 vs. $960). In fact, Britain had caught up with China in terms of its general standard of living as early as 1400.[98] A century later, Germany, Holland, and the southern Low Countries had caught up with or surpassed Italy, while the Chinese economy had grown only modestly (to $1,127).[99] In other words, the Great Divergence had already begun to take shape around 1500. By comparing grain wages to silver wages, Stephen Broadberry and Bishnupriya Gupta found that already in the second half of the 1500s unskilled southern Indian workers earned eighty-three percent as much as their English counterparts in grain payments, but only twenty-one percent as much in silver wages. Unskilled laborers in the Yangzi Delta region in 1550–1649 took home eighty-seven percent as much as their English counterparts in grain wages, but only thirty-nine percent as much in silver wages.[100] It is not surprising that grain wages were relatively high in both southern India and the Yangzi Delta, given the highly favorable agricultural conditions in those regions. Significantly higher silver wages, however, made for a superior standard of living, because one could purchase many goods with silver, aside from grain.

In the late Ming and early Qing eras, the Chinese state and society "were failing to cope" with the twin pressures of population increase and environmental deterioration.[101] This led, according to Patrick O'Brien and Kent Deng, to "a significant decline in caloric consumption in the early 1600s," even in the most advanced region of China, Jiangnan in the Yangzi Delta, a decline that continued into the mid-1700s.[102] Then, ordinary laborers in the region earned only about a quarter as much as their counterparts in London or Amsterdam.[103] True, the average caloric intake in England declined from its high around 1770 to a low point in the mid-1800s, yet by this point English grain wages for unskilled laborers were still seventy-one percent higher than those in southern India and sixty-two percent higher than those in the Yangzi Delta.[104] Thus, even during England's "Hungry Forties," the standard of living of ordinary people remained far higher than in the most advanced regions of China and India. As Europe's industrial economies prospered in the second half of the nineteenth century, the divergence grew to enormous proportions.

CONCLUSION

What did Europe make modern?

All early humans learned everything learnable from their natural environments. Each plant, animal, mineral, and feature of landscape was known and to the extent possible put to use. Connecting with other peoples, learning from them, and exchanging with them helped each culture to advance and flourish.[1] Those cultures thrived most stupendously that formed from the achievements of many cultures a new and powerful synthesis. The greatest of these emerged in ancient Greece, Golden Age Islamdom, and early modern Europe. The first two fell into decline. The European cultural synthesis has continued to develop to the present day. It gave birth to what one calls the modern world.

What specific inputs of medieval and early modern Europeans contributed to the emergence of the modern world? Among the most important were efficient, secular, and impersonal systems of law; a penchant for travel and exploration resulting in the knitting together of all the continents and regions of the globe into one interconnected sphere of exchange; an unbridled, independent, prodigious, and all-encompassing publishing enterprise; the concept and practice of steadily expanding individual and collective rights; a universal community of disciplined, objective, methodical, and self-regulating scholars and scientists dedicated to systematically unlocking the secrets of nature; a commitment to continuously expand knowledge, share information, and disinterestedly increase human understanding; a love of artistic experimentation and novelty; a dramatically rising capacity to project military power; emancipation of women from traditional constraints; the systematic harnessing of non-muscle power; and a steadily rising material standard of living.

All societies develop rules and customs for governing the interactions of persons and groups. Over time and in various cultures these rules grew more systematic and occasionally crystallized into written rulebooks or law codes. Some early ones, such as the Talmudic and Islamic, were firmly anchored in religious belief and practice. The first purely secular legal system,

Roman civil law, was also the most sophisticated. Centuries after the Roman Empire declined, its law was little used outside the Byzantine Empire. Early medieval Europe had fallen into political fragmentation and warlordism. Intellectually, it was to a large extent a *tabula rasa* upon which selected ideas and institutions could be inscribed. In the context of eleventh-century power struggles between the only institution with authority throughout Europe, the church, and local and regional warlords, papal jurists recovered and adapted Roman law. The first European university was founded in 1080 primarily to study and teach the law. In the following centuries, university-trained lawyers throughout Europe developed two secular legal systems, Continental civil law and English common law—the two most widespread and efficient legal systems in the world today. Ancient Egyptian, Middle Eastern, Greek, Roman, Golden Age Islamic, and, less directly, insights and achievements from other parts of Eurasia contributed to these developments as they did to many medieval and early modern European advancements, because Europeans beginning in the Middle Ages exhibited uncommon openness to learning from other cultures.

Although humans have wandered widely since our ancestors evolved into Homo sapiens tens of thousands of years ago, the first to journey systematically and leave written records of what they saw and experienced were ancient Greeks. Muslims of the first centuries after the founding of Islam voyaged great distances within Afro-Eurasia—further than any peoples before. In the early 1400s, Chinese mariners sailed immense fleets throughout the Indian Ocean. In 1433, however, the Chinese Emperor put a halt to these voyages. Because of imperial prohibitions, no such explorations were ever again undertaken by the Chinese in the premodern era. From the early medieval era, Europeans traveled widely within their continent and occasionally beyond, typically on pilgrimage to the Near East. By the late Middle Ages, they had mastered seamanship, thanks to their ready access to navigable waterways, to borrowings of technology and know-how from their Muslim neighbors, and to continuous experimentation and innovation. In the same decades when the Chinese were turning inward, Portuguese mariners began sailing down the coast of Africa. At the end of the 1400s, European seafarers developed blue-water navigation and sailed across the Atlantic Ocean to the Americas and around the Cape of Good Hope to India. European political fragmentation gave entrepreneurs like Columbus options. Whereas the one Chinese Emperor could forbid overseas exploration, Columbus was able to shop his idea from monarch to monarch until he found willing backers in Ferdinand and Isabella of Spain. A fever of

Conclusion

exploration soon gripped the continent, as hundreds of fleets sailed to all the corners of the earth, and entrepreneurs, explorers, missionaries, naturalists, and adventurers built up networks of cultural, economic, and technological exchange, thus laying a foundation for our interconnected modern world.

Humans have used spoken language for tens of thousands of years, writing systems for five thousand, alphabets for three, paper for two, and printing for over one. Chinese artisans, the most creative in the premodern era, devised both paper and printing, which permitted their society to flourish more dynamically than any other in the Song (960–1279) and early Ming (1368–1644) eras. In these same years, an expansion of educational opportunities, rising literacy rates, and slow but fitful economic growth in early modern Europe spurred a search for ways to mechanize printing. The mechanical printing press, devised by Gutenberg around 1450, was soon producing hundreds of thousands and then millions of books: close to 30,000 titles in 20 million copies by 1500 and another 200 million volumes a century later. This output dwarfed the relatively advanced Chinese printing industry by a factor of 100 or even more. As vastly more information became available to scholars, artisans, merchants, entrepreneurs, and experts, economic, technological, scientific, and intellectual development accelerated and dramatically transformed Europe. Europeans still eagerly assimilated learning and knowledge from the other developed cultures of Eurasia, as well as eyewitness accounts written by European explorers and other travelers, but gradually more and more European intellectuals opened new pathways of understanding and innovation, putting countless volumes of precious knowledge into the public domain.

Just as decentralized printing culture in Europe placed vastly more information in the hands of ever-expanding circles of readers, so the decentralization of power endowed more and more Europeans with rights, privileges, immunities, and liberties than any other peoples in history. The main reason was the comparative weakness of political leadership in Europe, where public order broke down almost completely in the two centuries after Charlemagne's death in 814. The continent's political authority divided among hundreds of kings and princes, and power devolved further to thousands of secular and ecclesiastical lords. Thousands of towns and cities, beginning in 1066, received charters of liberty, guaranteeing them political, economic, and social rights. Representatives of towns were summoned to take part in royal councils all across Europe, beginning in 1188 in Léon in northwestern Spain. The idea that good counsel depended on numbers and representativeness found its way into church governance as well with the conciliar movement. The first general church council convened on this principle in 1378. Grassroots and intellectual reform movements also arose in the church and culminated in the Protestant Reformation of the early 1500s. Martin Luther's doctrine of a priesthood of all believers with the ability to interpret Holy Scripture for themselves invested in ordinary people more authority than ever before in history. All these practices, combined with theories of political resistance dating to the early medieval era, laid the foundation for the emergence of modern rights, both political and civil.

Investigations and interpretations of how nature works are as old as civilization itself. The ancient Greeks developed a systematic approach, logical tools of analysis, and mental categories of classification and applied them systematically to natural phenomena. Their Hellenistic and Islamic successors over the following centuries did so as well. Natural philosophers in ancient China and India developed parallel but less robust methods and fruits of natural philosophy. Building on all these achievements—and assisted by the power of mechanical printing, the flourishing of technical illustration, worldwide networks of information flooding in from travelers' and colonizers' observations, the humanistic emphasis on returning to sources, and a critical mindset fostered by the Reformation—early modern European natural philosophers developed the modern scientific enterprise involving empirical research, detailed record-keeping, methodical analysis of data, peer review, sharing and testing of results, the development of powerful mathematical tools, imaginative hypothesizing, and the articulation of laws of nature.

Sharing results of their investigations and collaborating on intellectual projects, early modern European scholars developed what they called a "Republic of Letters." Its "citizens" built up networks of correspondence, felt deep bonds of allegiance across time and space, founded learned societies and journals, brought into the public domain knowledge in every sphere of human endeavor, and supported each other's challenges to tradition and received wisdom. As access to schooling became more widespread, the levels of literacy and numeracy, first in the northwest and then throughout Europe, exceeded those of any other major culture. Ordinary people began to enter into this public sphere through the reading of newspapers, other periodicals, and pamphlets; going to coffee shops to debate political and cultural topics and to share and obtain the latest economic, political, scholarly, and social information; and attending popular scientific lectures. In early modern Europe, more than anyplace else in history, intellectuals, merchants, artisans, and entrepreneurs—in a word, mental and practical workers—joined forces,

Conclusion

learning from one another, putting their heads together, collaborating, pooling talents and resources, and bridging the gulfs of incomprehension and contempt typical of all premodern societies. The result was the unleashing of more human creativity and the forging of more pathways of learning, leading to more and more innovation and breakthroughs.

Breaking free from tradition, custom, established approaches, and deeply rooted institutions became a hallmark of medieval and early modern Europe and ultimately of the modern world. Medieval visionaries conceived, designed, and built the world's tallest buildings. Renaissance artists radically parted ways with their mentors, leading to a Europewide trend of ceaseless experimentation in painting and sculpture. Incessant military competition among hundreds of European states drove a series of military revolutions endowing those states with an ability to project more power both continentally and abroad than any other peoples in history. Women gained more agency, authority, and influence, thanks to higher rates of literacy, numeracy, labor-force participation, delayed marriage, and personal decision-making opportunities, than in any other major culture or region. Finally, early modern Europeans developed and harnessed laborsaving devices, other means of increasing labor productivity, and fossil fuel more extensively than ever before, leading to the then-highest standard of living, especially in northwestern Europe, in world history. In all these ways, and doubtless many others, "Europe made the modern world."

How did Europe do it?

Why did Europe and not China, the Ottoman Empire, or India make the leap to the modern age? Scholars have put forward many interpretations. The most convincing ones emphasize Europe's political fragmentation, its interconnectedness with—and learning from—other cultures, "gifts" of backwardness and weakness, an early rise in literacy and numeracy, the lack of an indigenous or religiously grounded legal system, a Christian worldview centered on God as both Creator and Incarnate, and a tendency to experiment with radically new ways to address old problems.

One of the most widespread and robust arguments for early modern Europe's success emphasizes its political fragmentation (see Map 4.1, p. 67). With dozens of medium-sized and hundreds of small polities all competing for resources, both human and material, rulers could seldom afford to mistreat their most talented subjects, for fear of driving them into the arms of hostile competitors. In an age of dramatic transformations, failing to show regard for enterprising individuals could mean the difference between conquering most of South America (Spain thanks to Ferdinand and Isabella's willingness to support the voyages of Columbus) and conquering only a small part (Portugal, whose ruler refused to back him).[2] Such outcomes, though not always on such a monumental scale, doubtless recurred thousands and even millions of times, as schemes to innovate were tried or not tried throughout Europe and other parts of the early modern world. Moreover, not only did political fragmentation and decentralization in Europe permit entrepreneurs, organizers, dreamers, and schemers to find their voices, undertake projects, join forces, and launch bold ventures, European rulers often promoted and even took part in them. They granted royal charters to companies, bestowing on them limited liability and monopoly status, and personally sponsored commercial expeditions and voyages of exploration.

Political fragmentation had a big impact on the development of warfare in Europe, as well. Many rulers in Eurasia, in particular in China and the Ottoman Empire, developed large armies and gunpowder weaponry and in the modern era were able to project power far from their frontiers. Other regions were divided into smaller polities, such as India. But only in Europe did competing polities roughly match each other in strength and also systematically and steadily improve their military technology, technique, and fighting capacity, both in competition within Europe and in advancing their interests abroad. The British navy defeated the vastly bigger, more populous, and richer Chinese Empire in the First Opium War (1839–1842), but all of the major European colonial powers were vastly more able than any non-European countries to project power far from their shores as early as the 1500s—that is, long before the Great Divergence.

Another important recent line of argumentation holds that Europe's success was made possible by the "interconnected and sociologically co-constitutive nature of Europe."[3] It was a great boon for Europe to develop centuries after the major Eurasian cultures had completed their rise to regional preeminence and had achieved extraordinary advances in "mathematics, navigational invention, arts of war, and significant military technologies,"[4] among many others. Europeans creatively appropriated such advances—and many others—and linked together the great existing overland and maritime trade routes of the Indian Ocean world to continuously expanding oceanic routes the Europeans themselves opened for the first time in history. One can also argue that Europe benefited from

Conclusion

many historical accidents and particular developments in Eurasia. Mongol control of most of Eurasia opened up secure trade routes permitting the transfer of both leading-edge technologies, including gunpowder weapons, and devastating disease. Demographic catastrophe inflicted by the Black Death weakened the Chinese Empire but in Europe drove up wages and stimulated economic development. Increasing labor productivity in European agriculture, thanks to increased use of animal power and manure, as well as new techniques and technologies, gradually liberated more and more workers to take part in urban handicraft industries.[5] By contrast, low labor costs induced Chinese entrepreneurs to invest fewer resources in laborsaving technologies.[6] It seems, likewise, that higher labor costs drove European legislators to partially pare back rules governing apprenticeships and the establishment of workshops and manufacturing concerns, a development with no apparent counterpart in the Eastern Mediterranean region.[7] The centralized Ottoman Empire stifled commercial development and therefore weakened potential competitors of Europe while also threatening southeastern Europe militarily, to the advantage of the northwestern region. Ottoman control of the eastern Mediterranean also drove enterprising European merchant-warriors to seek alternative trade routes to the East. These were just some of the many ways in which trans-Eurasian interconnections influenced Europe's development.

One can thus speak of a "gift of backwardness." The Europeans skipped stages of development by appropriating breakthroughs of other cultures. Likewise, lacking deeply rooted traditions and institutions, they could also build up entirely new and extraordinarily flexible cultures. At the same time, the other advanced peoples of Eurasia failed to recognize Europe's early achievements, to learn from them, and to fear them. For a host of reasons, few Muslims, Indians, or Chinese felt compelled to travel to Europe until a century or so ago. By contrast, Europeans, at first deeply aware of their relative backwardness and later never losing the sense that other peoples had much to teach and offer them, nurtured an abiding passion for travel and exploration until it became a habit and a way of life, until Europeans had created the interconnected modern world.

The lack of a deeply rooted and interlocking set of customs and institutional patterns in Europe enabled Europeans not only to develop an extraordinarily flexible culture but also to undergo continuous transformation under the impact of a whole series of breakthroughs, borrowings, and discoveries, both endogenous and from abroad. Paper, gunpowder, the philosophy of Ibn Rushd, the compass, the discovery of the

Americas, printing, the Reformation, the scientific method: each one of these breakthroughs, many of them achieved in China and the Islamic world, had a revolutionary impact in Europe but not elsewhere. In all these cases, Europe showed itself more open to radical change and self-transformation than any other culture in world history. The printing revolution is an obvious example of a very early divergence of Europe from the other developed Eurasian societies. Already by 1500, many Europeans were gaining access to vastly more information on the widest variety of topics than ever before in history, which dramatically empowered the highly educated and growing literate segments of society and paved the way toward modern life with its unprecedented information economy.

Rights and liberties are an integral and precious feature of modern societies, yet they only began to emerge in medieval Europe thanks to the weakness of established rulers and governments. This is another way in which Europe's political fragmentation can be called a "gift." China, India, and the Islamic world all boasted many cities and craft guilds, but, largely because of centralized political power, they were unable to demand and assert political authority. In Europe, by contrast, comparatively weak rulers, the devolution of power to local and regional lords, the vibrancy of towns, a language and discourse of rights, and political and economic competition among diverse centers of power made possible the steady development of a complex architecture of checks and balances and rights and liberties so necessary for modern society.

China's ancient, all-pervading, and flexible culture emphasized harmonious resolution of conflict, forestalling the emergence of sophisticated civil law. Nor could Chinese jurists simply appropriate the elaborate remnants of the legal system of a disintegrated empire, the way Roman law could be adapted in Europe. Rigorous legal training, while not wholly absent from the formation of Chinese scholar-officials, was never in and of itself a guarantee of advancement in the political and economic spheres as it was in Europe. The fact that the law in Europe was not conceived of as revealed by God, as in Islamic sharia, meant that jurists could think critically about it and, therefore, that it could evolve on the bases of practicality and rationality. Thus, the extraordinarily important concepts of legal personhood and limited liability could emerge in medieval Europe but not, until quite recently, in the Islamic world. Such powerful instrumental use of the law enabled Europeans to discover, organize, and deploy resources, both human and material, far more efficiently and effectively than other peoples. Since the law was not deeply rooted in an ancient culture, and because the Roman

Conclusion

law needed to be reconciled with a host of other legal approaches, scholars felt compelled to work out systematic methods for testing, organizing, and applying the law. These methods were almost immediately put to use in other intellectual spheres, in particular in theology and philosophy, including natural philosophy, often with stupendous results.

European scholars and thinkers, starting in the Middle Ages, studied nature enthusiastically for many reasons. They believed that God created all things, and therefore they sought to study the "book of nature" in search of clues as to his intentions. Their faith taught the validation of the world of ordinary reality through the incarnation of God. The law as a concept and an institution central to their culture inspired a search for physical regularities in nature. The medieval Christian conceptualization of nature as an object divinely bestowed upon humanity for its use gave rise to objective and mechanistic approaches to the natural world. This conception seems also to have weakened the traditional and ubiquitous occupational division between mental and physical work in Europe more than in other advanced Eurasian cultures, such that intellectuals, artisans, entrepreneurs, and professionals began to collaborate and learn from one another in an accelerating pattern beginning in the Middle Ages.

Literacy and numeracy expanded among both men and women far earlier in Europe than in other developed regions of Eurasia. Christian reform movements, which advocated personal religious awakening through individual and collective reading of Holy Scripture, urged believers to learn their letters. Economic expansion beginning in the Renaissance increased the material value of education and promoted the opening of schools, starting in northern Italy. The Reformation greatly accelerated this process in northern Europe and the English colonies of North America. Higher rates of literacy, continued economic growth, a dramatic increase in available information, and political fragmentation all contributed to the emergence and steady development of spheres of public debate, exchange, learning, collaboration, and intellectual advancement. In no other world society did people come together to share information, learn from one another, and work together to solve problems and advance agendas so readily and effectively as did early modern Europeans. This process culminated in the European Enlightenment, a movement that was fully fledged before the Industrial Revolution and the Great Divergence. Throughout the early modern era, European intellectuals conceptualized and implemented radically new ways of organizing society, politics, economics, and the law. Among their achievements were ideas and practices of human rights, written constitutions, checks and balances, limited government, free enterprise, international law, penal reform, and making punishments fit the crime, to name only a few.

If unleashing inherent human creativity is the key ingredient in the success of human civilization, as has been argued throughout this book, then the emancipation of women, and in particular the greater realization of female potential through expanding literacy, numeracy, and participation in the public sphere, must be considered an important factor in Europe's rise and making of the modern world.

Another ingredient in the rise of Europe was its ability to break the power barrier, to substitute fossil fuel and mechanized laborsaving devices for muscle power. Earlier societies had made such transitions episodically and fitfully but only in northwestern Europe did the trend commence and steadily accelerate already beginning in the early modern era, at least a century or two before the Great Divergence. It was such advances, coupled with financial and commercial developments, as well as—and perhaps most importantly—continual improvements in the development of human capital, that enabled Europeans in the most advanced regions of their continent to attain a higher standard of living than people in the most advanced regions of China already in the 1500s and, more broadly, to gain continuously in wealth, power, knowledge, and organizational ability and thus to "make the modern world."

That this achievement required Europeans to draw on accomplishments of other peoples makes it no less original—any more than Apple Computer, Inc., was unoriginal because it built the iPod around a storage device invented in Japan. A prime feature of inventiveness is the willingness to gather ideas and inspiration from every direction and then to combine them, like an alchemist, into a new creation.

Once Europe brought to life the modern world, there was no stopping other peoples from adapting the necessary suite of innovations and developing their own versions of modernity. The Dutch historian Peer Vries was presumably right that "the chance that Qing China might have become the world's first industrial nation . . . was about nil."[8] Yet in the same way that many European countries, and especially those in the northwestern region, had long been laying the foundations for their stupendous leap to modernity, centuries of steady economic and technological development in China's Yangzi Delta had been preparing that country for its recent extraordinary economic ascent. By the eighteenth and nineteenth centuries, the Yangzi region boasted a "hardworking, readily trainable, and well-disciplined labor force and a large number of entrepreneurs, professionals and skillful merchants." The availability of such invaluable human capital, according to the Chinese historian Bozhong Li, "partly explains why the Yangzi Delta performed much better than most regions of China in economic modernization after modern technology and institutions were introduced from the West in the late nineteenth century."[9] Modernity is a universal condition of the world, now shared to a large extent by nearly all countries and peoples, but it emerged first in Europe, as this book has endeavored to show.

To some extent the "why Europe" question will remain murky and unanswerable, since so many factors contributed to its rise and the making of the modern world. For this reason, the alchemical metaphor, as articulated in the Introduction, is apt. Alchemists somewhat blindly, though often systematically, sought out, dabbled with, combined, and otherwise experimented on diverse materials and ingredients, hoping for positive results, based on past experiences of what was possible. Human cultures evolved in a similar manner, as people made contacts, imitated achievements, adapted insights, and in general learned from one another. Ironically it seems that one of the most modern technologies—artificial intelligence (AI) or machine learning algorithms, in which computers learn through trial and error—can be readily conceived as "a form of 'alchemy,'" meaning, a mysterious process of trial and error, as Ali Rahimi, an AI researcher at Google, and Ben Recht, a computer scientist at the University of California, Berkeley, argued in April 2018.[10] There is indeed no reason why it should be less difficult to understand why Europe made the modern world rather than China, Islamdom, or India, as it is to understand why this or that tweak to a machine learning algorithm improves its performance.

NOTES

Preface

1. See Maarten Bosker, Eltjo Buringh, and Jan Luiten van Zanden, "From Baghdad to London: Unraveling Urban Development in Europe, the Middle East, and North Africa, 800–1800," *Review of Economics and Statistics* 95, no. 4 (October 2013): 1423.
2. See Kenneth Pomeranz, *The Great Divergence: Europe, China, and the Making of the Modern World Economy* (Princeton, NJ: Princeton University Press, 2000).
3. See Robert Marks, *The Origins of the Modern World: A Global and Ecological Narrative* (Lanham, MD: Rowman and Littlefield, 2002).
4. A decade later, Pomeranz conceded that the divergence more likely began in 1750 or even 1700. See Kenneth Pomeranz, "Ten Years After: Responses and Reconsiderations," *Historically Speaking* 12, no. 4 (September 2011): 24.
5. Pomeranz, *The Great Divergence*, 68.
6. Marks, *The Origins of the Modern World*, 101.
7. Peter C. Perdue, *China Marches West: The Qing Conquest of Central Eurasia* (Cambridge, MA, and London: The Belknap Press of Harvard University Press, 2005), 537.
8. See, for example, Stephen Broadberry, Hanhui Guan, and David Daokui Li, "China, Europe and the Great Divergence: A Study in Historical National Accounting, 980–1850," *Journal of Economic History* 78, no. 4 (December 2018): 1–46.
9. Joseph E. Inikori, *Africans and the Industrial Revolution in England: A Study in International Trade and Economic Development* (Cambridge: Cambridge University Press, 2002), seeks to demonstrate that slave-holding and the slave trade were a major cause of the Industrial Revolution; David Eltis and Stanley L. Engerman, "Importance of Slavery and the Slave Trade to Industrializing Britain," *Journal of Economic History* 60, no. 1 (March 2000): 123–44, and Kenneth Morgan, *Slavery and the British Empire: From Africa to America* (Oxford: Oxford University Press, 2007), argue the contrary.
10. Jonathan Daly *The Rise of Western Power: A Comparative History of Western Civilization* (London and New York: Bloomsbury, 2014).
11. For some of this literature, see my *Historians Debate the Rise of the West* (London and New York: Routledge, 2015).

Notes

Introduction

1. For an optimistic assessment of the contemporary world, see Johan Norberg, *Progress: Ten Reasons to Look Forward to the Future* (London: Oneworld, 2016).
2. On this phenomenon, see Deirdre McCloskey, *Bourgeois Equality: How Ideas, Not Capital or Institutions, Enriched the World* (Chicago: University of Chicago Press, 2016), Chaps. 1–5.
3. I outline a couple dozen such interpretations in *Historians Debate the Rise of the West* (London and New York: Routledge, 2015).
4. As quoted from Andre Gunder Frank, *ReOrient: Global Economy in the Asian Age* (Berkeley, CA: University of California Press, 1998), xxv.
5. The true size of the Soviet economy was undoubtedly smaller than official statistics suggested. See Lev Navrozov, "Assessing the CIA's Soviet Economic Indices," in *The Soviet Economy on the Brink of Reform: Essays in Honor of Alec Nove*, ed. P.J.D. Wiles (Boston: Unwin & Hyman, 1988), 112–52.
6. Statistic cited from Diane Rowland and Alexandre V. Telyukov, "Soviet Health Care from Two Perspectives," *Health Affairs* (Fall 1991): 72.
7. Aristotle, *Politics*, Book 3, Sections 10–13.
8. See, for example, Lawrence M. Principe and William R. Newman, "Some Problems with the Historiography of Alchemy," in *Secrets of Nature: Astrology and Alchemy in Early Modern Europe*, ed. William R. Newman and Anthony Grafton (Cambridge, MA: MIT Press, 2001), 385–432.
9. Lawrence M. Principe, *The Secrets of Alchemy* (Chicago: University of Chicago Press, 2012).
10. This interpretation is developed by Charles Birch and John B. Cobb, Jr., in *The Liberation of Life: From the Cell to the Community* (Cambridge and New York: Cambridge University Press, 1981).
11. Jared Diamond, *Guns, Germs, and Steel: The Fates of Human Societies* (New York: W.W. Norton, 1997), 19–22.
12. See John Edward Huth, *The Lost Art of Finding Our Way* (Cambridge, MA: The Belknap Press of Harvard University Press, 2013), Chap. 7.
13. As quoted in Charles C. Mann, *1491: New Revelations of the Americas Before Columbus*, 2nd Vintage Books ed. (New York: Vintage, 2011), 223.
14. See Gregory Curtis, *The Cave Painters: Probing the Mysteries of the World's First Artists* (New York: Anchor Books, 2006).
15. For recent interpretations, see Robert N. Bellah and Hans Joas, eds., *The Axial Age and Its Consequences* (Cambridge, MA: Harvard University Press, 2012).
16. See Majid Fakhry, *A History of Islamic Philosophy*, 3rd ed. (New York: Columbia University Press, 2004), xxiv–xxv.
17. Diamond, *Guns, Germs, and Steel*, 139–42, 159–60.
18. Diamond, *Guns, Germs, and Steel*, 53.

19. See Marcia Ascher, *Ethnomathematics: A Multicultural View of Mathematical Ideas* (Belmont, CA: Brooks-Cole, 1991), 15–29.
20. As quoted from Ascher, *Ethnomathematics*, 31.

Chapter 1

1. This and the following two paragraphs draw on H. Patrick Glenn, *Legal Traditions of the World: Sustainable Diversity in Law*, 5th ed. (Oxford: Oxford University Press, 2014).
2. Plato, *Laws*, 628c
3. Randall Peerenboom, *China's Long March toward Rule of Law* (Cambridge: Cambridge University Press, 2002), Chap. 2.
4. As quoted from Jiang Yonglin, *The Mandate of Heaven and the Great Ming Code* (Seattle: University of Washington Press, 2011), 13. See also Paul R. Katz, *Divine Justice: Religion and the Development of Chinese Legal Culture* (New York: Routledge, 2009), 13.
5. See Geoffrey MacCormack, *Traditional Chinese Penal Law* (Edinburgh: Edinburgh University Press, 1990).
6. See Philip C.C. Huang, *Civil Justice in China: Representation and Practice in the Qing* (Stanford, CA: Stanford University Press, 1996).
7. See Linxia Liang, *Delivering Justice in Qing China: Civil Trials in the Magistrate's Court* (Oxford: Oxford University Press, 2007).
8. See Katz, *Divine Justice*, Chaps. 3 and 4.
9. See Glenn, *Legal Traditions of the World*, Chap. 5.
10. See, for example, Thomas N. Bisson, *The Crisis of the Twelfth Century: Power, Lordship, and the Origins of European Government* (Princeton, NJ: Princeton University Press, 2008).
11. See Harold J. Berman, *Law and Revolution: The Formation of the Western Legal Tradition* (Cambridge, MA, and London: Harvard University Press, 1983), 303–15. For a different interpretation, see Susan Reynolds, *Fiefs and Vassals: The Medieval Evidence Reinterpreted* (Oxford: Oxford University Press, 1994).
12. See Berman, *Law and Revolution*, 316–32.
13. See Susan Reynolds "The Emergence of Professional Law in the Long Twelfth Century," *Law and History Review* 21, no. 2 (Summer 2003): 347–66.
14. Most recently, see Geoffrey Koziol, *The Peace of God* (Leeds: ARC Humanities Press, 2018).
15. See Kathleen G. Cushing, *Reform and the Papacy in the Eleventh Century: Spirituality and Social Change* (Manchester and New York: Manchester University Press, 2005).

Notes

16. See Peter Landau, "The Development of Law," in *The New Cambridge Medieval History*, Volume 4: *c.1024–c.1198*, pt. 1, ed. David Luscombe and Jonathan Riley-Smith (Cambridge: Cambridge University Press, 2004), 113–47.
17. See Harold J. Berman, "The Origins of Western Legal Science," *Harvard Law Review* 90, no. 5 (March 1977): 894–943.
18. See Berman, *Law and Revolution*, 132–35.
19. See Alex J. Novikoff, "Anselm, Dialogue, and the Rise of Scholastic Disputation," *Speculum* 86 (2011): 387–418.
20. For some of the pathways by which work by Muslim philosophers was received into medieval Europe, see Charles Butterworth and Blake A. Kessel, eds., *The Introduction of Arabic Philosophy into Europe* (New York: E.J. Brill, 1994).
21. See Roy Lowe and Yoshihito Yasuhara, *The Origins of Higher Learning: Knowledge Networks and the Early Development of Universities* (London and New York: Routledge, 2017), Chap. 8.
22. See Berman, *Law and Revolution*, 143–51.
23. Édouard Jeauneau, *Rethinking the School of Chartres*, trans. Claude Paul Desmarais (Toronto: University of Toronto Press, 2009), Chap. 2.
24. Marsha L. Colish, "Haskins's *Renaissance* Seventy Years Later: Beyond Anti-Burkhardtianism," *Haskins Society Journal*, ed. Stephen Morillo, Volume 11 (2003): 10.
25. See Alex J. Novikoff, *The Medieval Culture of Disputation: Pedagogy, Practice, and Performance* (Philadelphia: University of Pennsylvania Press, 2013).
26. As quoted from Alex J. Novikoff, ed., *The Twelfth-Century Renaissance: A Reader* (Toronto: University of Toronto Press, 2017), 89.
27. See Saint Thomas Aquinas, *Summa Theologica*, 22 Volumes, trans. Fathers of the English Dominican Province (New York: Benziger Brothers, 1911–1925).
28. On non-European higher learning, see Lowe and Yasuhara, *The Origins of Higher Learning*, Chaps. 1–7.
29. See George Makdisi, "Madrasa and University in the Middle Ages," *Studia Islamica* 32 (1970): 255–64; idem., *The Rise of Colleges: Institutions of Learning in Islam and the West* (Edinburgh: Edinburgh University Press, 1981).
30. See Berman, *Law and Revolution*, 143–48.
31. As quoted in Berman, "The Origins of Western Legal Science," 923.
32. As quoted from Maria Dobozy, trans. and ed., *The Saxon Mirror: A "Sachsenspiegel" of the Fourteenth Century* (Philadelphia: University of Pennsylvania Press, 1999), 67.
33. See Berman, *Law and Revolution*, Chaps. 9–13.
34. See Reynolds "The Emergence of Professional Law in the Long Twelfth Century."
35. Quoted from James Q. Whitman, *The Origins of Reasonable Doubt: Theological Roots of the Criminal Trial* (New Haven, CT: Yale University Press, 2008), 53.

Notes

36. On English common law, see Glenn, *Legal Traditions of the World*, Chap. 7.
37. As quoted from John A. Makdisi, "The Islamic Origins of the Common Law," *North Carolina Law Review* 77, no. 5 (1999): 1723. For more on Muslim influences in Sicily both before and after the Norman conquest in the late 1000s, see Alex Metcalfe, *The Muslims of Medieval Italy* (Edinburgh: Edinburgh University Press, 2009).
38. Quoted from Whitman, *The Origins of Reasonable Doubt*, 54.
39. Harold J. Berman, "Religious Foundations of Law in the West: An Historical Perspective," *Journal of Law and Religion* 1 (Summer 1983): 11.
40. See Glenn, *Legal Traditions of the World*, Chap. 6.
41. See Joseph Needham with the research assistance of Wang Ling, *Science and Civilization in China*, Volume 2: *History of Scientific Thought* (Cambridge: Cambridge University Press, 1956), 519–31, 543–45, 572–82.
42. As quoted from Avner Greif, *Institutions and the Path to the Modern Economy: Lessons from Medieval Trade* (Cambridge: Cambridge University Press, 2006), 390.
43. So argues Monica M. Gaudiosi, "The Influence of the Islamic Law of Waqf on the Development of the Trust in England: The Case of Merton College," *University of Pennsylvania Law Review* 136, no. 4 (April 1988): 1231–61.
44. On English trusts, see Alan Macfarlane, *The Making of the Modern World: Visions from the West and East* (Basingstoke, UK, and New York: Palgrave, 2002), 83–105.
45. On the Islamic world, see Timur Kuran, *The Long Divergence: How Islamic Law Held Back the Middle East* (Princeton, NJ: Princeton University Press, 2011), Chap. 6. On China, see Tingmei Fu, "Legal Person in China: Essence and Limits," *The American Journal of Comparative Law* 41, no. 2 (Spring 1993): 262. In premodern India, only actual persons enjoyed rights in a court of law, yet the joint-family enterprise in Hindu culture "held de facto personhood in its daily interactions." As quoted from Timur Kuran and Anantdeep Singh, "Economic Modernization in Late British India: Hindu-Muslim Differences," *Economic Development and Cultural Change* 61, no. 3 (April 2013): 509.
46. The largest Hindu joint-family enterprises had over fifty branches across South Asia, yet they were far less able to raise capital than the Western joint-stock companies and corporations. Anantdeep Singh email to the author, November 8, 2018. In his review of Kuran's *The Long Divergence*, Abdul Azim Islahi suggests that "overall development in the region" may have been more determinant than specific legal impediments, since "in the Islamic Shariah there is provision of joint ownership," which could have been deployed to work around prohibitions on fictive personhood. See *JKAU: Islamic Economics* 25, no. 2 (2012): 253–61 [here: 257–58]. Kaveh Yazdani kindly brought this review to my attention.
47. Berman, *Law and Revolution*, 348–56.
48. As quoted from Hans-Bernd Schäfer and Alexander J. Wulf, "Jurists, Clerics, and Merchants: The Rise of Learned Law in Medieval Europe and Its Impact on Economic Growth," *Journal of Empirical Legal Studies* 11, no. 2 (June 2014): 299.

Notes

49. See Kuran, *The Long Divergence*, Chap. 5.
50. As quoted from Kuran, *The Long Divergence*, 76.

Chapter 2

1. Quoted in David Dobbs, "Restless Genes," *National Geographic* 223, no. 1 (January 2013): 45.
2. Kim M. Phillips makes this point in "Travelers East and West," *Journal of the Economic and Social History of the Orient* 53, no. 3 (2010): 506.
3. See Robert B. Strassler, ed., *The Landmark Herodotus: The Histories*, trans. Andrea L. Purvis, intro. Rosalind Thomas (New York: Pantheon Books, 2007).
4. See J. Lennart Berggren and Alexander Jones, ed. and trans., *Ptolemy's Geography: An Annotated Translation of the Theoretical Chapters* (Princeton, NJ: Princeton University Press, 2000).
5. See Tansen Sen, "The Travel Records of Chinese Pilgrims Faxian, Xuanzang, and Yijing: Sources for Cross-Cultural Encounters between Ancient China and Ancient India," *Education about Asia* 11, no. 3 (Winter 2006): 24–33.
6. See Houari Touati, *Islam and Travel in the Middle Ages*, trans. Lydia G. Cochrane (Chicago: University of Chicago Press, 2010), 8–9n22.
7. See John M. Hobson, *The Eastern Origins of Western Civilisation* (Cambridge: Cambridge University Press, 2004), 122.
8. See Cong Ellen Zhang, *Transformative Journeys: Travel and Culture in Song China* (Honolulu: University of Hawai'i Press, 2011).
9. See Stewart Gordon, *When Asia Was the World: Traveling Merchants, Scholars, Warriors, and Monks Who Created the "Riches of the East"* (Cambridge, MA: Da Capo Press, 2008).
10. See Janet L. Abu-Lughod, *Before European Hegemony: The World System A.D. 1250–1350* (New York: Oxford University Press, 1989).
11. As quoted from Tansen Sen, "The Impact of Zheng He's Expeditions on Indian Ocean Interactions," *Bulletin of the School of Oriental and African Studies* 79, no. 3 (2016): 632.
12. See Sally Church, "Zheng He: An Investigation into the Plausibility of 450-ft Treasure Ships," *Monumenta Serica: Journal of Oriental Studies* 53, no. 1 (January 2005): 1–42.
13. See Andre Gunder Frank, *ReOrient: Global Economy in the Asian Age* (Berkeley, CA: University of California Press, 1998), 197.
14. Gang Deng, *Chinese Maritime Activities and Socioeconomic Development, c. 2100 B.C.–1900 A.D.* (Westport, CT: Greenwood Press, 1997), 50.
15. As quoted from Felipe Fernández-Armesto, *Pathfinders: A Global History of Exploration* (New York: W.W. Norton, 2007), 115.

Notes

16. See Niall Ferguson, *Civilization: The West and the Rest* (New York: Penguin Press, 2011), 32.
17. As quoted from Robert Finlay, "The Voyages of Zheng He: Ideology, State Power, and Maritime Trade in Ming China," *Journal of The Historical Society* 8, no. 3 (September 2008): 338.
18. See Deng, *Chinese Maritime Activities and Socioeconomic Development*, 54–58.
19. See Deng, *Chinese Maritime Activities and Socioeconomic Development*, 88–94, 154.
20. As quoted from Fernández-Armesto, *Pathfinders*, 116.
21. See Kent G. Deng, "Development and Its Deadlock in Imperial China, 221 B.C.–1840 A.D.," *Economic Development and Cultural Change* 51 (January 2003): 479–522.
22. Quoted from Romila Thapar, *Early India, From the Origins to AD 1300* (Berkeley and Los Angeles, CA: University of California Press, 2002), 383.
23. As quoted from Kaveh Yazdani, *India, Modernity and the Great Divergence: Mysore and Gujarat (17th to 19th C.)* (Leiden and Boston: Brill, 2017), 261.
24. See Richard N. Frye, trans. and ed., *Ibn Fadlan's Journey to Russia: A Tenth-century Traveler from Baghdad to the Volga River* (Princeton, NJ: Markus Wiener Publishers, 2005).
25. See Kenneth Garden, "The Rihla and Self-Reinvention of Abu Bakr Ibn al-'Arabī," *Journal of the American Oriental Society* 135, no. 1 (January–March 2015): 7.
26. See Brian A. Catlos, *Muslims of Medieval Latin Christendom, c. 1050–1614* (Cambridge: Cambridge University Press, 2014), 256n123.
27. See Natalie Zemon Davis, *Trickster Travels: A Sixteenth-Century Muslim Between Worlds* (New York: Hill & Wang, 2006).
28. This is the subject of Catlos, *Muslims of Medieval Latin Christendom*.
29. As quoted from Catlos, *Muslims of Medieval Latin Christendom*, 279.
30. See Maarten Bosker, Eltjo Buringh, and Jan Luiten van Zanden, "From Baghdad to London: Unraveling Urban Development in Europe, the Middle East, and North Africa, 800–1800," *Review of Economics and Statistics* 95, no. 4 (October 2013): 1429.
31. See Catlos, *Muslims of Medieval Latin Christendom*, 257, 414–16.
32. See Catlos, *Muslims of Medieval Latin Christendom*, 228.
33. See Olivia Remie Constable, "Muslims in Medieval Europe," in *A Companion to the Medieval World*, ed. Carol Lansing and Edward D. English (Chichester, UK: Blackwell Publishing, 2013), 320; Catlos, *Muslims of Medieval Latin Christendom*, 250.
34. See Nabil Matar, *Europe through Arab Eyes, 1578–1727* (New York: Routledge, 2009).
35. As quoted from Constable, "Muslims in Medieval Europe," 320.

Notes

36. Samar Attar, "Conflicting Accounts on the Fear of Strangers: Muslim and Arab Perceptions of Europeans in Medieval Geographical Literature," *Arab Studies Quarterly* 27, no. 4 (Fall 2005): 17–29.
37. Catlos, *Muslims of Medieval Latin Christendom*, 229.
38. See Bernard Lewis, *The Muslim Discovery of Europe* (New York: W.W. Norton & Company, 2001), 91.
39. Catlos, *Muslims of Medieval Latin Christendom*, 261.
40. Touati, *Islam and Travel in the Middle Ages*, 3.
41. See Antony Black, *The West and Islam: Religion and Political Thought in World History* (New York: Oxford University Press, 2008), 115.
42. Romedio Schmitz-Esser, "Travel and Exploration in the Middle Ages," in *Handbook of Medieval Culture: Fundamental Aspects and Conditions of the European Middle Ages*, 3 Volumes, ed. Albrecht Classen (Berlin and New York: De Gruyter, 2010), 3:1702.
43. See Yazdani, *India, Modernity*, 292.
44. See John Wilkinson, trans. and ed., *Jerusalem Pilgrims before the Crusades* (Warminster, UK: Aris & Phillip, 2002).
45. See Schmitz-Esser, "Travel and Exploration in the Middle Ages," 3:1683.
46. As quoted in Bernard Hamilton, "'Knowing the Enemy': Western Understanding of Islam at the Time of the Crusades," *Journal of the Royal Asiatic Society* 7, no. 3 (November 1997): 373.
47. On the Crusades, see Jonathan Riley-Smith, *The Crusades: A History*, 3rd ed. (London: Bloomsbury Publishing, 2014).
48. See Nicholas Morton, *Encountering Islam on the First Crusade* (Cambridge: Cambridge University Press, 2016), 238–44, 278–80 (quotation: 279).
49. See Schmitz-Esser, "Travel and Exploration in the Middle Ages," 1684.
50. See Catlos, *Muslims of Medieval Latin Christendom*, 333.
51. See Christopher MacEvitt, "Martyrdom and the Muslim World Through Franciscan Eyes," *Catholic Historical Review* 97, no. 1 (January 2011): 11–12.
52. See Evelyn Edson, *The World Map, 1300–1493: The Persistence of Tradition and Transformation* (Baltimore, MD: Johns Hopkins University Press, 2007), 92–98.
53. See Alexander C. Wolfe, "Marco Polo: Factotum, Auditor: Language and Political Culture in the Mongol World Empire," *Literature Compass* 11, no. 7 (2014): 417.
54. See Gang Zhou, "Small Talk: A New Reading of Marco Polo's *Il Milione*," *Modern Language Notes* 124, no. 1 (January 2009): 1–22.
55. Quoted from Hans Ulrich Vogel, *Marco Polo Was in China: New Evidence from Currencies, Salts and Revenues* (Leiden: Brill, 2013), 29.
56. Quoted from John Larner, *Marco Polo and the Discovery of the World* (New Haven, CT, and London: Yale University Press, 1999), 97.

Notes

57. See Zhou, "Small Talk," 2.
58. David Waines, *The Odyssey of Ibn Battuta: Uncommon Tales of a Medieval Adventurer* (London and New York: I.B. Tauris, and Co., 2010), 6; Larner, *Marco Polo and the Discovery of the World*, 184.
59. John Larner, "Plucking Hairs from the Great Cham's Beard: Marco Polo, Jan de Langhe, and Sir John Mandeville", in *Marco Polo and the Encounter of East and West*, ed. Suzanne Conklin Akbari and Amilcare Iannucci (Toronto: University of Toronto Press, 2008), 133–55.
60. See Catlos, *Muslims of Medieval Latin Christendom*, 349.
61. Edson, *The World Map*, 108 (acceptance), 109 (manuscripts).
62. Hamilton, "'Knowing the Enemy,'" 386–87; Jo Ann Hoeppner Moran Cruz, "Popular Attitudes Toward Islam in Medieval Europe," in *Travellers, Intellectuals, and the World beyond Medieval Europe*, ed. David R. Blanks and Michael Frassetto (New York: Palgrave Macmillan, 1999), 62.
63. See Schmitz-Esser, "Travel and Exploration in the Middle Ages," 1697.
64. See Edson, *The World Map*, 33–39.
65. As quoted from Timothy Runyan, "Ships and Seafaring," in Classen, ed., *Handbook of Medieval Culture*, 3:1631.
66. See Lawrence V. Mott, "A Three-Masted Ship Depiction from 1409," *International Journal of Nautical Archeology* 23, no. 1 (February 1994): 39–40.
67. To take two examples, John Hobson argues that the lateen sail may have been invented by "Persians or Arabs" and that the sternpost rudder was "undoubtedly" a Chinese invention subsequent adopted by European mariners. See his *The Eastern Origins of Western Civilisation*,125.
68. See Jeffrey Burton Russell, *Inventing the Flat Earth: Columbus and Modern Historians* (Westport, CT, and London: Praeger, 1991).
69. Edson, *The World Map*, 132.
70. Robert Friedel, *A Culture of Improvement: Technology and the Western Millennium* (Cambridge, MA: MIT Press, 2010).
71. As quoted from Zhuang Guotu, "China's Policies on Chinese Overseas: Past and Present," in *Routledge Handbook of the Chinese Diaspora*, ed. Chee-Beng Tan (London and New York: Routledge, 2013), 32.
72. See Peter Edward Russell, *Prince Henry "The Navigator": A Life* (New Haven, CT: Yale University Press, 2000), Chaps. 4-5.
73. The claim by Gavin Menzies, in *1421: The Year China Discovered America* (New York: William Morrow, 2003), that Chinese ships discovered the Americas before Columbus, is not taken seriously by scholars.
74. Erik Ringmar, "Audience for a Giraffe: European Expansionism and the Quest for the Exotic," *Journal of World History* 17, no. 4 (December 2006): 391 (unicorn), 395 (journey).

Notes

75. See John Francis Guilmartin, "The Earliest Shipboard Gunpowder Ordnance: An Analysis of Its Technical Parameters and Tactical Capabilities," *Journal of Military History* 71, no. 3 (July 2007): 660–67.
76. See Edson, *The World Map*, 121.
77. As quoted in Larry Stewart, "Other Centres of Calculation, or, Where the Royal Society Didn't Count: Commerce, Coffee-Houses and Natural Philosophy in Early Modern London," *British Journal for the History of Science* 32, no. 2 (June 1999): 134.
78. As quoted in Ricardo Duchesne, "A Civilization of Explorers," *Academic Questions* 25, no. 1 (March 2012): 91.
79. See Jan Luiten van Zanden and Milja van Tielhof, "Roots of Growth and Productivity Change in Dutch Shipping Industry, 1500–1800," *Explorations in Economic History* 46, no. 4 (2009): 390–92, 399.
80. See Jared Diamond, *Guns, Germs, and Steel: The Fates of Human Societies* (New York: W.W. Norton, 1997), 210–12.
81. See Brian Tierney, *The Idea of Natural Rights: Studies on Natural Rights, Natural Law and Church Law, 1150–1625* (Atlanta, GA: Scholars Press, 1997), Chaps. 10–11.
82. See, for example, George Huppert, *The Style of Paris: Renaissance Origins of the French Enlightenment* (Bloomington, IN: Indiana University Press, 1999).
83. See Alfred W. Crosby, Jr., *The Columbian Exchange: Biological and Cultural Consequences of 1492*, Thirtieth Anniversary ed. (Westport, CT: ABC-CLIO, 2003).
84. Jeremy Black makes this point in *Kings, Nobles and Commoners: States and Societies in Early Modern Europe, a Revisionist History* (London: I.B. Tauris, 2004), 157.
85. See Greg Clark, *Global Cities: A Short History* (Washington, DC: Brookings Institution Press, 2016).
86. Edson, *The World Map*, 73–86.
87. Statistic in Robert Karrow, "Centers of Map Publishing in Europe, 1472–1600," in *The History of Cartography*, Volume 3: *Cartography in the European Renaissance*, ed. David Woodward (Chicago and London: University of Chicago Press, 2007), 621.
88. See Nicholas Crane, *Mercator: The Man Who Mapped the Planet* (New York: Henry Holt and Company, 2003).
89. See Benjamin A. Elman, *On Their Own Terms: Science in China, 1550–1900* (Cambridge, MA: Harvard University Press, 2005), 127–33.
90. As quoted from David Woodward, Cordell D. K. Lee, and Joseph E. Schwartzberg, "Concluding Remarks," in *The History of Cartography*, Volume 2, Book 2: *Cartography in the Traditional East and Southeast Asian Societies*, ed. J.B. Harley and David Woodward (Chicago and London: University of Chicago Press, 1994), 845.

Notes

91. Quoted from John Rennie Short, *Making Space: Revisioning the World, 1475–1600* (Syracuse, NY: Syracuse University Press, 2004), 6–7.
92. See Majid Fakhry, "Philosophy and Theology: From the Eighth Century C.E. to the Present," in *The Oxford History of Islam*, ed. John L. Esposito (Oxford and New York: Oxford University Press, 1999), 302.
93. See Steven Harvey, "Jewish and Muslim Philosophy: Similarities and Differences," in *A History of Jewish-Muslim Relations: From the Origins to the Present Day*, ed. Abdelwahab Meddeb and Benjamin Stora (Princeton, NJ: Princeton University Press, 2013), 751.
94. Averroism retained strong intellectual appeal in Europe for centuries. See Anna Akasoy and Guido Giglioni, eds., *Renaissance Averroism and Its Aftermath: Arabic Philosophy in Early Modern Europe* (Dordrecht: Springer, 2013).

Chapter 3

1. On the alphabet's still-obscure origins, see Brian E. Colless, "The Origin of the Alphabet," *Antiguo Oriente* 12 (2014): 71–104.
2. See John Man, *Alpha Beta: How 26 Letters Shaped the Western World* (New York: Wiley, 2000).
3. Statistic cited in Roy Lowe and Yoshihito Yasuhara, *The Origins of Higher Learning: Knowledge Networks and the Early Development of Universities* (London and New York: Routledge, 2017), 19.
4. See Alexander Monro, *The Paper Trail: An Unexpected History of the World's Greatest Invention* (New York: Alfred A. Knopf, 2016).
5. See Mark Kurlansky, *Paper: Paging Through History* (New York: W.W. Norton, 2016).
6. Statistic cited in Lowe and Yasuhara, *The Origins of Higher Learning*, 135.
7. Quoted from Seung-Hwan Mun, "Printing Press without Copyright: A Historical Analysis of Printing and Publishing in Song, China," *Chinese Journal of Communication* 6, no. 1 (2013): 5.
8. Cynthia J. Brokaw, "On the History of the Book in China," in *Printing and Book Culture in Late Imperial China*, ed. Cynthia J. Brokaw and Kai-wing Chow (Berkeley, CA: University of California Press, 2005), 8.
9. As quoted from Susan Cherniack, "Book Culture and Textual Transmission in Sung China," *Harvard Journal of Asiatic Studies* 54, no. 1 (June 1994): 102.
10. As quoted from Joseph McDermott, "The Ascendance of the Imprint in China," in Brokaw and Chow, eds., *Printing and Book Culture in Late Imperial China*, 59.
11. Quotations from McDermott, "The Ascendance of the Imprint in China," 92.
12. See Christopher de Hamel, "The European Medieval Book," in *The Book: A Global History*, ed. Michael F. Suarez and H.R. Woudhuysen (Oxford and New York: Oxford University Press, 2013), 59–79.

Notes

13. Statistics from Timothy J. Reiss, *Knowledge, Discovery and Imagination in Early Modern Europe: The Rise of Aesthetic Rationalism* (Cambridge: Cambridge University Press, 1997), 140.

14. See Şevket Pamuk, "The Black Death and the Origins of the 'Great Divergence' across Europe, 1300–1600," *European Review of Economic History* 11, no. 3 (December 2007): 310.

15. See Robert Friedel, *A Culture of Improvement: Technology and the Western Millennium* (Cambridge, MA: The MIT Press, 2007), 115.

16. On Gutenberg and his invention, see John Man, *Gutenberg: How One Man Remade the World with Words* (New York: John Wiley & Sons, 2002).

17. On the early spread of printing, see Stephan Füssel, *Gutenberg and the Impact of Printing*, trans. Douglas Martin (Aldershot, UK, and Burlington, VT: Ashgate Publishing Co., 2005), 59–70; Lotta Helinga, "The Gutenberg Revolutions," in *A Companion to the History of the Book*, ed. Simon Eliot and Jonathan Rose (Malden, MA: Blackwell Pub., 2007), 207–19.

18. Statistic from S.H. Steinberg, *Five Hundred Years of Printing* (London: British Library, 1996), 114.

19. See Susan Dackerman, ed., *Prints and the Pursuit of Knowledge in Early Modern Europe* (Cambridge, MA: Harvard University Art Museums, 2011).

20. Statistic cited in R.A. Houston, *Literacy in Early Modern Europe: Culture and Education, 1500–1800*, 2nd ed. (London and New York: Routledge, 2013), 175.

21. See Margaret Zeegers and Deirdre Barron, *Gatekeepers of Knowledge: A Consideration of the Library, the Book and the Scholar in the Western World* (Oxford, Cambridge, and New Delhi: Chandos Publishing, 2010), 54.

22. See Fred Lerner, *The Story of Libraries: From the Invention of Writing to the Computer Age* (London and New York: Continuum, 2001), 86.

23. As quoted in George Huppert, *The Style of Paris: Renaissance Origins of the French Enlightenment* (Bloomington, IN: Indiana University Press, 1999), 63.

24. See Bill Katz, *Cuneiform to Computer: A History of Reference Sources* (Lanham, MD, and London: The Scarecrow Press, 1998), 3–4.

25. See Geoffrey Roper, "The History of the Book in the Muslim World," in Suarez and Woudhuysen, eds., *The Book*, 541–53.

26. Johannes Pedersen, *The Arabic Book*, trans. Geoffrey French, ed. Robert Hillenbrand (Princeton, NJ: Princeton University Press, 1984), 133.

27. As quoted from Metin M. Coşgel, Thomas J. Miceli, and Jared Rubin, "The Political Economy of Mass Printing: Legitimacy and Technological Change in the Ottoman Empire," *Journal of Comparative Economics* 40, no. 3 (August 2012): 364.

28. Jan Luiten van Zanden makes this point in *The Long Road to the Industrial Revolution: The European Economy in a Global Perspective, 1000–1800* (Leiden: Brill, 2009), 187.

Notes

29. As argued by Coşgel, Miceli, and Rubin, "The Political Economy of Mass Printing," 365.
30. See Kaveh Yazdani, *India, Modernity and the Great Divergence: Mysore and Gujarat (17th to 19th C.)* (Leiden and Boston: Brill, 2017), 105–7.
31. Statistics in van Zanden, *The Long Road to the Industrial Revolution*, 188.
32. See Luis Angeles, "The Great Divergence and the Economics of Printing," *Economic History Review* 70, no. 1 (February 2017): 49–50.
33. Statistics and hypothesis from Eltjo Buringh and Jan Luiten van Zanden, "Charting the 'Rise of the West': Manuscripts and Printed Books in Europe, a Long-Term Perspective from the Sixth through Eighteenth Centuries," *Journal of Economic History* 69, no. 2 (June 2009): 437.
34. See Mun, "Printing Press without Copyright," 5–7.
35. See Harriet T. Zurndorfer, "The Passion to Collect, Select, and Protect: Fifteen Hundred Years of the Chinese Encyclopedia," in *Encyclopaedism from Antiquity to the Renaissance*, ed. Jason König and Greg Woolf (Cambridge: Cambridge University Press, 2013), 515–16.
36. As quoted from Mun, "Printing Press without Copyright," 3.
37. Quoted from Susan Cherniack, "Book Culture and Textual Transmission in Sung China," 29–30.
38. Quotations from McDermott, "The Ascendance of the Imprint in China," 93.
39. As quoted from Benjamin A. Elman, *On Their Own Terms: Science in China, 1550–1900* (Cambridge, MA: Harvard University Press, 2005), 19.
40. Quotation from Lynn White, Jr., *Machina ex Deo: Essays in the Dynamism of Western Culture* (Cambridge, MA: MIT Press, 1968), 65.
41. As quoted from Thomas P. Hughes, *Human-Built World: How to Think about Technology and Culture* (Chicago: University of Chicago Press, 2005), 21.
42. See Tamara Albertini, "Mathematics and Astronomy," in *Introducing Nicholas of Cusa: A Guide to a Renaissance Man*, ed. Christopher M. Bellitto and Thomas M. Izbicki (New York: Paulist Press, 2004), 388–91.
43. See Alfred W. Crosby, *The Measure of Reality: Quantification and Western Society, 1250–1600* (Cambridge and New York: Cambridge University Press, 1996).

Chapter 4

1. See, for example, Victoria Tin-bor Hui, *War and State Formation in Ancient China and Early Modern Europe* (New York: Cambridge University Press, 2005).
2. See Daniel Pipes, *Slave Soldiers and Islam: The Genesis of a Military System* (New Haven, CT, and London: Yale University Press, 1981), 140–48.

Notes

3. Quotation from Patricia Crone, *Slaves on Horses: The Evolution of the Islamic Polity* (Cambridge: Cambridge University Press, 2003), 81.
4. As quoted from Claude Cahen, "Economy, Society, Institutions," in *Islamic Society and Civilization*, ed. P.M. Holt, Ann K.S. Lambton, and Bernard Lewis (Cambridge: Cambridge University Press, 1970), 536.
5. For abundant documents illuminating feudal social relations in one corner of France, see Theodore Evergates, ed. and trans., *Feudal Society in Medieval France: Documents from the County of Champagne* (Philadelphia: University of Pennsylvania Press, 1993).
6. For this argument, see Lisa Blaydes and Eric Chaney, "The Feudal Revolution and Europe's Rise: Political Divergence of the Christian West and the Muslim World before 1500 CE," *American Political Science Review* 107, no. 1 (February 2013): 16–34.
7. As quoted in Alan Harding, "Political Liberty in the Middle Ages," *Speculum* 55, no. 3 (July 1980): 426.
8. See Janet Nelson, "Rulers and Government," in *The New Cambridge Medieval History*, Volume 3: *c.900–c.1024*, ed. Timothy Reuter (Cambridge: Cambridge University Press, 1999), 100.
9. See Harding, "Political Liberty in the Middle Ages," 433.
10. See David M. Nicholas, *The Growth of the Medieval City: From Late Antiquity to the Early Fourteenth Century* (London and New York: Longman, 1997), 80.
11. See Maarten Bosker, Eltjo Buringh, and Jan Luiten van Zanden, "From Baghdad to London: Unraveling Urban Development in Europe, the Middle East, and North Africa, 800–1800," *Review of Economics and Statistics* 95, no. 4 (October 2013): 1432.
12. Alan Harding, *Medieval Law and the Foundations of the State* (Oxford and New York: Oxford University Press, 2002), 72–79.
13. See, for example, Joseph F. O'Callaghan, *The Cortes of Castile-León, 1188–1350* (Philadelphia: University of Pennsylvania Press, 1989), 11–14.
14. See Nicholas, *The Growth of the Medieval City*, 113–24.
15. See O'Callaghan, *The Cortes of Castile-León*, 15–16, 194.
16. See Nicholas, *The Growth of the Medieval City*, 144, 146, 150–51.
17. As quoted from Harding, "Political Liberty in the Middle Ages," 430.
18. On the enduring impact of Magna Carta, see Zachary Elkins, Tom Ginsburg, and James Melton, "On the Influence of Magna Carta and Other Cultural Relics," *International Review of Law and Economics* 47 (2016): 3–9.
19. See John Witte, Jr., and Justin Latterell, "Christianity and Human Rights: Past Contributions and Future Challenges," *Journal of Law and Religion* 30, no. 3 (2015): 361–69.
20. Steven A. Epstein, *An Economic and Social History of Later Medieval Europe, 1000–1500* (Cambridge: Cambridge University Press, 2009), Chaps. 1–3.

Notes

21. See Nicholas, *The Growth of the Medieval City*, 149.
22. See Marshall Hodgson, *The Venture of Islam: Conscience and History in a World Civilization*, 3 Volumes. (Chicago: University of Chicago Press, 1974), 3:93.
23. See Marshall G.S. Hodgson, "Cultural Patterning in Islamdom and the Occident," in *Rethinking World History: Essays on Europe, Islam, and World History*, ed. Edmund Burke III (Cambridge: Cambridge University Press, 1993), 159.
24. As quoted from Cahen, "Economy, Society, Institutions," 520.
25. See Bosker, Buringh, and van Zanden, "From Baghdad to London," 1433.
26. See Şevket Pamuk, "Institutional Change and the Longevity of the Ottoman Empire, 1500–1800," *Journal of Interdisciplinary History* 35, no. 2 (Autumn 2004): 225–47.
27. See Nicholas, *The Growth of the Medieval City*, 168.
28. On Chinese cities and guilds, see Aidan Southall, *The City in Time and Space* (Cambridge and New York: Cambridge University Press, 1998), 38–44, 125–58. On one of the most advanced regions, see Yoshinobu Shiba, "On the Emergence and Intensification of the Pattern of Rural-Urban Continuum in Late Imperial Jiangnan Society," in *The Economy of Lower Yangzi Delta in Late Imperial China*, ed. Billy K.L. So (London and New York: Routledge, 2013), 149–207.
29. See Romila Thapar, *Early India: From the Origins to AD 1300* (Berkeley and Los Angeles, CA: University of California Press, 2002), 385; Kaveh Yazdani, *India, Modernity and the Great Divergence: Mysore and Gujarat (17th to 19th C.)* (Leiden and Boston: Brill, 2017), 401–31.
30. See Nicholas, *The Growth of the Medieval City*, 212 (encroachments), 287 (succeeded), 292–317 (shifted).
31. Harding, "Political Liberty in the Middle Ages," 434–37 (quotation: 442).
32. See Diane Martin, "Prosecution of the Statutes of Provisors and Premunire in the King's Bench, 1377–1394," in *Fourteenth Century England*, Volume 4, ed. J.S. Hamilton (Rochester, NY: Boydell & Brewer, 2006), 109–23.
33. As argued by Jan Luiten van Zanden, Eltjo Buringh, and Maarten Bosker, "The Rise and Decline of European Parliaments, 1188–1789," *Economic History Review* 65, no. 3 (2012): 837.
34. As quoted from Nelson, "Rulers and Government," 124.
35. See O'Callaghan, *The Cortes of Castile-León*.
36. Quotations from Joseph F. O'Callaghan, "The Beginnings of the Cortes in León-Castile," *American Historical Review* 74, no. 5 (June 1969): 1503–37 [here: 1514–15].
37. As quoted from O'Callaghan, "The Beginnings of the Cortes in León-Castile," 1533.
38. See O'Callaghan, *The Cortes of Castile-León*, 75–76.
39. See van Zanden, Buringh, and Bosker, "The Rise and Decline of European Parliaments," 839.

Notes

40. See O'Callaghan, *The Cortes of Castile-León*, 39–40, 58–59, 77, 93–94, 110–11, 128–29, 150–51.

41. See van Zanden, Buringh, and Bosker, "The Rise and Decline of European Parliaments," 846.

42. This argument in advanced in David Stasavage, "When Distance Mattered: Geographic Scale and the Development of European Representative Assemblies," *American Political Science Review* 104, no. 4 (2010): 625–43.

43. As demonstrated in K. Kivanç Karaman and Şevket Pamuk, "Different Paths to the Modern State in Europe: The Interaction Between Warfare, Economic Structure, and Political Regime," *American Political Science Review* 107, no. 3 (August 2013): 603–26.

44. See Antony Black, "The Conciliar Movement," in *The Cambridge History of Medieval Political Thought c.350–c.1450*, ed. J.H. Burns (Cambridge: Cambridge University Press, 1988), 573–87.

45. As quoted in Black, "The Conciliar Movement," 576.

46. As quoted from Black, "The Conciliar Movement," 579.

47. As quoted from Michael D. Breidenbach, "Conciliarism and the American Founding," *William and Mary Quarterly* 73, no. 3 (July 2016): 499.

48. Timothy George, *Theology of the Reformers*, rev. ed. (Nashville: Broadman and Holman, 2013), 34–38.

49. See Carter Lindberg, *The European Reformations*, 2nd ed. (Oxford: Wiley-Blackwell, 2010).

50. Quoted from Toby E. Huff, "Law and Science," *Academic Questions* 25, no. 1 (March 2012): 57–58.

51. Mark U. Edwards, Jr., *Printing, Propaganda, and Martin Luther* (Berkeley, CA: University of California Press, 1994), 1–2.

52. As quoted from Lindberg, *The European Reformations*, 84.

53. As noted in John Witte, Jr., "Introduction," in *Christianity and Human Rights: An Introduction*, ed. John Witte, Jr., and Frank S. Alexander (Cambridge: Cambridge University Press, 2010), 39.

54. See Gerrit Voogt, "'Anyone Who Can Read May Be a Preacher': Sixteenth-Century Roots of the Collegiants," *Nederlands archief voor kerkgeschiedenis* 85, no. 1 (2005): 424.

55. As quoted from Lynn Hunt, *Inventing Human Rights: A History* (New York: W.W. Norton, 2007), 147.

56. This paragraph draws on Atle Grahl-Madsen, "The European Tradition of Asylum and the Development of Refugee Law," *Journal of Peace Research* 3 (1966): 278–89.

57. As quoted in David Gordon Newcombe, *Henry VIII and the English Reformation* (London: Routledge, 1995), 45.

Notes

58. As quoted in Joshua Aaron Chafetz, *Democracy's Privileged Few: Legislative Privilege and Democratic Norms in the British and American Constitutions* (New Haven, CT, and London: Yale University Press, 2007), 117.
59. See Cary J. Nederman and Catherine Campbell, "Priests, Kings, and Tyrants: Spiritual and Temporal Power in John of Salisbury's *Policraticus*," *Speculum* 66 (July 1991): 572–90.
60. See Edward Rubin, "Judicial Review and the Right to Resist," *Georgetown Law Journal* 96 (November 2008): 72–75 (quotation: 72).
61. See Anne McClaren, "Rethinking Republicanism: *Vindiciae, Contra Tyrannos* in Context," *Historical Journal* 49, no. 1 (March 2006): 23–52.
62. See Quentin Skinner, *The Foundations of Modern Political Thought*, Volume 2: *The Age of Reformation* (Cambridge: Cambridge University Press, 1978), 201–37.
63. See John Locke, *Second Treatise of Civil Government*, Chap. 7.

Chapter 5

1. See David Lindberg, *The Beginnings of Western Science: The European Scientific Tradition in Philosophical, Religious, and Institutional Context, 600 BC. to AD. 1450* (Chicago: University of Chicago Press, 1992), Chap. 1.
2. See Daniel W. Graham, "Matter," in *A Companion to Science, Technology, and Medicine in Ancient Greece and Rome*, 2 Volumes, ed. Georgia L. Irby (Chichester, UK, and Malden, MA: Wiley Blackwell, 2016), 1:29–31.
3. Details and argument from Wen-yuan Qian, *The Great Inertia: Scientific Stagnation in Traditional China* (London and Dover, NH: Croom Helm, 1985), 75–76.
4. See Bryan E. Penprase, *The Power of Stars: How Celestial Observations Have Shaped Civilization* (New York: Springer Verlag, 2011), 110–12.
5. For a still authoritative study, see G.E.R. Lloyd, *Greek Science after Aristotle* (New York: Norton, 1973).
6. See John North, *Cosmos: An Illustrated History of Astronomy and Cosmology* (Chicago and London: The University of Chicago Press, 2008), 67–80.
7. On the methods and works of Aristotle, see Christopher Shields, ed., *The Oxford Handbook of Aristotle* (Oxford and New York: Oxford University Press, 2012); Lindberg, *The Beginnings of Western Science*, Chap. 3.
8. See North, *Cosmos*, 85.
9. See Lindberg, *The Beginnings of Western Science*, Chap. 6; George Sarton, *Hellenistic Science and Culture in the Last Three Centuries B.C.* (New York: Dover Publications, 1993), Chaps. 8–9, 22.

Notes

10. As quoted in Stephen Gaukroger, *The Emergence of a Scientific Culture: Science and the Shaping of Modernity, 1210–1685* (Oxford: Clarendon Press, 2006), 34n87.
11. See Thorsten Fögen, "Roman Responses to Greek Science and Scholarship as a Cultural and Political Phenomenon," in Irby, ed., *A Companion to Science, Technology, and Medicine in Ancient Greece and Rome*, 1:958–72.
12. See Jason König and Greg Woolf, "Encyclopaedism in the Roman Empire," in *Encyclopaedism from Antiquity to the Renaissance*, ed. Jason König and Greg Woolf (Cambridge: Cambridge University Press, 2013), 23–63.
13. On early Chinese science, see Yongxiang Lu, ed., *A History of Chinese Science and Technology*, Volume 1 (Shanghai: Shanghai Jiao Tong University Press; Heidelberg: Springer, 2015).
14. For a scholarly assessment of this monumental work, see Robert Finlay, "China, the West, and World History in Joseph Needham's *Science and Civilisation in China*," *Journal of World History* 11 (Fall 2000): 265–303. I am grateful to Paula Dempsey, Head Librarian, Research Services and Resources, at the University of Illinois at Chicago, for establishing the precise number of volumes.
15. Joseph Needham summarizes his findings in *The Grand Titration: Science and Society in East and West* (London: Allen & Unwin, 1969); idem., *Science in Traditional China: A Comparative Perspective* (Cambridge, MA: Harvard University Press; Hong Kong: The Chinese University Press, 1981). For an abridgement, see Colin A. Ronan, *The Shorter Science and Civilisation in China: An Abridgement of Joseph Needham's Original Text*, 5 Volumes (Cambridge: Cambridge University Press, 1978–1995).
16. See Dengjian Jin, *The Great Knowledge Transcendence: The Rise of Western Science and Technology Reframed* (Basingstoke, UK, and New York: Palgrave Macmillan, 2016), 25.
17. See Tables 2.1 and 2.2 in Jin, *The Great Knowledge Transcendence*, as well as pp. 130–34.
18. For a fuller list of Chinese scientific and technological advances, see Simon Winchester, *The Man Who Loved China: The Fantastic Story of the Eccentric Scientist Who Unlocked the Mysteries of the Middle Kingdom* (New York: Harper Perennial, 2008), 267–77.
19. See G.E.R. Lloyd, *The Ambitions of Curiosity: Understanding the World in Ancient Greece and China* (New York: Cambridge University Press, 2002).
20. As quoted from North, *Cosmos*, 141.
21. See Benjamin A. Elman, *On Their Own Terms: Science in China, 1550–1900* (Cambridge, MA: Harvard University Press, 2005), 7–9.
22. On early Indian science, see Debiprasad Chattopadhyaya, *History of Science and Technology in Ancient India*, 3 Volumes (Calcutta: Firma K.L. Mukhopadhyaya, 1988–1996).
23. See Roy Lowe and Yoshihito Yasuhara, *The Origins of Higher Learning: Knowledge Networks and the Early Development of Universities* (London and New York: Routledge, 2017), 35–54 (quotations: 42, 54).

Notes

24. See Kim Plofker, *Mathematics in India* (Princeton, NJ, and Oxford: Princeton University Press, 2009); T.K. Puttaswamy, *Mathematical Achievements of Premodern Indian Mathematicians* (London: Elsevier, 2012).
25. As quoted in North, *Cosmos*, 180.
26. As quoted from Roy W. Perrett, "History, Time, and Knowledge in Ancient India," *History and Theory* 38, no. 3 (October 1999): 320.
27. See the discussion of the phenomenon and the term in Giorgio Riello, *Cotton: The Fabric that Made the Modern World* (Cambridge and New York: Cambridge University Press, 2013), 112–16.
28. See Kaveh Yazdani, *India, Modernity and the Great Divergence: Mysore and Gujarat (17th to 19th C.)* (Leiden and Boston: Brill, 2017).
29. See Jacques Sesiano, *An Introduction to the History of Algebra: Solving Equations from Mesopotamian Times to the Renaissance*, trans. Anna Pierrehumbert (Providence, RI: American Mathematical Society, 2009), Chap. 3.
30. See Lawrence M. Principe, *The Secrets of Alchemy* (Chicago: University of Chicago Press, 2012), Chap. 2.
31. See Ahmad Dallal, "Science, Medicine, and Technology: The Making of a Scientific Culture," in *The Oxford History of Islam*, ed. John L. Esposito (Oxford: Oxford and New York, 1999), 155–214.
32. See Brian A. Catlos, *Muslims of Medieval Latin Christendom, c. 1050–1614* (Cambridge: Cambridge University Press, 2014), 434.
33. See Edward Grant, *A History of Natural Philosophy: From the Ancient World to the Nineteenth Century* (Cambridge: Cambridge University Press, 2007), 78–84.
34. See Grant, *A History of Natural Philosophy*, 87–90; Antony Black, *The West and Islam: Religion and Political Thought in World History* (New York: Oxford University Press, 2008), 119–24.
35. See F.J. Ragep, "Copernicus and His Islamic Predecessors: Some Historical Remarks," *History of Science* 45 (March 2007): 65–81.
36. See Catlos, *Muslims of Medieval Latin Christendom*, 432–34.
37. See, for example, William Eamon, *Science and the Secrets of Nature: Books of Secrets in Medieval and Early Modern Culture* (Princeton, NJ: Princeton University Press, 1994).
38. See Toby E. Huff, *The Rise of Early Modern Science: Islam, China, and the West*, 3rd ed. (Cambridge: Cambridge University Press, 2017), 176.
39. As quoted in Richard C. Taylor, "Ibn Rushd/Averroes and 'Islamic' Rationalism," *Medieval Encounters* 15 (2009): 232.
40. See Anna Akasoy and Guido Giglioni, eds., *Renaissance Averroism and Its Aftermath: Arabic Philosophy in Early Modern Europe* (Dordrecht: Springer, 2013).
41. Quoted from Edward Grant, ed., *A Source Book in Medieval Science* (Cambridge, MA: Harvard University Press, 1974), 199–200.

Notes

42. As quoted in Arthur Hyman, James J. Walsh, and Thomas Williams, eds., *Philosophy in the Middle Ages: The Christian, Islamic, and Jewish Traditions*, 3rd ed. (Indianapolis and Cambridge, MA: Hackett Publishing Co., 2010), 542.
43. See David Park, *The How and the Why: An Essay on the Origins and Development of Physical Theory* (Princeton, NJ: Princeton University Press, 1988), 136–39.
44. See Lindberg, *The Beginnings of Western Science*, 300–6.
45. On Oresme and Buridan, see Lindberg, *The Beginnings of Western Science*, 282–85; Grant, *A History of Natural Philosophy*, 192–200.
46. See Principe, *The Secrets of Alchemy*, 54–62.
47. As quoted from Luis-Alfonso Arráez-Aybar, José-L. Bueno-López, and Nicolas Raio, "Toledo School of Translators and Their Influence on Anatomical Terminology," *Annals of Anatomy* 198 (March 2015): 25.
48. See William H. York, *Health and Wellness in Antiquity through the Middle Ages* (Santa Barbara, CA: Greenwood, 2012), 227.
49. See Hawa Edriss, et al., "Islamic Medicine in the Middle Ages," *American Journal of the Medical Sciences* 354, no. 3 (September 2017): 227.
50. Sanjib Kumar Ghosh, "Human Cadaveric Dissection: A Historical Account from Ancient Greece to the Modern Era," *Anatomy & Cell Biology* 48 (2015): 155.
51. On the re-emergence of anatomical dissection, see Daniel D. Cavalcanti, William Feindel, James T. Goodrich, T. Forcht Dagi, Charles J. Prestigiacomo, and Mark C. Preul, "Anatomy, Technology, Art, and Culture: Toward a Realistic Perspective of the Brain," *Neurosurgical Focus* 27 (September 2009): 1–22.
52. See Paula Findlen, "Anatomy Theaters, Botanical Gardens, and Natural History Collections," in *The Cambridge History of Science*, Volume 3: *Early Modern Science*, ed. Katharine Park and Lorraine Daston (Cambridge: Cambridge University Press, 2006), 275–77.
53. See Gavin Moodie, *Universities, Disruptive Technologies, and Continuity in Higher Education: The Impact of Information Revolutions* (New York: Palgrave Macmillan, 2016), 99.
54. See Paula Findlen, "Natural History," in Park and Daston, eds., *The Cambridge History of Science*, Volume 3: *Early Modern Science*, 447–48.
55. See Findlen, "Anatomy Theaters, Botanical Gardens, and Natural History Collections," 273–74, 280–83.
56. See Carmen Nekrasz and Claudia Swan, "Art," in Park and Daston, eds., *The Cambridge History of Science*, Volume 3: *Early Modern Science*, 780, 780n21.
57. As quoted in Elizabeth L. Eisenstein, *The Printing Revolution in Early Modern Europe*, 2nd ed. (Cambridge: Cambridge University Press, 2005), 220.
58. See Cavalcanti, et al., "Anatomy, Technology, Art, and Culture," 13–15.

Notes

59. See Klaus Hentschel, *Visual Cultures in Science and Technology: A Comparative History* (Oxford and New York: Oxford University Press, 2014), 216.
60. See Zaheer Baber, "The Plants of Empire: Botanic Gardens, Colonial Power and Botanical Knowledge," *Journal of Contemporary Asia* 46, no. 4 (September 2016): 674.
61. See Findlen, "Natural History," 459.
62. As quoted from Baber, "The Plants of Empire," 672.
63. See Kirsti Andersen, *The Geometry of an Art: The History of the Mathematical Theory of Perspective from Alberti to Monge* (New York: Springer, 2007), 93–94.
64. See Elizabeth L. Eisenstein, *Divine Art, Infernal Machine: The Reception of Printing in the West from First Impressions to the Sense of an Ending* (Philadelphia and Oxford: University of Pennsylvania Press, 2011), 94.
65. Pamela H. Smith, "Laboratories," in Park and Daston, eds., *The Cambridge History of Science*, Volume 3: *Early Modern Science*, 304–5.
66. See Bernard Goldstein, "Copernicus and the Origin of His Heliocentric System," *Journal for the History of Astronomy* 33, no. 3 (August 2002): 219–35.
67. See Jin, *The Great Knowledge Transcendence*, 176–80 (quotation 178).
68. Richard S. Westfall, "The Scientific Revolution of the Seventeenth Century: The Construction of a New World View," in *The Concept of Nature: The Herbert Spencer Lectures*, ed. John Torrance (Oxford: Clarendon Press, 1992), 66.
69. On the Tychonic system, see Michael J. Crowe, *Theories of the World from Antiquity to the Copernican Revolution* (New York: Dover Publications, 1990), Chap. 7.
70. See Peter Machamer, "Galileo's Machines, His Mathematics, and His Experiments," in *The Cambridge Companion to Galileo*, ed. Peter Machamer (Cambridge: Cambridge University Press, 1998), 53–79.
71. See William R. Shea and Mariano Artigas, *Galileo in Rome: The Rise and Fall of a Troublesome Genius* (Oxford and New York: Oxford University Press, 2003), Chap. 6.
72. See Machamer, "Galileo's Machines," 53-55.
73. As quoted in Alfred W. Crosby, *The Measure of Reality: Quantification and Western Society, 1250–1600* (Cambridge: Cambridge University Press, 1996), 126.
74. Alexandre Koyré, *The Astronomical Revolution: Copernicus, Kepler, Borelli*, trans. R.E.W. Maddison (Paris: Hermann, 1973), 183.
75. See André Charrak, "The Mathematical Model of Creation According to Kepler," in *Mathematics and the Divine: A Historical Study*, ed. T. Koetsier and L. Bergmans (Amsterdam: Elsevier B.V., 2005), 361–74.
76. Mohammed T. Numan, "Ibn Al Nafis: His Seminal Contributions to Cardiology," *Pediatric Cardiology* 35, no. 7 (October 2014): 1089.

Notes

77. See John B. West, "Ibn al-Nafis, the Pulmonary Circulation, and the Islamic Golden Age," *Journal of Applied Physiology* 105, no. 6 (December 2008): 1877–80.
78. See Jole Shackelford, *William Harvey and the Mechanics of the Heart* (Oxford and New York: Oxford University Press, 2003), Chap. 2.
79. See Westfall, "The Scientific Revolution of the Seventeenth Century," 68.
80. See Madeline M. Muntersbjorn, "Francis Bacon's Philosophy of Science: *Machina Intellectus* and *Forma Indita*," *Philosophy of Science* 70 (December 2003): 1137–48.
81. As quoted from Francis Bacon, *The New Organon*, ed. Lisa Jardine and Michael Silverthorne (Cambridge: Cambridge University Press, 2000), 92, 106.
82. René Descartes, *A Discourse on the Method*, trans. Ian Maclean (Oxford: Oxford University Press, 2006), 28. This phrase is often translated as "I think, therefore I am."
83. See René Descartes, *Meditations on First Philosophy: With Selections from the Objections and Replies*, ed. John Cottingham (Cambridge: Cambridge University Press, 1996). Descartes develops this idea in his Sixth Meditation.
84. See William R. Shea, *The Magic of Numbers and Motion: The Scientific Career of René Descartes* (Canton, MA: Science History Publications, 1991).
85. As quoted in Gerald James Holton and Stephen G. Brush, *Physics, the Human Adventure: From Copernicus to Einstein and Beyond* (New Brunswick, NJ: Rutgers University Press, 2001), 152.
86. See I. Bernard Cohen, "Newton's Concepts of Force and Mass, with Notes on the Laws of Motion," in *The Cambridge Companion to Newton*, 2nd ed., ed. Rob Iliffe and George E. Smith (Cambridge: Cambridge University Press, 2016), 61–92.
87. See Stephen J. Harris, "Networks of Travel, Correspondence, and Exchange," in Park and Daston, *The Cambridge History of Science*, Volume 3: *Early Modern Science*, eds., 346–47.
88. See Jack Goldstone, *Why Europe? The Rise of the West in World History, 1500–1850* (Boston: McGraw Hill, 2009), 153.
89. See John B. West, "Robert Boyle's Landmark Book of 1660 with the First Experiments on Rarified Air," *Journal of Applied Physiology* 98 (2005): 31–39.
90. Quoted from Westfall, "The Scientific Revolution of the Seventeenth Century," 75.
91. Statistic in Westfall, "The Scientific Revolution of the Seventeenth Century," 85.
92. See Harris, "Networks of Travel, Correspondence, and Exchange," 344.
93. See Alan H. Cook, *Edmond Halley: Charting the Heavens and the Seas* (Oxford: Clarendon Press, 1998), 81–88.
94. See P. Fontes da Costa, "The Culture of Curiosity at The Royal Society in the First Half of the Eighteenth Century," *Notes and Records of the Royal Society of London* 56 (May 2002): 152–53.

Notes

95. This paragraph also draws upon Michael Brian Schiffer, *Draw the Lightning Down: Benjamin Franklin and Electrical Technology in the Age of Enlightenment* (Berkeley, CA: University of California Press, 2003).
96. See J.B. Gough, "Lavoisier and the Fulfillment of the Stahlian Revolution," *Osiris* 4 (1988): 15–33; Arthur Donovan, "Lavoisier and the Origins of Modern Chemistry," in ibid., 214–31.
97. For details on their discovery, see John Emsley, *Nature's Building Blocks: An A-Z Guide to the Elements*, 2nd ed. (Oxford: Oxford University Press, 2011).
98. See Diederick Raven, "What Needs to Be Explained about Modern Science?" *British Journal for the History of Science* 44, no. 3 (September 2011): 453.
99. As quoted from Sachiko Kusukawa, "Nature's Regularity in Some Protestant Natural Philosophy Textbooks, 1530–1630," in *Natural Law and Laws of Nature in Early Modern Europe: Jurisprudence, Theology, Moral and Natural Philosophy*, ed. Lorraine Daston and Michael Stolleis (Farnham, UK, and Burlington, VT: Ashgate Pub., 2008), 121.
100. See Harold J. Berman, *Law and Revolution: The Formation of the Western Legal Tradition* (Cambridge, MA, and London: Harvard University Press, 1983).
101. See Alan Macfarlane, *The Making of the Modern World: Visions from the West and East* (Basingstoke, UK, and New York: Palgrave, 2002), 224.
102. See Jin, *The Great Knowledge Transcendence*, 105–17.
103. As quoted from Jin, *The Great Knowledge Transcendence*, 114.
104. As quoted from Jin, *The Great Knowledge Transcendence*, 158, 165, 171.
105. See Jin, *The Great Knowledge Transcendence*, 202–3.
106. For proposed explanations, see Jonathan Daly, *Historians Debate the Rise of the West* (London and New York: Routledge, 2014), Chap. 5.
107. As quoted from Mark Elvin, *The Pattern of the Chinese Past* (Stanford, CA: Stanford University Press, 1973), 233.
108. As quoted from Joseph Needham, with the research assistance of Wang Ling, *Science and Civilization in China*, Volume 2: *History of Scientific Thought* (Cambridge: Cambridge University Press, 1956), 543.
109. As quoted from Peter J. Golas, *Picturing Technology in China: From Earliest Times to the Nineteenth Century* (Hong Kong: Hong Kong University Press, 2015), 173.
110. See Elman, *On Their Own Terms*, 63–149.

Chapter 6

1. As quoted from Joel Mokyr, "Institutions and the Origins of the Great Enrichment," *Atlantic Economic Journal* 44, no. 2 (June 2016): 244.

Notes

2. See Mokyr, "Institutions and the Origins of the Great Enrichment," 248 (transnational), 254 (market).
3. Quoted from Joel Mokyr, "Peer Vries's Great Divergence," *Tijdschrift voor Sociale en Economische Geschiedenis/The Low Countries Journal of Social and Economic History* 12, no. 2 (June 2015): 99.
4. See S.A. Farmer, *Syncretism in the West: Pico's 900 Theses (1486): The Evolution of Traditional Religious and Philosophical Systems*, trans. S.A. Farmer (Tempe, AZ: Medieval & Renaissance Texts & Studies, 1998), x-xi.
5. See Anthony Grafton, *Worlds Made by Words: Scholarship and Community in the Modern West* (Cambridge, MA: Harvard University Press, 2009), 19.
6. See Mokyr, "Institutions and the Origins of the Great Enrichment," 248n7.
7. As quoted from Anne Goldgar, *Impolite Learning: Conduct and Community in the Republic of Letters, 1680–1750* (New Haven, CT, and London: Yale University Press, 1995), 7.
8. See Londa Schiebinger, "Women of Natural Knowledge," in *The Cambridge History of Science*, Volume 3: *Early Modern Science*, ed. Katharine Park and Lorraine Daston (Cambridge: Cambridge University Press, 2006), 196.
9. As quoted in Schiebinger, "Women of Natural Knowledge," 198.
10. See Merry E. Wiesner-Hanks, *Women and Gender in Early Modern Europe*, 3rd ed. (Cambridge: Cambridge University Press, 2008), 199.
11. See Schiebinger, "Women of Natural Knowledge," 199–203.
12. See James McClellan III, "Scientific Organisations and the Organisation of Science," in *The Cambridge History of Science*, Volume 4: *The Eighteenth-Century*, ed. Roy Porter (Cambridge: Cambridge University Press, 2003), 102.
13. See James Van Horn Melton, *The Rise of the Public in Enlightenment Europe* (Cambridge: Cambridge University Press, 2001), 150 (quotation), 153 (idealized).
14. As quoted from Stephen J. Harris, "Networks of Travel, Correspondence, and Exchange," in Park and Daston, eds., *The Cambridge History of Science*, Volume 3: *Early modern Science*, 348.
15. As noted in Gabriella Del Lungo Camiciotti, "Letters and Letter Writing in Early Modern Culture: An Introduction," *Journal of Early Modern Studies* 3 (March 2014): 24.
16. See Steven G. Marks, *The Information Nexus: Global Capitalism from the Renaissance to the Present* (Cambridge: Cambridge University Press, 2016), 81, 105; Mokyr, "Institutions and the Origins of the Great Enrichment," 253.
17. Statistic in Andrew Pettegree, *The Invention of News: How the World Came to Know about Itself* (New Haven, CT: Yale University Press, 2014), 318.
18. See Camiciotti, "Letters and Letter Writing in Early Modern Culture," 24.
19. See Gideon Burton, "From *Ars dictaminis* to *Ars conscribendi epistolis*: Renaissance Letter-Writing Manuals in the Context of Humanism," in *Letter-Writing Manuals*

Notes

and Instruction from Antiquity to the Present, ed. Carol Poster and Linda C. Mitchell (Columbia, SC: University of South Carolina Press, 2007), 88–101.

20. See Egbertus van Gulik, *Erasmus and His Books* (Toronto, Buffalo, and London: University of Toronto Press, 2018), 116, 116n41.
21. As quoted from Grafton, *Worlds Made by Words*, 22.
22. As quoted in Goldgar, *Impolite Learning*, 21.
23. See Harris, "Networks of Travel, Correspondence, and Exchange," 361.
24. As quoted from Alexander Bevilacqua, *The Republic of Arabic Letters: Islam and the European Enlightenment* (Cambridge, MA: Harvard University Press, 2018), 112.
25. See Samar Attar, *The Vital Roots of European Enlightenment: Ibn Tufayl's Influence on Modern Western Thought* (Lanham, MD: Rowman and Littlefield Publishers, 2007), Chap. 2.
26. As quoted in Anthony Grafton, "Libraries and Lecture Halls," in Park and Daston, eds., *The Cambridge History of Science*, Volume 3: *Early Modern Science*, 245.
27. David S. Lux and Harold J. Cook, "Closed Circles or Open Networks?: Communicating at a Distance during the Scientific Revolution," *History of Science* 36 (1998): 184–85.
28. See McClellan, "Scientific Organisations and the Organisation of Science," 87.
29. See Schiebinger, "Women of Natural Knowledge," 194.
30. See McClellan, "Scientific Organisations and the Organisation of Science," 88.
31. See Bruce T. Moran, "Courts and Academies," in Park and Daston, eds., *The Cambridge History of Science*, Volume 3: *Early Modern Science*, 251–71.
32. As quoted from Grafton, *Worlds Made by Words*, 2.
33. See Adrian Johns, "Coffeehouses and Print Shops," in Park and Daston, eds., *The Cambridge History of Science*, Volume 3: *Early Modern Science*, 325.
34. Larry Stewart, "Other Centres of Calculation, or, Where the Royal Society Didn't Count: Commerce, Coffee-Houses and Natural Philosophy in Early Modern London," *British Journal for the History of Science* 32, no. 2 (June 1999): 136–37.
35. See Dengjian Jin, *The Great Knowledge Transcendence: The Rise of Western Science and Technology Reframed* (Basingstoke, UK, and New York: Palgrave Macmillan, 2016), 224.
36. See Johns, "Coffeehouses and Print Shops," 329–30.
37. See McClellan, "Scientific Organisations and the Organisation of Science," 91 (seventy), 94 (colonies).
38. See McClellan, "Scientific Organisations and the Organisation of Science," 98.
39. See Lux and Cook, "Closed Circles or Open Networks?," 183–84 (Busschoff), 188–89 (van Leeuwenhoek).
40. See Goldgar, *Impolite Learning*, 56.

Notes

41. See McClellan, "Scientific Organisations and the Organisation of Science," 95.
42. See Andrea Rusnock, "Correspondence Networks and the Royal Society, 1700–1750," *British Journal for the History of Science* 32, no. 2 (June 1999): 157 (committees), 164–66 (collaboration).
43. As quoted from Jin, *The Great Knowledge Transcendence*, 230.
44. As quoted from Frederic Wakeman, Jr., "Boundaries of the Public Sphere in Ming and Qing China," *Daedalus* 127, no. 3 (Summer 1998): 175.
45. See Wakeman, "Boundaries of the Public Sphere in Ming and Qing China," 177–79.
46. See John A. Hall, *Powers and Liberties: The Causes and Consequences of the Rise of the West* (Oxford: Basil Blackwell, 1985), 78.
47. Statistics in Eltjo Buringh and Jan Luiten van Zanden, "Charting the 'Rise of the West': Manuscripts and Printed Books in Europe, a Long-Term Perspective from the Sixth through Eighteenth Centuries," *Journal of Economic History* 69, no. 2 (June 2009): 421.
48. See Luis Angeles, "The Great Divergence and the Economics of Printing," *Economic History Review* 70, no. 1 (February 2017): 49.
49. As quoted from İ. Semih Akçomak, Dinand Webbink, and Bas ter Weel, "Why Did the Netherlands Develop So Early? The Legacy of the Brethren of the Common Life," *Economic Journal* 126, no. 593 (June 2016): 821.
50. See Harvey J. Graff, *The Legacies of Literacy: Continuities and Contradictions in Western Culture and Society* (Bloomington, IN: Indiana University Press, 1991), 163–70.
51. Statistics from Robert C. Allen, "Progress and Poverty in Early Modern Europe," *Economic History Review* 56, no. 3 (August 2003): 415.
52. See Jessica Otis, "'Set Them to the Cyphering Schoole': Reading, Writing, and Arithmetical Education, circa 1540–1700," *Journal of British Studies* 56 (July 2017): 458.
53. See Melton, *The Rise of the Public in Enlightenment Europe*, 85.
54. Statistics in Rab Houston, "Literacy and Society in the West, 1500–1850," *Social History* 8, no. 3 (October 1983): 270, 275 (schooling).
55. Statistics from Victor Lieberman, *Strange Parallels: Southeast Asia in Global Context, c. 800–1830*, Volume 2: *Mainland Mirrors: Europe, Japan, China, South Asia, and the Islands* (New York: Cambridge University Press, 2009), 678, 678n118.
56. See Evelyn Sakakida Rawski, *Education and Popular Literacy in Ch'ing China* (Ann Arbor: University of Michigan Press, 1979), 140.
57. Statistics from UNESCO, *Progress of Literacy in Various Countries: A Preliminary Statistical Study of Available Census Data since 1900* (Paris: UNESCO, 1953), 170–71.
58. See Akçomak, Webbink, and ter Weel, "Why Did the Netherlands Develop So Early?" 821–60.
59. See Otis, "'Set Them to the Cyphering Schoole,'" 473–74.

Notes

60. John W. O'Malley, *Four Cultures of the West* (Cambridge, MA: The Belknap Press of Harvard University Press, 2004), 154, 163-64.
61. See Marks, *The Information Nexus*, 84.
62. As quoted from Otis, "'Set Them to the Cyphering Schoole,'" 454.
63. Quotation from Tine De Moor and Jan Luiten van Zanden, "'Every Woman Counts': A Gender-Analysis of Numeracy in the Low Countries during the Early Modern Period," *Journal of Interdisciplinary History* 41, no. 2 (Autumn 2010): 20.
64. See Brian A'Hearn, Jörg Baten, and Dorothee Crayen, "Quantifying Quantitative Literacy: Age Heaping and the History of Human Capital," *Journal of Economic History* 69, no. 3 (September 2009): 794 (data sets), 803 (statistic).
65. Statistics from Gerrit Verhoeven, "'Le pays où on ne sait pas lire': Literacy, Numeracy and Human Capital in the Commercial Hub of the Austrian Netherlands (1715-75)," *European History Quarterly* 44, no. 2 (2014): 228, 230.
66. This claim is advanced in Franziska Tollnek and Joerg Baten, "Farmers at the Heart of the 'Human Capital Revolution'? Decomposing the Numeracy Increase in Early Modern Europe," *Economic History Review* 70, no. 3 (2017): 779.
67. Statistics from Jörg Baten and Johan Fourie, "Numeracy of Africans, Asians, and Europeans during the Early Modern Period: New Evidence from Cape Colony Court Registers," *Economic History Review* 68, no. 2 (May 2015): 648.
68. As quoted from Anthony Smith, *The Newspaper: An International History* (London: Thames and Hudson, 1979), 13.
69. See Marks, *The Information Nexus*, 112.
70. Statistic from Andrew Pettegree, *The Invention of News*, 8.
71. See Smith, *The Newspaper*, 32-40.
72. See Joad Raymond, *Pamphlets and Pamphleteering in Early Modern Britain* (New York: Cambridge University Press, 2003), 298 (statistics), 381 (quotation).
73. As quoted from David Zaret, "Petitions and the 'Invention' of Public Opinion in the English Revolution," *American Journal of Sociology* 101, no. 6 (May 1996): 1532.
74. See Marks, *The Information Nexus*, 109.
75. As quoted from Melton, *The Rise of the Public in Enlightenment Europe*, 20-21, 25.
76. See Marks, *The Information Nexus*, 122.
77. As quoted from Pettegree, *The Invention of News*, 12.
78. See, for example, Oscar Gelderblom and Joost Jonker, "Completing a Financial Revolution: The Finance of the Dutch East India Trade and the Rise of the Amsterdam Capital Market, 1595-1612," *Journal of Economic History* 64 (September 2004): 641-72.
79. As noted in Marks, *The Information Nexus*, 109 (customs), 113 (price).
80. See Marks, *The Information Nexus*, 107-8; Harris, "Networks of Travel, Correspondence, and Exchange," 358-59.

Notes

81. See Jeffrey R. Wigelsworth, *Selling Science in the Age of Newton: Advertising and the Commoditization of Knowledge* (Farnham, UK: Ashgate, 2010).

82. See George Boyce, James Curran, and Pauline Wingate, eds., *Newspaper History from the Seventeenth Century to the Present Day* (London: Constable, 1978).

83. Marks, *The Information Nexus*, 93–94.

84. Quotation from James E. Baldwin, "Petitioning the Sultan in Ottoman Egypt," *Bulletin of the School of Oriental and African Studies* 75, no. 3 (2012): 509.

85. See Li Jia, "Conflicts Between Monarch and Ministers: A Political and Cultural Interpretation of the Ming-Dynasty Officials' Collective 'Petitions to the Palace,'" *Chinese Studies in History* 44, no. 3 (Spring 2011): 72–89.

86. See Emİnegül Karababa and Gülİz Ger, "Early Modern Ottoman Coffeehouse Culture and the Formation of the Consumer Subject," *Journal of Consumer Research* 37, no. 5 (February 2011): 744.

87. Statistic from Ralph S. Hattox, *Coffee and Coffeehouses: The Origins of a Social Beverage in the Medieval Near East* (Seattle: University of Washington Press, 1985), 81.

88. See Karababa and Ger, "Early Modern Ottoman Coffeehouse Culture," 744–46.

89. Quotation and argument from Karababa and Ger, "Early Modern Ottoman Coffeehouse Culture," 748.

90. As quoted from Karababa and Ger, "Early Modern Ottoman Coffeehouse Culture," 756.

91. Quotations from James Grehan, "Smoking and 'Early Modern' Sociability: The Great Tobacco Debate in the Ottoman Middle East (Seventeenth to Eighteenth Centuries)," *American Historical Review* 111, no. 5 (December 2006): 1375.

92. This paragraph draws on Melton, *The Rise of the Public in Enlightenment Europe*, 240–46.

93. On women in coffee houses, see Markman Ellis, "An Introduction to the Coffee-house: A Discursive Model," *Language & Communication* 28 (2008): 162. Women were not present at all in Middle Eastern coffeehouses. See Alan Mikhail, "The Heart's Desire: Gender, Urban Space and the Ottoman Coffee House," in *Ottoman Tulips, Ottoman Coffee: Leisure and Lifestyle in the Eighteenth Century*, ed. Dana Sajdi (London: I.B. Tauris, 2007), 169.

94. See, for example, Karababa and Ger, "Early Modern Ottoman Coffeehouse Culture," 738.

95. As quoted from Markman Ellis, "Coffee-House Libraries in Mid-Eighteenth-Century London," *The Library: The Transactions of the Bibliographical Society* 10, no. 1 (March 2009): 3.

96. As quoted from Johns, "Coffeehouses and Print Shops," 333.

Notes

97. See Ellis, "Coffee-House Libraries," 15–17.
98. On the founding of the Society, see Johns, "Coffeehouses and Print Shops," 320.
99. As quoted from Ellis, "An Introduction to the Coffee-house," 160–61.
100. As quoted from Ellis, "Coffee-House Libraries," 4. See also Richard Dale, *The First Crash: Lessons from the South Sea Bubble* (Princeton, NJ: Princeton University Press, 2004), 10.
101. See Herbert Lederer, "The Vienna Coffeehouse: History and Cultural Significance," in *The Thinking Space: The Café as a Cultural Institution in Paris, Italy and Vienna*, ed. Leona Rittner, W. Scott Haine, and Jeffrey H. Jackson (Farnham, UK: Ashgate, 2013), 31.
102. Such are the findings of Ellis, "Coffee-House Libraries," 21–25, 31–34, 37–38, 40 (quotation).
103. See Ellis, "Coffee-House Libraries," 38–39.
104. Quotations from Larry Stewart, "Other Centres of Calculation," 142–43.
105. As quoted from Stewart, "Other Centres of Calculation," 149–50.
106. See Melton, *The Rise of the Public in Enlightenment Europe*, 93 (reviews).
107. See Melton, *The Rise of the Public in Enlightenment Europe*, 104–7; Ellis, "Coffee-House Libraries," 35–36.
108. See K. A. Manley, "Infidel Books and 'Factories of the Enlightenment': Censorship and Surveillance in Subscription and Circulating Libraries in an Age of Revolutions, 1790–1850," *Book History* 19 (2016): 170–75.
109. See Mark Overton, *Agricultural Revolution in England: The Transformation of the Agrarian Economy, 1500–1850* (Cambridge: Cambridge University Press, 1996), 130.
110. See Manley, "Infidel Books and 'Factories of the Enlightenment,'" 175–91.
111. As quoted from Dena Goodman, *The Republic of Letters: A Cultural History of the French Enlightenment* (Ithaca, NY: Cornell University Press, 1994), 91.
112. As quoted from Melton, *The Rise of the Public in Enlightenment Europe*, 207.
113. As quoted from Wiesner-Hanks, *Women and Gender in Early Modern Europe*, 170.
114. See Melton, *The Rise of the Public in Enlightenment Europe*, 208–15.
115. See Goodman, *The Republic of Letters*, 240.
116. See, for example, Stefan-Ludwig Hoffmann, *Civil Society, 1750–1914* (Houndmills, UK: Palgrave Macmillan, 2006), 11–16; Goodman, *The Republic of Letters*, 253–58.
117. Statistics from Melton, *The Rise of the Public in Enlightenment Europe*, 255.
118. As argued in Alan Macfarlane, *Invention of the Modern World* (Les Brouzils, France: Odd Volumes of the Fortnightly Review, 2014), 118.

Notes

119. See, for example, Johann N. Neem, *Creating a Nation of Joiners: Democracy and Civil Society in Early National Massachusetts* (Cambridge, MA, and London: Harvard University Press, 2008).
120. Thus, argues Alexis de Tocqueville, *Democracy in America*, trans. George Lawrence, ed. J.P. Mayer (Garden City, NY: Doubleday, 1969), 513.
121. As quoted from Kaveh Yazdani, *India, Modernity and the Great Divergence: Mysore and Gujarat (17th to 19th C.)* (Leiden and Boston: Brill, 2017), 416.
122. Quotations from Şevket Pamuk, "Institutional Change and the Longevity of the Ottoman Empire, 1500–1800," *Journal of Interdisciplinary History* 35, no. 2 (Autumn 2004): 228–29.
123. Şevket Pamuk, "The Black Death and the Origins of the 'Great Divergence' across Europe, 1300–1600," *European Review of Economic History* 11, no. 3 (December 2007): 309–11.
124. Statistics from Angus Maddison, *Contours of the World Economy, 1–2030 A.D.: Essays in Macroeconomic History* (Oxford: Oxford University Press, 2007), 43.
125. As quoted from Randall A. Dodgen, "Salvaging Kaifeng: Natural Calamity and Urban Community in Late Imperial China," *Journal of Urban History* 21, no. 6 (September 1995): 734.
126. As quoted from R. Bin Wong, "The Political Ambiguity of Voluntary Associations in Late Imperial and Modern China: Chinese Forms of Cultural Hegemony, Coercion and Social Control in Comparative Perspective," *Global Economic Review* 31, no. 1 (2002): 32.
127. Quotations from Nadir Özbek, "Defining the Public Sphere during the Late Ottoman Empire: War, Mass Mobilization and the Young Turk Regime (1908–18)," *Middle Eastern Studies* 43, no. 5 (September 2007): 796, 797.
128. As quoted from Robert Iliffe, "Material Doubts: Hooke, Artisan Culture, and the Exchange of Information in 1670s London," *British Journal for the History of Science* 28, no. 3 (September 1995): 286.
129. See Larry Stewart, *The Rise of Public Science: Rhetoric, Technology, and Natural Philosophy in Newtonian Britain, 1660–1750* (Cambridge: Cambridge University Press, 1992), 183–211.
130. See Daniel K. Headrick, *When Information Came of Age: Technologies of Knowledge in the Age of Reason and Revolution, 1700–1850* (New York: Oxford University Press, 2000), 178.
131. As quoted from Stewart, "Other Centres of Calculation," 146.
132. See Dava Sobel, *Longitude: The True Story of a Lone Genius Who Solved the Greatest Scientific Problem of His Time* (New York: Walker, 1995).
133. See Simon Winchester, *The Map That Changed the World: William Smith and the Birth of Modern Geology* (New York: Perennial, 2001).
134. See Peter Watson, *Ideas: A History of Thought and Invention, from Fire to Freud* (New York: HarperCollins, 2005), 529–31.

Notes

135. As quoted from Michael Adas, *Machines as the Measure of Men: Science, Technology, and Ideologies of Western Dominance* (Ithaca, NY, and London: Cornell University Press, 1989), 92.
136. See Deirdre McCloskey, *Bourgeois Dignity: Why Economics Can't Explain the Modern World* (Chicago: University of Chicago Press, 2010), 392.
137. See Robert E. Schofield, *The Lunar Society of Birmingham: A Social History of Provincial Science and Industry in Eighteenth-Century England* (Oxford: Clarendon Press, 1963).
138. See David Philip Miller, "The Usefulness of Natural Philosophy: The Royal Society and the Culture of Practical Utility in the Later Eighteenth Century," *British Journal for the History of Science* 32, no. 2 (June 1999): 193.
139. As quoted from Miller, "The Usefulness of Natural Philosophy," 186.
140. As quoted from Lux and Cook, "Closed Circles or Open Networks?," 180.
141. See McCloskey, *Bourgeois Dignity*.
142. See Mokyr, "Institutions and the Origins of the Great Enrichment," 257.
143. See Hamid Hosseini, "Seeking the Roots of Adam Smith's Division of Labor in Medieval Persia," *History of Political Economy* 30, no. 4 (January 1998): 653–81.
144. See Karel Davids, *Religion, Technology, and the Great and Little Divergences: China and Europe Compared, c. 700–1800* (Leiden: Brill, 2014), 119–67.
145. As quoted from Davids, *Religion, Technology, and the Great and Little Divergences*, 140.
146. As quoted from Davids, *Religion, Technology, and the Great and Little Divergences*, 123.
147. See Cem Karayalçin, "Divided We Stand, United We Fall: The Hume-North-Jones Mechanism for the Rise of Europe," *International Economic Review* 49, no. 3 (August 2008): 986–89.
148. See Carlo Marco Belfanti, "Guilds, Patents, and the Circulation of Technical Knowledge: Northern Italy during the Early Modern Age," *Technology and Culture* 45, no. 3 (July 2004): 569–89.
149. As quoted from Davids, *Religion, Technology, and the Great and Little Divergences*, 159.
150. As quoted in Davids, *Religion, Technology, and the Great and Little Divergences*, 162.

Chapter 7

1. For this recent discovery, see D.L. Hoffmann, et al., "U-Th Dating of Carbonate Crusts Reveals Neandertal Origin of Iberian Cave Art," *Science* 359, no. 6378 (February 23, 2018): 912–15.

Notes

2. See M. Aubert, et al., "Pleistocene Cave Art from Sulawesi, Indonesia," *Nature* 514 (October 9, 2014): 223–27.

3. Quotation in Mark Pagel, *Wired for Culture: Origins of the Human Social Mind* (New York: W.W. Norton, 2012), 111.

4. See Jinli He, "Continuity and Evolution: The Idea of 'Co-creativity' in Chinese Art," *ASIANetwork Exchange: A Journal for Asian Studies in the Liberal Arts* 21, no. 2 (2014): 15–23.

5. As quoted from F.W. Mote, "The Arts and the 'Theorizing Mode' of the Civilization," in *Artists and Traditions: Uses of the Past in Chinese Culture*, ed. Christian F. Murck (Princeton, NJ: The Art Museum, Princeton University, 1976), 6.

6. As quoted in Stephen G. Nichols, "Senses of the Imagination: Pseudo-Dionysius, Suger, and Saint-Denis," *Romanistisches Jahrbuch* 61 (November 2011): 232.

7. See Lindy Grant, *Abbot Suger of St-Denis: Church and State in Early Twelfth-Century France* (London and New York: Longman, 1998), 23.

8. As quoted in Andreas Speer, "Is There a Theology of the Gothic Cathedral? A Rereading of Abbot Suger's Writings on the Abbey Church of St.-Denis," in *The Mind's Eye: Art and Theological Argument in the Middle Ages*, ed. Jeffrey F. Hamburger and Anne-Marie Bouché (Princeton, NJ: Princeton University Press, 2006), 69.

9. As quoted from Conrad Rudolph, "Inventing the Exegetical Stained-Glass Window: Suger, Hugh, and a New Elite Art," *Art Bulletin* 93, no. 4 (2011): 418.

10. See Robert Bork, "Rock, Spires, Paper: Technical Aspects of Gothic Spires," in *Villard's Legacy: Studies in Medieval Technology, Science, and Art in Memory of Jean Gimpel*, ed. Marie-Thérèse Zenner (Aldershot, UK, and Burlington, VT: Ashgate, 2004), 135n1, 146–47.

11. As quoted from Christopher Wilson, *The Gothic Cathedral: The Architecture of the Great Church, 1130–1530* (New York and London: Thames and Hudson, 1990), 84.

12. This paragraph relies on Michael Levey, *From Giotto to Cézanne: A Concise History of Painting* (London: Thames and Hudson, 1968), especially Chap. 1.

13. As quoted in Marc Gotlieb, "The Painter's Secret: Invention and Rivalry from Vasari to Balzac," *Art Bulletin* 84, no. 3 (September 2002): 470.

14. See Martin Kemp, *The Science of Art: Optical Themes in Western Art from Brunelleschi to Seurat* (New Haven, CT: Yale University Press, 1992), Chap. 1.

15. Daniel D. Cavalcanti, William Feindel, James T. Goodrich, T. Forcht Dagi, Charles J. Prestigiacomo, and Mark C. Preul, "Anatomy, Technology, Art, and Culture: Toward a Realistic Perspective of the Brain," *Neurosurgical Focus* 27 (September 2009): 2.

16. As quoted from Cavalcanti, Feindel, Goodrich, Dagi, Prestigiacomo, and Preul, "Anatomy, Technology, Art, and Culture," 20.

Notes

17. See Stefano Di Bella, Fabrizio Taglietti, Andrea Iacobuzio, Emma Johnson, Andrea Baiocchini, and Nicola Petrosillo, "The 'Delivery' of Adam," *Mayo Clinic Proceedings* 90, no. 4 (2015): 505–8; Katherine Park, "Masaccio's Skeleton: Art and Anatomy in Early Renaissance Italy," in *Masaccio's Trinity*, ed. Rona Goffen (Cambridge: Cambridge University Press, 1998), 119–40.

18. See Rona Goffen, *Renaissance Rivals: Michelangelo, Leonardo, Raphael, Titian* (New Haven, CT: Yale University Press, 2004).

19. Joanna Woods-Marsden, *Renaissance Self-Portraiture: The Visual Construction of Identity and the Social Status of the Artist* (New Haven, CT: Yale University Press, 1998).

20. This paragraph draws on J. Peter Burkholder, Donald Jay Grout, and Claude V. Palisca, *A History of Western Music*, 9th ed. (New York and London: W.W. Norton, 2014), especially Chaps. 5 and 6.

21. See David Maw, "Machaut and the 'Critical' Phase of Medieval Polyphony," *Music & Letters* 87, no. 2 (May 2006): 262.

22. See Thomas Forrest Kelly, *Capturing Music: The Story of Notation* (New York: W.W. Norton, 2015).

23. On the very complicated development of the musical staff, see John Haines, "The Origins of the Musical Staff," *Musical Quarterly* 91, no. 3/4 (Fall–Winter 2008): 327–78.

24. See Burkholder, Grout, and Palisca, *A History of Western Music*, 114.

25. See D. Kern Holoman, *Berlioz: A Musical Biography of the Creative Genius of the Romantic Era* (Cambridge, MA: Harvard University Press, 1989), 308–11.

26. As quoted from Bernard Lewis, *What Went Wrong? Western Impact and Middle Eastern Response* (Oxford: Oxford University Press, 2002), 128–29.

27. For reliable surveys, see Alfred W. Crosby, *Throwing Fire: Projectile Technology through History* (New York: Cambridge University Press, 2002); Jack Kelly, *Gunpowder: Alchemy, Bombards, and Pyrotechnics: The History of the Explosive That Changed the World* (New York: Basic Books, 2004).

28. See Clifford J. Rogers, "The Military Revolutions of the Hundred Years' War," *Journal of Military History* 57 (April 1993): 261.

29. See, for example, William E. Wallace, "'Dal disegno allo spazio': Michelangelo's Drawings for the Fortifications of Florence," *Journal of the Society of Architectural Historians* 46 (June 1987): 119–34.

30. As quoted from Jan Glete, *War and the State in Early Modern Europe: Spain, the Dutch Republic and Sweden as Fiscal-Military States, 1500–1660* (London: Routledge, 2002), 172.

31. See David Stasavage, *States of Credit: Size, Power, and the Development of European Polities* (Princeton, NJ: Princeton University Press, 2011).

32. See Geoffrey Parker, "The Limits to Revolutions in Military Affairs: Maurice of Nassau, the Battle of Nieuwpoort (1600), and the Legacy," *Journal of Military History* 71 (April 2007): 331–72.

Notes

33. See William H. McNeill, *Keeping Together in Time: Dance and Drill in Human History* (Cambridge, MA: Harvard University Press, 1995), 128–31.
34. See Kenneth Chase, *Firearms: A Global History to 1700* (New York: Cambridge University Press, 2003), 200–1.
35. See Jeremy Black, *War and the World: Military Power and the Fate of Continents, 1450–2000* (New Haven, CT: Yale University Press, 1998), 127–28.
36. As quoted from Peter Lorge, *War, Politics, and Society in Early Modern China, 900–1795* (London and New York: Routledge, 2005), 6.
37. As quoted from Tonio Andrade, *The Gunpowder Age: China, Military Innovation, and the Rise of the West in World History* (Princeton, NJ: Princeton University Press, 2016), 275.
38. See Lorge, *War, Politics and Society in Early Modern China*, 176 (quotation), 178 (execution).
39. Joel Mokyr, *The Lever of Riches: Technological Creativity and Economic Progress* (New York: Oxford University Press, 1990), 233.
40. As quoted from Philip T. Hoffman, *Why Did Europe Conquer the World?* (Princeton, NJ: Princeton University Press, 2015), 15.
41. See Hoffman, *Why Did Europe Conquer the World?* 62.
42. Statistics in Hoffman, *Why Did Europe Conquer the World?* 97.
43. See Iqtidar Alam Khan, *Gunpowder and Firearms: Warfare in Medieval India* (New Delhi: Oxford University Press, 2004).
44. As quoted from Pepijn Brandon, *War, Capital and the Dutch State (1588–1795)* (Chicago: Haymarket Books, 2016), 207.
45. See Şevket Pamuk, "The Black Death and the Origins of the 'Great Divergence' across Europe, 1300–1600," *European Review of Economic History* 11, no. 3 (December 2007): 311.
46. See, for example, Karel Davids and Bert De Munck, "Innovation and Creativity in Late Medieval and Early Modern European Cities: An Introduction," in *Innovation and Creativity in Late Medieval and Early Modern European Cities*, ed. Karel Davids and Bert De Munck (London: Routledge, 2016), 1–35.
47. See Mark Dincecco and Massimiliano G. Onorato, *From Warfare to Wealth: The Military Origins of Urban Prosperity in Europe* (New York: Cambridge University Press, 2018).
48. Quotation from R.B. Wong, "China before Capitalism," in *The Cambridge History of Capitalism, Volume 1: The Rise of Capitalism: From Ancient Origins to 1848*, ed. Larry Neal and Jeffrey G. Williamson (Cambridge: Cambridge University Press, 2014), 154.
49. See Nico Voigtländer and Hans-Joachim Voth, "Gifts of Mars: Warfare and Europe's Early Rise to Riches," *Journal of Economic Perspectives* 27, no. 4 (Fall 2013): 165–86.

Notes

50. Quoted from Ann Towns, "The Status of Women as a Standard of Civilization," *European Journal of International Relations* 15, no. 4 (December 2009): 694.
51. As quoted from Alexis de Tocqueville, *Democracy in America*, trans. George Lawrence, ed. J.P. Mayer (Garden City, NY: Doubleday, 1969), 603.
52. See Merry E. Wiesner-Hanks, *Women and Gender in Early Modern Europe*, 3rd ed. (Cambridge: Cambridge University Press, 2008), 12.
53. See Tracy Dennison and Sheilagh Ogilvie, "Does the European Marriage Pattern Explain Economic Growth?" *Journal of Economic History* 74, no. 3 (September 2014): 651–93; Sarah G. Carmichael, Alexandra de Pleijt, Jan Luiten van Zanden, and Tine De Moor, "The European Marriage Pattern and Its Measurement," *Journal of Economic History* 76, no. 1 (March 2016): 196–204.
54. Statistics cited in Tine De Moor and Jan Luiten van Zanden, "Girl Power: The European Marriage Pattern and Labour Markets in the North Sea Region in the Late Medieval and Early Modern Period," *Economic History Review* 63, no. 1 (February 2010): 12–13.
55. See Wiesner-Hanks, *Women and Gender in Early Modern Europe*, 134.
56. See De Moor and van Zanden, "Girl Power," 14–22.
57. Statistics from Stephen Broadberry, Bruce M.S. Campbell, Alexander Klein, Mark Overton, and Bas van Leeuwen, *British Economic Growth, 1270–1870* (Cambridge: Cambridge University Press, 2015), 390.
58. See Alexandra M. de Pleijt, Jan Luiten van Zanden, and Sarah Guilland Carmichael, "Gender Relations and Economic Development: Hypotheses about the Reversal of Fortune in EurAsia," in *Cliometrics and the Family: Global Patterns and their Impact on Diverging Development*, ed. Claude Diebolt, Auke Rijpma, Sarah Carmichael, Selin Dilli, and Charlotte Störmer (Berlin: Springer Verlag, 2019).
59. As quoted from Joseph Henrich, Robert Boyd, and Peter J. Richerson, "The Puzzle of Monogamous Marriage," *Philosophical Transactions of the Royal Society B: Biological Sciences* 367, no. 1589 (March 2012): 658.
60. See Melissa J. Brown, Laurel Bossen, Hill Gates, and Damian Satterthwaite-Phillips, "Marriage Mobility and Footbinding in Pre-1949 Rural China: A Reconsideration of Gender, Economics, and Meaning in Social Causation," *Journal of Asian Studies* 71, no. 4 (November 2012): 1036–39.
61. See Dorothy Ko, "Pursuing Talent and Virtue: Education and Women's Culture in Seventeenth- and Eighteenth-Century China," *Late Imperial China* 13, no. 1 (June 1992): 17 (suicide), 18 (quotation).
62. As quoted from Vincent Goossaert, "Irrepressible Female Piety: Late Imperial Bans on Women Visiting Temples," *Nan Nü* 10 (2008): 215.
63. See Maya Shatzmiller, "The Female Body in Islamic Law and Medicine: Obstetrics, Gynecology, and Pediatrics," in *Attending to Early Modern Women: Conflict and Concord*, ed. Karen Nelson (Newark, DE: University of Delaware Press, 2013), 98–101.

Notes

64. See Maya Shatzmiller, "Aspects of Women's Participation in the Economic Life of Later Medieval Islam: Occupations and Mentalities," *Arabica* 35 (March 1988): 52.

65. As quoted from Maya Shatzmiller, *Her Day in Court: Women's Property Rights in Fifteenth-Century Granada* (Cambridge, MA: Islamic Legal Studies Program, Harvard Law School, 2007), 191.

66. See Madeline Zilfi, "Thoughts on Women and Slavery in the Ottoman Era and Historical Sources," in *Beyond the Exotic: Women's Histories in Islamic Societies*, ed. Amira El Azhary Sonbol (Syracuse, NY: Syracuse University Press, 2005), 131–38.

67. As quoted from Jonathan Berkey, "Women and Gender in Islamic Traditions," in *The Oxford Handbook of Women and Gender in Medieval Europe*, ed. Judith M. Bennett and Ruth Mazo Karras (Oxford: Oxford University Press, 2013), 62 (quotation) 64 (hadith and Sufi).

68. See Kaveh Yazdani, *India, Modernity and the Great Divergence: Mysore and Gujarat (17th to 19th C.)* (Leiden and Boston: Brill, 2017), 502–9 (quotation: 502n599).

69. See Robert Hartwell, "A Revolution in the Chinese Iron and Coal Industries during the Northern Sung, 960–1126 A.D.," *Journal of Asian Studies* 21 (February 1962): 155; idem., "A Cycle of Economic Change in Imperial China: Coal and Iron in Northeast China, 750–1350," *Journal of the Economic and Social History of the Orient* 10, no. 1 (July 1967): 104.

70. Statistic cited in Hartwell, "A Cycle of Economic Change in Imperial China," 121–22, 122n1.

71. Donald B. Wagner, "The Administration of the Iron Industry in Eleventh-Century China," *Journal of the Economic and Social History of the Orient* 44, no. 2 (2001): 191.

72. Hartwell gave his numbers in U.S. short tons, while other scholars calculate in terms of metric tons, which are 10 percent heavier. Nevertheless, the margins of error for all premodern Chinese iron and coal production statistics greatly exceed that discrepancy. As a result, no distinction will be made between short and metric tons in this survey.

73. Statistics supplied in Tim Wright, "An Economic Cycle in Imperial China? Revisiting Robert Hartwell on Iron and Coal," *Journal of the Economic and Social History of the Orient* 50, no. 4 (2007): 404.

74. As quoted from Hartwell, "A Cycle of Economic Change in Imperial China," 141.

75. As quoted from Hartwell, "A Cycle of Economic Change in Imperial China," 162.

76. As quoted from Jack A. Goldstone, "Efflorescences and Economic Growth in World History: Rethinking the 'Rise of the West' and the Industrial Revolution," *Journal of World History* 13, no. 2 (Fall 2002): 379.

Notes

77. See William Guanglin Liu, "The Making of a Fiscal State in Song China, 960–1279," *Economic History Review* 68, no. 1 (2015): 48–78.
78. See Kenneth Pomeranz, *The Great Divergence: China, Europe and the Making of the Modern World Economy* (Princeton, NJ: Princeton University Press, 2000), 62–68, 181–83, 239–41; Bozhong Li, "The Early Modern Economy of the Yangzi Delta in a New Perspective," *Social Sciences in China* 36, no. 1 (2015): 106.
79. Statistic cited in William M. Cavert, "Industrial Coal Consumption in Early Modern London," *Urban History* 44, no. 3 (August 2017): 427.
80. Quotation from Cavert, "Industrial Coal Consumption in Early Modern London," 442–44.
81. See Jack A. Goldstone, "Why and Where Did Modern Economic Growth Begin?" *Tijdschrift voor Sociale en Economische Geschiedenis/The Low Countries Journal of Social and Economic History* 12, no. 2 (June 2015): 20.
82. Statistics from Peter King, "The Production and Consumption of Bar Iron in Early Modern England and Wales," *Economic History Review* 58, no. 1 (2005): 7.
83. See Pomeranz, *The Great Divergence*, 63.
84. "Medieval Europe was perhaps the first society to build an economy on non-human power" wrote Mokyr in *The Lever of Riches*, 35.
85. See Adam Robert Lucas, "Industrial Milling in the Ancient and Medieval Worlds: A Survey of the Evidence for an Industrial Revolution in Medieval Europe," *Technology and Culture* 46, no. 1 (January 2005): 10–11.
86. Quotation from John Langdon, *Mills in the Medieval Economy: England 1300–1540* (New York: Oxford University Press, 2004), 299.
87. As quoted from Lucas, "Industrial Milling in the Ancient and Medieval Worlds," 26.
88. See Adam Lucas, *Wind, Water, Work: Ancient and Medieval Milling Technology* (Leiden: Brill, 2006), 262.
89. See Bas van Bavel, Eltjo Buringh, and Jessica Dijkman, "Mills, Cranes, and the Great Divergence: The Use of Immovable Capital Goods in Western Europe and the Middle East, Ninth to Sixteenth Centuries," *Economic History Review* 71, no. 1 (2018): 31–54.
90. See Karel Davids, "Successful and Failed Transitions: A Comparison of Innovations in Windmill-Technology in Britain and the Netherlands in the Early Modern Period," *History and Technology* 14 (1998): 227–28.
91. See Peter Boomgaard, "Technologies of a Trading Empire: Dutch Introduction of Water- and Windmills in Early-Modern Asia, 1650s–1800," *History and Technology* 24, no. 1 (March 2008): 43–55.
92. See Davids, "Successful and Failed Transitions," 229–32.
93. As quoted from Eric L. Jones, *Locating the Industrial Revolution: Inducement and Response* (Singapore: World Scientific, 2010), 23.

Notes

94. See van Bavel, Buringh, and Dijkman, "Mills, Cranes, and the Great Divergence," 51–52.
95. Quotation from Goldstone, "Why and Where Did Modern Economic Growth Begin?" 17.
96. As quoted from Benjamin A. Elman, *On Their Own Terms: Science in China, 1550-1900* (Cambridge, MA: Harvard University Press, 2005), xxxi.
97. As quoted from Eric L. Jones, "England as the Source of the Great Divergence," *Tijdschrift voor Sociale en Economische Geschiedenis/The Low Countries Journal of Social and Economic History* 12, no. 2 (June 2015): 91.
98. See Stephen Broadberry, Hanhui Guan, and David Daokui Li, "China, Europe and the Great Divergence: A Study in Historical National Accounting, 980–1850," *Journal of Economic History* 78, no. 4 (December 2018): 957, 988.
99. Statistics from Bruce Campbell, *The Great Transition: Climate, Disease and Society in the Late-Medieval World* (Cambridge: Cambridge University Press, 2016), 378–80.
100. Statistics in Stephen Broadberry and Bishnupriya Gupta, "The Early Modern Great Divergence: Wages, Prices, and Economic Development in Europe and Asia, 1500–1800," *Economic History Review* 59, no. 1 (2006): 17, 19.
101. As quoted from Patrick O'Brien and Kent Deng, "Can the Debate on the Great Divergence Be Located within the Kuznetsian Paradigm for an Empirical Form of Global Economic History?" *Tijdschrift voor Sociale en Economische Geschiedenis/ The Low Countries Journal of Social and Economic History* 12, no. 2 (June 2015): 73.
102. Kent Deng and Patrick O'Brien, "Nutritional Standards of Living in England and the Yangzi Delta (Jiangnan), circa 1644–circa 1840: Clarifying Data for Reciprocal Comparisons," *Journal of World History* 26, no. 2 (June 2015): 248 (quotation), 249 (1700s).
103. See Robert C. Allen, Jean-Pascal Bassino, Debin Ma, Christine Moll-Murata, and Jan Luiten van Zanden, "Wages, Prices, and Living Standards in China, 1738–1925: In Comparison with Europe, Japan, and India," *Economic History Review* 64, no. 1 (2011): 30.
104. See David Meredith and Deborah Oxley, "Food and Fodder: Feeding England, 1700–1900," *Past and Present*, no. 222 (February 2014): 210–12; Broadberry and Gupta, "The Early Modern Great Divergence," 17, 19.

Conclusion

1. Thus, argues William H. McNeill throughout his classic *The Rise of the West: A History of the Human Community* (Chicago: University of Chicago Press, 1963).
2. For this argument, see Cem Karayalçin, "Divided We Stand, United We Fall: The Hume-North-Jones Mechanism for the Rise of Europe," *International Economic Review* 49, no. 3 (August 2008): 973–97.

Notes

3. As quoted from Alexander Anievas and Kerem Nişancioğlu, *How the West Came to Rule: The Geopolitical Origins of Capitalism* (London: Pluto Press, 2015), 43.
4. Quotation from Anievas and Nişancioğlu, *How the West Came to Rule*, 67.
5. See Philip C.C. Huang, "Development or Involution in Eighteenth-Century Britain and China? A Review of Kenneth Pomeranz's 'The Great Divergence: China, Europe, and the Making of the Modern World Economy,'" *Journal of Asian Studies* 61 (May 2002): 534.
6. Thus, argue Bozhong Li and Jan Luiten van Zanden, "Before the Great Divergence? Comparing the Yangzi Delta and the Netherlands at the Beginning of the Nineteenth Century," *Journal of Economic History* 72, no. 4 (December 2012), 981.
7. See Şevket Pamuk, "The Black Death and the Origins of the 'Great Divergence' across Europe, 1300–1600," *European Review of Economic History* 11, no. 3 (December 2007): 310.
8. As quoted from Peer Vries, *Escaping Poverty: The Origins of Modern Economic Growth* (Vienna and Göttingen: Vienna University Press and V & R Unipress, 2013), 401.
9. As quoted from Bozhong Li, "The Early Modern Economy of the Yangzi Delta in a New Perspective," *Social Sciences in China* 36, no. 1 (2015): 105.
10. See Matthew Hutson, "AI Researchers Allege that Machine Learning Is Alchemy," *Science* 360, no. 6388 (May 3, 2018): 478.

WORKS CITED

A'Hearn, Brian, Jörg Baten, and Dorothee Crayen. "Quantifying Quantitative Literacy: Age Heaping and the History of Human Capital." *Journal of Economic History* 69, no. 3 (September 2009): 783–808.

Abu-Lughod, Janet L. *Before European Hegemony: The World System A.D. 1250–1350*. New York: Oxford University Press, 1989.

Adas, Michael. *Machines as the Measure of Men: Science, Technology, and Ideologies of Western Dominance*. Ithaca, NY, and London: Cornell University Press, 1989.

Akasoy, Anna, and Guido Giglioni, eds. *Renaissance Averroism and Its Aftermath: Arabic Philosophy in Early Modern Europe*. Dordrecht: Springer, 2013.

Akçomak, İ. Semih, Dinand Webbink, and Bas ter Weel. "Why Did the Netherlands Develop So Early? The Legacy of the Brethren of the Common Life." *Economic Journal* 126, no. 593 (June 2016): 821–60.

Albertini, Tamara. "Mathematics and Astronomy." In *Introducing Nicholas of Cusa: A Guide to a Renaissance Man*. Edited by Christopher M. Bellitto and Thomas M. Izbicki. New York: Paulist Press, 2004. Pp. 373–408.

Allen, Robert C. "Progress and Poverty in Early Modern Europe." *Economic History Review* 56, no. 3 (August 2003): 403–43.

Allen, Robert C., Jean-Pascal Bassino, Debin Ma, Christine Moll-Murata, and Jan Luiten van Zanden. "Wages, Prices, and Living Standards in China, 1738–1925: In Comparison with Europe, Japan, and India." *Economic History Review* 64, no. 1 (2011): 8–38.

Andersen, Kirsti. *The Geometry of an Art: The History of the Mathematical Theory of Perspective from Alberti to Monge*. New York: Springer, 2007.

Andrade, Tonio. *The Gunpowder Age: China, Military Innovation, and the Rise of the West in World History*. Princeton, NJ: Princeton University Press, 2016.

Angeles, Luis. "The Great Divergence and the Economics of Printing." *Economic History Review* 70, no. 1 (February 2017): 30–51.

Anievas, Alexander, and Kerem Nişancioğlu. *How the West Came to Rule: The Geopolitical Origins of Capitalism*. London: Pluto Press, 2015.

Arráez-Aybar, Luis-Alfonso, José-L. Bueno-López, and Nicolas Raio. "Toledo School of Translators and Their Influence on Anatomical Terminology." *Annals of Anatomy* 198 (March 2015): 21–33.

Aquinas, Saint Thomas. *Summa Theologica*. 22 Volumes. Translated by Fathers of the English Dominican Province. New York: Benziger Brothers, 1911–1925.

Ascher, Marcia. *Ethnomathematics: A Multicultural View of Mathematical Ideas*. Belmont, CA: Brooks-Cole, 1991.

Attar, Samar. "Conflicting Accounts on the Fear of Strangers: Muslim and Arab Perceptions of Europeans in Medieval Geographical Literature." *Arab Studies Quarterly* 27, no. 4 (Fall 2005): 17–29.

Works Cited

Attar, Samar. *The Vital Roots of European Enlightenment: Ibn Tufayl's Influence on Modern Western Thought*. Lanham, MD: Rowman and Littlefield Publishers, 2007.
Aubert, M., et al. "Pleistocene Cave Art from Sulawesi, Indonesia." *Nature* 514 (October 9, 2014): 223–27.
Baber, Zaheer. "The Plants of Empire: Botanic Gardens, Colonial Power and Botanical Knowledge." *Journal of Contemporary Asia* 46, no. 4 (September 2016): 659–79.
Bacon, Francis. *The New Organon*. Edited by Lisa Jardine and Michael Silverthorne. Cambridge: Cambridge University Press, 2000.
Baldwin, James E. "Petitioning the Sultan in Ottoman Egypt." *Bulletin of the School of Oriental and African Studies* 75, no. 3 (2012): 499–524.
Baten, Jörg, and Johan Fourie. "Numeracy of Africans, Asians, and Europeans during the Early Modern Period: New Evidence from Cape Colony Court Registers." *Economic History Review* 68, no. 2 (May 2015): 632–56.
Belfanti, Carlo Marco. "Guilds, Patents, and the Circulation of Technical Knowledge: Northern Italy during the Early Modern Age." *Technology and Culture* 45, no. 3 (July 2004): 569–89.
Bellah, Robert N., and Hans Joas, eds. *The Axial Age and Its Consequences*. Cambridge, MA: Harvard University Press, 2012.
Berggren, J. Lennart, and Alexander Jones, ed. and trans. *Ptolemy's Geography: An Annotated Translation of the Theoretical Chapters*. Princeton, NJ: Princeton University Press, 2000.
Berkey, Jonathan. "Women and Gender in Islamic Traditions." In *The Oxford Handbook of Women and Gender in Medieval Europe*. Edited by Judith M. Bennett and Ruth Mazo Karras. Oxford: Oxford University Press, 2013. Pp. 52–67.
Berman, Harold J. "Religious Foundations of Law in the West: An Historical Perspective." *Journal of Law and Religion* 1 (Summer 1983): 3–43.
Berman, Harold J. "The Origins of Western Legal Science." *Harvard Law Review* 90, no. 5 (March 1977): 894–943.
Berman, Harold J. *Law and Revolution: The Formation of the Western Legal Tradition*. Cambridge, MA, and London: Harvard University Press, 1983.
Bevilacqua, Alexander. *The Republic of Arabic Letters: Islam and the European Enlightenment*. Cambridge, MA: Harvard University Press, 2018.
Birch, Charles, and John B. Cobb, Jr. *The Liberation of Life: From the Cell to the Community*. Cambridge and New York: Cambridge University Press, 1981.
Bisson, Thomas N. *The Crisis of the Twelfth Century: Power, Lordship, and the Origins of European Government*. Princeton, NJ: Princeton University Press, 2008.
Black, Antony. "The Conciliar Movement." In *The Cambridge History of Medieval Political Thought c.350–c.1450*. Edited by J.H. Burns. Cambridge: Cambridge University Press, 1988. Pp. 573–87.
Black, Antony. *The West and Islam: Religion and Political Thought in World History*. New York: Oxford University Press, 2008.
Black, Jeremy. *War and the World: Military Power and the Fate of Continents, 1450–2000*. New Haven, CT: Yale University Press, 1998.
Black, Jeremy. *Kings, Nobles and Commoners: States and Societies in Early Modern Europe, a Revisionist History*. London: I.B. Tauris, 2004.

Works Cited

Blaydes, Lisa, and Eric Chaney. "The Feudal Revolution and Europe's Rise: Political Divergence of the Christian West and the Muslim World before 1500 CE." *American Political Science Review* 107, no. 1 (February 2013): 16–34.

Boomgaard, Peter. "Technologies of a Trading Empire: Dutch Introduction of Water- and Windmills in Early-Modern Asia, 1650s–1800." *History and Technology* 24, no. 1 (March 2008): 41–59.

Bork, Robert. "Rock, Spires, Paper: Technical Aspects of Gothic Spires." In *Villard's Legacy: Studies in Medieval Technology, Science, and Art in Memory of Jean Gimpel*. Edited by Marie-Thérèse Zenner. Aldershot, UK, and Burlington, VT: Ashgate, 2004. Pp. 135–56.

Bosker, Maarten, Eltjo Buringh, and Jan Luiten van Zanden. "From Baghdad to London: Unraveling Urban Development in Europe, the Middle East, and North Africa, 800–1800." *Review of Economics and Statistics* 95, no. 4 (October 2013): 1418–37.

Boyce, George, James Curran, and Pauline Wingate, eds. *Newspaper History from the Seventeenth Century to the Present Day*. London: Constable, 1978.

Brandon, Pepijn. *War, Capital and the Dutch State (1588–1795)*. Chicago: Haymarket Books, 2016.

Breidenbach, Michael D. "Conciliarism and the American Founding." *William and Mary Quarterly* 73, no. 3 (July 2016): 467–500.

Broadberry, Stephen, and Bishnupriya Gupta. "The Early Modern Great Divergence: Wages, Prices, and Economic Development in Europe and Asia, 1500–1800." *Economic History Review* 59, no. 1 (2006): 2–31.

Broadberry, Stephen, Bruce M.S. Campbell, Alexander Klein, Mark Overton, and Bas van Leeuwen. *British Economic Growth, 1270–1870*. Cambridge: Cambridge University Press, 2015.

Broadberry, Stephen, Hanhui Guan, and David Daokui Li. "China, Europe and the Great Divergence: A Study in Historical National Accounting, 980–1850." *Journal of Economic History* 78, no. 4 (December 2018): 955–1000.

Brokaw, Cynthia J. "On the History of the Book in China." In *Printing and Book Culture in Late Imperial China*. Edited by Cynthia J. Brokaw and Kai-wing Chow. Berkeley, CA: University of California Press, 2005. Pp. 3–54.

Brown, Melissa J., Laurel Bossen, Hill Gates, and Damian Satterthwaite-Phillips. "Marriage Mobility and Footbinding in Pre-1949 Rural China: A Reconsideration of Gender, Economics, and Meaning in Social Causation." *Journal of Asian Studies* 71, no. 4 (November 2012): 1035–67.

Buringh, Eltjo, and Jan Luiten van Zanden. "Charting the 'Rise of the West': Manuscripts and Printed Books in Europe, a Long-Term Perspective from the Sixth through Eighteenth Centuries." *Journal of Economic History* 69, no. 2 (June 2009): 409–45.

Burkholder, J. Peter, Donald Jay Grout, and Claude V. Palisca. *A History of Western Music*. 9th ed. New York and London: W.W. Norton, 2014.

Burton, Gideon. "From *Ars dictaminis* to *Ars conscribendi epistolis*: Renaissance Letter-Writing Manuals in the Context of Humanism." In *Letter-Writing Manuals and Instruction from Antiquity to the Present*. Edited by Carol Poster and Linda C. Mitchell. Columbia, SC: University of South Carolina Press, 2007. Pp. 88–101.

Works Cited

Butterworth, Charles, and Blake A. Kessel, eds. *The Introduction of Arabic Philosophy into Europe.* New York: E.J. Brill, 1994.

Cahen, Claude. "Economy, Society, Institutions." In *Islamic Society and Civilization.* Edited by P.M. Holt, Ann K.S. Lambton, and Bernard Lewis. Cambridge: Cambridge University Press, 1970. Pp. 511–38.

Camiciotti, Gabriella Del Lungo. "Letters and Letter Writing in Early Modern Culture: An Introduction." *Journal of Early Modern Studies* 3 (March 2014): 17–35.

Campbell, Bruce. *The Great Transition: Climate, Disease and Society in the Late-Medieval World.* Cambridge: Cambridge University Press, 2016.

Carmichael, Sarah G., Alexandra de Pleijt, Jan Luiten van Zanden, and Tine De Moor. "The European Marriage Pattern and Its Measurement." *Journal of Economic History* 76, no. 1 (March 2016): 196–204.

Catlos, Brian A. *Muslims of Medieval Latin Christendom, c. 1050–1614.* Cambridge: Cambridge University Press, 2014.

Cavalcanti, Daniel D., William Feindel, James T. Goodrich, T. Forcht Dagi, Charles J. Prestigiacomo, and Mark C. Preul. "Anatomy, Technology, Art, and Culture: Toward a Realistic Perspective of the Brain." *Neurosurgical Focus* 27 (September 2009): 1–22.

Cavert, William M. "Industrial Coal Consumption in Early Modern London." *Urban History* 44, no. 3 (August 2017): 424–43.

Chafetz, Joshua Aaron. *Democracy's Privileged Few: Legislative Privilege and Democratic Norms in the British and American Constitutions.* New Haven, CT, and London: Yale University Press, 2007.

Charrak, André. "The Mathematical Model of Creation According to Kepler." In *Mathematics and the Divine: A Historical Study.* Edited by T. Koetsier and L. Bergmans. Amsterdam: Elsevier B.V., 2005. Pp. 361–74.

Chase, Kenneth. *Firearms: A Global History to 1700.* New York: Cambridge University Press, 2003.

Chattopadhyaya, Debiprasad. *History of Science and Technology in Ancient India.* 3 Volumes. Calcutta: Firma K.L. Mukhopadhyaya, 1988–1996.

Cherniack, Susan. "Book Culture and Textual Transmission in Sung China." *Harvard Journal of Asiatic Studies* 54, no. 1 (June 1994): 5–125.

Church, Sally. "Zheng He: An Investigation into the Plausibility of 450-ft Treasure Ships." *Monumenta Serica: Journal of Oriental Studies* 53, no. 1 (January 2005): 1–42.

Clark, Greg. *Global Cities: A Short History.* Washington, DC: Brookings Institution Press, 2016.

Cohen, I. Bernard. "Newton's Concepts of Force and Mass, with Notes on the Laws of Motion." In *The Cambridge Companion to Newton.* 2nd ed. Edited by Rob Iliffe and George E. Smith. Cambridge: Cambridge University Press, 2016. Pp. 61–92.

Colish, Marsha L. "Haskins's *Renaissance* Seventy Years Later: Beyond Anti-Burkhardtianism." *Haskins Society Journal.* Edited by Stephen Morillo. Volume 11 (2003): 1–15.

Colless, Brian E. "The Origin of the Alphabet." *Antiguo Oriente* 12 (2014): 71–104.

Constable, Olivia Remie. "Muslims in Medieval Europe." In *A Companion to the Medieval World*. Edited by Carol Lansing and Edward D. English. Chichester, UK: Blackwell Publishing, 2013. Pp. 313-32.

Cook, Alan H. *Edmond Halley: Charting the Heavens and the Seas*. Oxford: Clarendon Press, 1998.

Coşgel, Metin M., Thomas J. Miceli, and Jared Rubin, "The Political Economy of Mass Printing: Legitimacy and Technological Change in the Ottoman Empire." *Journal of Comparative Economics* 40, no. 3 (August 2012): 357-71.

Costa, P. Fontes da. "The Culture of Curiosity at The Royal Society in the First Half of the Eighteenth Century." *Notes and Records of the Royal Society of London* 56 (May 2002): 147-66.

Crane, Nicholas. *Mercator: The Man Who Mapped the Planet*. New York: Henry Holt and Company, 2003.

Crone, Patricia. *Slaves on Horses: The Evolution of the Islamic Polity*. Cambridge: Cambridge University Press, 2003.

Crosby, Alfred W. *The Measure of Reality: Quantification and Western Society, 1250-1600*. Cambridge: Cambridge University Press, 1996.

Crosby, Alfred W. *Throwing Fire: Projectile Technology through History*. New York: Cambridge University Press, 2002.

Crosby, Alfred W., Jr. *The Columbian Exchange: Biological and Cultural Consequences of 1492*. Thirtieth Anniversary ed. Westport, CT: ABC-CLIO, 2003.

Crowe, Michael J. *Theories of the World from Antiquity to the Copernican Revolution*. New York: Dover Publications, 1990.

Curtis, Gregory. *The Cave Painters: Probing the Mysteries of the World's First Artists*. New York: Anchor Books, 2006.

Cushing, Kathleen G. *Reform and the Papacy in the Eleventh Century: Spirituality and Social Change*. Manchester and New York: Manchester University Press, 2005.

Dackerman, Susan, ed. *Prints and the Pursuit of Knowledge in Early Modern Europe*. Cambridge, MA: Harvard University Art Museums, 2011.

Dale, Richard. *The First Crash: Lessons from the South Sea Bubble*. Princeton, NJ: Princeton University Press, 2004.

Dallal, Ahmad. "Science, Medicine, and Technology: The Making of a Scientific Culture." In *The Oxford History of Islam*. Edited by John L. Esposito. Oxford: Oxford and New York, 1999. Pp. 155-214.

Daly, Jonathan. *Historians Debate the Rise of the West*. London and New York: Routledge, 2015.

Daly, Jonathan. *The Rise of Western Power: A Comparative History of Western Civilization*. London and New York: Bloomsbury, 2014.

Davids, Karel, and Bert De Munck. "Innovation and Creativity in Late Medieval and Early Modern European Cities: An Introduction." In *Innovation and Creativity in Late Medieval and Early Modern European Cities*. Edited by Karel Davids and Bert De Munck. London: Routledge, 2016. Pp. 1-35.

Davids, Karel. "Successful and Failed Transitions: A Comparison of Innovations in Windmill-Technology in Britain and the Netherlands in the Early Modern Period." *History and Technology* 14 (1998): 225-47.

Works Cited

Davids, Karel. *Religion, Technology, and the Great and Little Divergences: China and Europe Compared, c. 700–1800*. Leiden: Brill, 2014.

Davis, Natalie Zemon. *Trickster Travels: A Sixteenth-Century Muslim Between Worlds*. New York: Hill & Wang, 2006.

de Hamel, Christopher. "The European Medieval Book." In *The Book: A Global History*. Edited by Michael F. Suarez and H.R. Woudhuysen. Oxford and New York: Oxford University Press, 2013. Pp. 59–79.

De Moor, Tine, and Jan Luiten van Zanden. "'Every Woman Counts': A Gender-Analysis of Numeracy in the Low Countries during the Early Modern Period." *Journal of Interdisciplinary History* 41, no. 2 (Autumn 2010): 179–208.

De Moor, Tine, and Jan Luiten van Zanden. "Girl Power: The European Marriage Pattern and Labour Markets in the North Sea Region in the Late Medieval and Early Modern Period." *Economic History Review* 63, no. 1 (February 2010): 1–33.

de Pleijt, Alexandra M., Jan Luiten van Zanden, and Sarah Guilland Carmichael. "Gender Relations and Economic Development: Hypotheses about the Reversal of Fortune in EurAsia." In *Cliometrics and the Family: Global Patterns and their Impact on Diverging Development*. Edited by Claude Diebolt, Auke Rijpma, Sarah Carmichael, Selin Dilli, and Charlotte Störmer. Berlin: Springer Verlag, 2019.

de Tocqueville, Alexis. *Democracy in America*. Translated by George Lawrence. Edited by J.P. Mayer. Garden City, NY: Doubleday, 1969.

Deng, Gang. *Chinese Maritime Activities and Socioeconomic Development, c. 2100 B.C.–1900 A.D.* Westport, CT: Greenwood Press, 1997.

Deng, Kent G. "Development and Its Deadlock in Imperial China, 221 B.C.–1840 A.D." *Economic Development and Cultural Change* 51 (January 2003): 479–522.

Deng, Kent, and Patrick O'Brien. "Nutritional Standards of Living in England and the Yangzi Delta (Jiangnan), circa 1644–circa 1840: Clarifying Data for Reciprocal Comparisons." *Journal of World History* 26, no. 2 (June 2015): 233–67.

Dennison, Tracy, and Sheilagh Ogilvie. "Does the European Marriage Pattern Explain Economic Growth?" *Journal of Economic History* 74, no. 3 (September 2014): 651–93.

Descartes, René. *A Discourse on the Method*. Translated by Ian Maclean. Oxford: Oxford University Press, 2006.

Descartes, René. *Meditations on First Philosophy: With Selections from the Objections and Replies*. Edited by John Cottingham. Cambridge: Cambridge University Press, 1996.

Di Bella, Stefano, Fabrizio Taglietti, Andrea Iacobuzio, Emma Johnson, Andrea Baiocchini, and Nicola Petrosillo. "The 'Delivery' of Adam." *Mayo Clinic Proceedings* 90, no. 4 (2015): 505–8.

Diamond, Jared. *Guns, Germs, and Steel: The Fates of Human Societies*. New York: W.W. Norton, 1997.

Dincecco, Mark, and Massimiliano G. Onorato. *From Warfare to Wealth: The Military Origins of Urban Prosperity in Europe*. New York: Cambridge University Press, 2018.

Dobbs, David. "Restless Genes." *National Geographic* 223, no. 1 (January 2013): 44–57.

Works Cited

Dobozy, Maria, trans. and ed. *The Saxon Mirror: A "Sachsenspiegel" of the Fourteenth Century*. Philadelphia: University of Pennsylvania Press, 1999.

Dodgen, Randall A. "Salvaging Kaifeng: Natural Calamity and Urban Community in Late Imperial China." *Journal of Urban History* 21, no. 6 (September 1995): 716–40.

Donovan, Arthur. "Lavoisier and the Origins of Modern Chemistry." *Osiris* 4 (1988): 214–31.

Duchesne, Ricardo. "A Civilization of Explorers." *Academic Questions* 25, no. 1 (March 2012): 65–93.

Eamon, William. *Science and the Secrets of Nature: Books of Secrets in Medieval and Early Modern Culture*. Princeton, NJ: Princeton University Press, 1994.

Edson, Evelyn. *The World Map, 1300–1493: The Persistence of Tradition and Transformation*. Baltimore, MD: Johns Hopkins University Press, 2007.

Edriss, Hawa, et al. "Islamic Medicine in the Middle Ages." *American Journal of the Medical Sciences* 354, no. 3 (September 2017): 223–29.

Edwards, Mark U., Jr. *Printing, Propaganda, and Martin Luther*. Berkeley, CA: University of California Press, 1994.

Eisenstein, Elizabeth L. *Divine Art, Infernal Machine: The Reception of Printing in the West from First Impressions to the Sense of an Ending*. Philadelphia and Oxford: University of Pennsylvania Press, 2011.

Eisenstein, Elizabeth L. *The Printing Revolution in Early Modern Europe*. 2nd ed. Cambridge: Cambridge University Press, 2005.

Elkins, Zachary, Tom Ginsburg, and James Melton, "On the Influence of Magna Carta and Other Cultural Relics." *International Review of Law and Economics* 47 (2016): 3–9.

Ellis, Markman. "An Introduction to the Coffee-house: A Discursive Model." *Language & Communication* 28 (2008): 156–64.

Ellis, Markman. "Coffee-House Libraries in Mid-Eighteenth-Century London." *The Library: Transactions of the Bibliographical Society* 10, no. 1 (March 2009): 3–40.

Elman, Benjamin A. *On Their Own Terms: Science in China, 1550–1900*. Cambridge, MA: Harvard University Press, 2005.

Eltis, David, and Stanley L. Engerman. "The Importance of Slavery and the Slave Trade to Industrializing Britain." *Journal of Economic History* 60, no. 1 (March 2000): 123–44.

Elvin, Mark. *The Pattern of the Chinese Past*. Stanford, CA: Stanford University Press, 1973.

Emsley, John. *Nature's Building Blocks: An A–Z Guide to the Elements*. 2nd ed. Oxford: Oxford University Press, 2011.

Epstein, Steven A. *An Economic and Social History of Later Medieval Europe, 1000–1500*. Cambridge: Cambridge University Press, 2009.

Evergates, Theodore, ed. and trans. *Feudal Society in Medieval France: Documents from the County of Champagne*. Philadelphia: University of Pennsylvania Press, 1993.

Fakhry, Majid. "Philosophy and Theology: From the Eighth Century C.E. to the Present." In *The Oxford History of Islam*. Edited by John L. Esposito. Oxford and New York: Oxford University Press, 1999. Pp. 269–305.

Works Cited

Fakhry, Majid. *A History of Islamic Philosophy*. 3rd ed. New York: Columbia University Press, 2004.

Farmer, S.A. *Syncretism in the West: Pico's 900 Theses (1486): The Evolution of Traditional Religious and Philosophical Systems*. Translated by S.A. Farmer. Tempe, AZ: Medieval & Renaissance Texts & Studies, 1998.

Ferguson, Niall. *Civilization: The West and the Rest*. New York: Penguin Press, 2011.

Fernández-Armesto, Felipe. *Pathfinders: A Global History of Exploration*. New York: W.W. Norton, 2007.

Findlen, Paula. "Anatomy Theaters, Botanical Gardens, and Natural History Collections." In *The Cambridge History of Science*. Volume 3: *Early Modern Science*. Edited by Katharine Park and Lorraine Daston. Cambridge: Cambridge University Press, 2006. Pp. 272–89.

Findlen, Paula. "Natural History." In *The Cambridge History of Science*. Volume 3: *Early Modern Science*. Edited by Katharine Park and Lorraine Daston. Cambridge: Cambridge University Press, 2006. Pp. 435–68.

Finlay, Robert. "China, the West, and World History in Joseph Needham's *Science and Civilisation in China*." *Journal of World History* 11 (Fall 2000): 265–303.

Finlay, Robert. "The Voyages of Zheng He: Ideology, State Power, and Maritime Trade in Ming China." *Journal of The Historical Society* 8, no. 3 (September 2008): 327–47.

Fögen, Thorsten. "Roman Responses to Greek Science and Scholarship as a Cultural and Political Phenomenon." In *A Companion to Science, Technology, and Medicine in Ancient Greece and Rome*. 2 Volumes. Edited by Georgia L. Irby. Chichester, UK, and Malden, MA: Wiley Blackwell, 2016. 1:958–72.

Frank, Andre Gunder. *ReOrient: Global Economy in the Asian Age*. Berkeley, CA: University of California Press, 1998.

Friedel, Robert. *A Culture of Improvement: Technology and the Western Millennium*. Cambridge, MA: MIT Press, 2010.

Frye, Richard N., trans. and ed. *Ibn Fadlan's Journey to Russia: A Tenth-century Traveler from Baghdad to the Volga River*. Princeton, NJ: Markus Wiener Publishers, 2005.

Fu, Tingmei. "Legal Person in China: Essence and Limits." *American Journal of Comparative Law* 41, no. 2 (Spring 1993): 261–97.

Füssel, Stephan. *Gutenberg and the Impact of Printing*. Translated by Douglas Martin. Aldershot, UK, and Burlington, VT: Ashgate Publishing Co., 2005.

Garden, Kenneth. "The Rihla and Self-Reinvention of Abu Bakr Ibn al-'Arabī." *Journal of the American Oriental Society* 135, no. 1 (January–March 2015): 1–17.

Gaudiosi, Monica M. "The Influence of the Islamic Law of Waqf on the Development of the Trust in England: The Case of Merton College." *University of Pennsylvania Law Review* 136, no. 4 (April 1988): 1231–61.

Gaukroger, Stephen. *The Emergence of a Scientific Culture: Science and the Shaping of Modernity, 1210–1685*. Oxford: Clarendon Press, 2006.

Gelderblom, Oscar, and Joost Jonker. "Completing a Financial Revolution: The Finance of the Dutch East India Trade and the Rise of the Amsterdam Capital Market, 1595–1612." *Journal of Economic History* 64 (September 2004): 641–72.

Works Cited

George, Timothy. *Theology of the Reformers.* Revised ed. Nashville: Broadman and Holman, 2013.

Ghosh, Sanjib Kumar. "Human Cadaveric Dissection: A Historical Account from Ancient Greece to the Modern Era." *Anatomy & Cell Biology* 48 (2015): 153–69.

Glenn, H. Patrick. *Legal Traditions of the World: Sustainable Diversity in Law.* 5th ed. Oxford: Oxford University Press, 2014.

Glete, Jan. *War and the State in Early Modern Europe: Spain, the Dutch Republic and Sweden as Fiscal-Military States, 1500–1660.* London: Routledge, 2002.

Goffen, Rona. *Renaissance Rivals: Michelangelo, Leonardo, Raphael, Titian.* New Haven, CT: Yale University Press, 2004.

Golas, Peter J. *Picturing Technology in China: From Earliest Times to the Nineteenth Century.* Hong Kong: Hong Kong University Press, 2015.

Goldgar, Anne. *Impolite Learning: Conduct and Community in the Republic of Letters, 1680–1750.* New Haven, CT, and London: Yale University Press, 1995.

Goldstein, Bernard. "Copernicus and the Origin of His Heliocentric System." *Journal for the History of Astronomy* 33, no. 3 (August 2002): 219–35.

Goldstone, Jack A. "Efflorescences and Economic Growth in World History: Rethinking the 'Rise of the West' and the Industrial Revolution." *Journal of World History* 13, no. 2 (Fall 2002): 323–89.

Goldstone, Jack. *Why Europe? The Rise of the West in World History, 1500–1850.* Boston: McGraw Hill, 2009.

Goldstone, Jack A. "Why and Where Did Modern Economic Growth Begin?" *Tijdschrift voor Sociale en Economische Geschiedenis/The Low Countries Journal of Social and Economic History* 12, no. 2 (June 2015): 17–30.

Goodman, Dena. *The Republic of Letters: A Cultural History of the French Enlightenment.* Ithaca, NY: Cornell University Press, 1994.

Goossaert, Vincent. "Irrepressible Female Piety: Late Imperial Bans on Women Visiting Temples." *Nan Nü* 10 (2008): 212–41.

Gordon, Stewart. *When Asia Was the World: Traveling Merchants, Scholars, Warriors, and Monks Who Created the "Riches of the East."* Cambridge, MA: Da Capo Press, 2008.

Gotlieb, Marc. "The Painter's Secret: Invention and Rivalry from Vasari to Balzac." *Art Bulletin* 84, no. 3 (September 2002): 469–90.

Gough, J.B. "Lavoisier and the Fulfillment of the Stahlian Revolution." *Osiris* 4 (1988): 15–33.

Graff, Harvey J. *The Legacies of Literacy: Continuities and Contradictions in Western Culture and Society.* Bloomington, IN: Indiana University Press, 1991.

Grafton, Anthony. "Libraries and Lecture Halls." In *The Cambridge History of Science.* Volume 3: *Early Modern Science.* Edited by Katharine Park and Lorraine Daston. Cambridge: Cambridge University Press, 2006. Pp. 238–50.

Grafton, Anthony. *Worlds Made by Words: Scholarship and Community in the Modern West.* Cambridge, MA: Harvard University Press, 2009.

Graham, Daniel W. "Matter." In *A Companion to Science, Technology, and Medicine in Ancient Greece and Rome.* 2 Volumes. Edited by Georgia L. Irby. Chichester, UK, and Malden, MA: Wiley Blackwell, 2016. 1:29–42.

Works Cited

Grahl-Madsen, Atle. "The European Tradition of Asylum and the Development of Refugee Law." *Journal of Peace Research* 3 (1966): 278–89.

Grant, Edward, ed. *A Source Book in Medieval Science*. Cambridge, MA: Harvard University Press, 1974.

Grant, Edward. *A History of Natural Philosophy: From the Ancient World to the Nineteenth Century*. Cambridge: Cambridge University Press, 2007.

Grant, Lindy. *Abbot Suger of St-Denis: Church and State in Early Twelfth-Century France*. London and New York: Longman, 1998.

Grehan, James. "Smoking and 'Early Modern' Sociability: The Great Tobacco Debate in the Ottoman Middle East (Seventeenth to Eighteenth Centuries)." *American Historical Review* 111, no. 5 (December 2006): 1352–77.

Greif, Avner. *Institutions and the Path to the Modern Economy: Lessons from Medieval Trade*. Cambridge: Cambridge University Press, 2006.

Guilmartin, John Francis. "The Earliest Shipboard Gunpowder Ordnance: An Analysis of Its Technical Parameters and Tactical Capabilities." *Journal of Military History* 71, no. 3 (July 2007): 649–69.

Guotu, Zhuang. "China's Policies on Chinese Overseas: Past and Present." In *Routledge Handbook of the Chinese Diaspora*. Edited by Chee-Beng Tan. London and New York: Routledge, 2013. Pp. 31–41.

Haines, John. "The Origins of the Musical Staff." *Musical Quarterly* 91, no. 3/4 (Fall-Winter 2008): 327–78.

Hall, John A. *Powers and Liberties: The Causes and Consequences of the Rise of the West*. Oxford: Basil Blackwell, 1985.

Hamilton, Bernard. "'Knowing the Enemy': Western Understanding of Islam at the Time of the Crusades." *Journal of the Royal Asiatic Society* 7, no. 3 (November 1997): 373–87.

Harding, Alan. "Political Liberty in the Middle Ages." *Speculum* 55, no. 3 (July 1980): 423–43.

Harding, Alan. *Medieval Law and the Foundations of the State*. Oxford and New York: Oxford University Press, 2002.

Harris, Stephen J. "Networks of Travel, Correspondence, and Exchange." In *The Cambridge History of Science*. Volume 3: *Early Modern Science*. Edited by Katharine Park and Lorraine Daston. Cambridge: Cambridge University Press, 2006. Pp. 341–62.

Hartwell, Robert. "A Revolution in the Chinese Iron and Coal Industries During the Northern Sung, 960–1126 A.D." *Journal of Asian Studies* 21 (February 1962): 153–62.

Hartwell, Robert. "A Cycle of Economic Change in Imperial China: Coal and Iron in Northeast China, 750–1350." *Journal of the Economic and Social History of the Orient* 10, no. 1 (July 1967): 102–59.

Harvey, Steven. "Jewish and Muslim Philosophy: Similarities and Differences." In *A History of Jewish-Muslim Relations: From the Origins to the Present Day*. Edited by Abdelwahab Meddeb and Benjamin Stora. Princeton, NJ: Princeton University Press, 2013. Pp. 737–63.

Hattox, Ralph S. *Coffee and Coffeehouses: The Origins of a Social Beverage in the Medieval Near East*. Seattle: University of Washington Press, 1985.

He, Jinli. "Continuity and Evolution: The Idea of 'Co-creativity' in Chinese Art." *ASIANetwork Exchange: A Journal for Asian Studies in the Liberal Arts* 21, no. 2 (2014): 15–23.

Headrick, Daniel K. *When Information Came of Age: Technologies of Knowledge in the Age of Reason and Revolution, 1700–1850.* New York: Oxford University Press, 2000.

Helinga, Lotta. "The Gutenberg Revolutions." In *A Companion to the History of the Book.* Edited by Simon Eliot and Jonathan Rose. Malden, MA: Blackwell Pub., 2007. Pp. 207–19.

Henrich, Joseph, Robert Boyd, and Peter J. Richerson. "The Puzzle of Monogamous Marriage." *Philosophical Transactions of the Royal Society B: Biological Sciences* 367, no. 1589 (March 2012): 657–69.

Hentschel, Klaus. *Visual Cultures in Science and Technology: A Comparative History.* Oxford and New York: Oxford University Press, 2014.

Hobson, John M. *The Eastern Origins of Western Civilisation.* Cambridge: Cambridge University Press, 2004.

Hodgson, Marshall. *The Venture of Islam: Conscience and History in a World Civilization.* 3 Volumes. Chicago: University of Chicago Press, 1974.

Hodgson, Marshall G.S. "Cultural Patterning in Islamdom and the Occident." In *Rethinking World History: Essays on Europe, Islam, and World History.* Edited by Edmund Burke III. Cambridge: Cambridge University Press, 1993. Pp. 126–70.

Hoffmann, D.L., et al. "U-Th Dating of Carbonate Crusts Reveals Neandertal Origin of Iberian Cave Art." *Science* 359, no. 6378 (February 23, 2018): 912–15.

Hoffman, Philip T. *Why Did Europe Conquer the World?* Princeton, NJ: Princeton University Press, 2015.

Hoffmann, Stefan-Ludwig. *Civil Society, 1750–1914.* Houndmills, UK: Palgrave Macmillan, 2006.

Holoman, D. Kern. *Berlioz: A Musical Biography of the Creative Genius of the Romantic Era.* Cambridge, MA: Harvard University Press, 1989.

Holton, Gerald James, and Stephen G. Brush, *Physics, the Human Adventure: From Copernicus to Einstein and Beyond.* New Brunswick, NJ: Rutgers University Press, 2001.

Hosseini, Hamid. "Seeking the Roots of Adam Smith's Division of Labor in Medieval Persia." *History of Political Economy* 30, no. 4 (January 1998): 653–81.

Houston, R.A. *Literacy in Early Modern Europe: Culture and Education, 1500–1800.* 2nd ed. London and New York: Routledge, 2013.

Houston, Rab. "Literacy and Society in the West, 1500–1850." *Social History* 8, no. 3 (October 1983): 269–93.

Huang, Philip C.C. "Development or Involution in Eighteenth-Century Britain and China? A Review of Kenneth Pomeranz's 'The Great Divergence: China, Europe, and the Making of the Modern World Economy.'" *Journal of Asian Studies* 61 (May 2002): 501–38.

Huang, Philip C.C. *Civil Justice in China: Representation and Practice in the Qing.* Stanford, CA: Stanford University Press, 1996.

Huff, Toby E. "Law and Science." *Academic Questions* 25, no. 1 (March 2012): 54–64.

Works Cited

Huff, Toby E. *The Rise of Early Modern Science: Islam, China, and the West.* 3rd ed. Cambridge: Cambridge University Press, 2017.

Hughes, Thomas P. *Human-Built World: How to Think about Technology and Culture.* Chicago: University of Chicago Press, 2005.

Hui, Victoria Tin-bor. *War and State Formation in Ancient China and Early Modern Europe.* New York: Cambridge University Press, 2005.

Hunt, Lynn. *Inventing Human Rights: A History.* New York: W.W. Norton, 2007.

Huppert, George. *The Style of Paris: Renaissance Origins of the French Enlightenment.* Bloomington, IN: Indiana University Press, 1999.

Huth, John Edward. *The Lost Art of Finding our Way.* Cambridge, MA: The Belknap Press of Harvard University Press, 2013.

Hutson, Matthew. "AI Researchers Allege that Machine Learning Is Alchemy." *Science* 360, no. 6388 (May 3, 2018): 478.

Hyman, Arthur, James J. Walsh, and Thomas Williams, eds. *Philosophy in the Middle Ages: The Christian, Islamic, and Jewish Traditions.* 3rd ed. Indianapolis and Cambridge, MA: Hackett Publishing Co., 2010.

Iliffe, Robert. "Material Doubts: Hooke, Artisan Culture, and the Exchange of Information in 1670s London." *British Journal for the History of Science* 28, no. 3 (September 1995): 285–318.

Inikori, Joseph E. *Africans and the Industrial Revolution in England: A Study in International Trade and Economic Development.* Cambridge: Cambridge University Press, 2002.

Jeauneau, Édouard. *Rethinking the School of Chartres.* Translated by Claude Paul Desmarais. Toronto: University of Toronto Press, 2009.

Jia, Li. "Conflicts Between Monarch and Ministers: A Political and Cultural Interpretation of the Ming-Dynasty Officials' Collective 'Petitions to the Palace.'" *Chinese Studies in History* 44, no. 3 (Spring 2011): 72–89.

Jin, Dengjian. *The Great Knowledge Transcendence: The Rise of Western Science and Technology Reframed.* Basingstoke, UK, and New York: Palgrave Macmillan, 2016.

Johns, Adrian. "Coffeehouses and Print Shops." In *The Cambridge History of Science. Volume 3: Early Modern Science.* Edited by Katharine Park and Lorraine Daston. Cambridge: Cambridge University Press, 2006. Pp. 320–40.

Jones, Eric L. "England as the Source of the Great Divergence." *Tijdschrift voor Sociale en Economische Geschiedenis/The Low Countries Journal of Social and Economic History* 12, no. 2 (June 2015): 79–92.

Jones, Eric L. *Locating the Industrial Revolution: Inducement and Response.* Singapore: World Scientific, 2010.

Karababa, Emİnegül, and Güliz Ger. "Early Modern Ottoman Coffeehouse Culture and the Formation of the Consumer Subject." *Journal of Consumer Research* 37, no. 5 (February 2011): 737–60.

Karaman, K. Kivanç, and Şevket Pamuk. "Different Paths to the Modern State in Europe: The Interaction Between Warfare, Economic Structure, and Political Regime." *American Political Science Review* 107, no. 3 (August 2013): 603–26.

Karayalçin, Cem. "Divided We Stand, United We Fall: The Hume-North-Jones Mechanism for the Rise of Europe." *International Economic Review* 49, no. 3 (August 2008): 973–97.

Works Cited

Karrow, Robert. "Centers of Map Publishing in Europe, 1472-1600." In *The History of Cartography*. Volume 3: *Cartography in the European Renaissance*. Edited by David Woodward. Chicago and London: University of Chicago Press, 2007. Pp. 611-21.

Katz, Bill. *Cuneiform to Computer: A History of Reference Sources*. Lanham, MD, and London: The Scarecrow Press, 1998.

Katz, Paul R. *Divine Justice: Religion and the Development of Chinese Legal Culture*. New York: Routledge, 2009.

Kelly, Jack. *Gunpowder: Alchemy, Bombards, and Pyrotechnics: The History of the Explosive That Changed the World*. New York: Basic Books, 2004.

Kelly, Thomas Forrest. *Capturing Music: The Story of Notation*. New York: W.W. Norton, 2015.

Kemp, Martin. *The Science of Art: Optical Themes in Western Art from Brunelleschi to Seurat*. New Haven, CT: Yale University Press, 1992.

Khan, Iqtidar Alam. *Gunpowder and Firearms: Warfare in Medieval India*. New Delhi: Oxford University Press, 2004.

King, Peter. "The Production and Consumption of Bar Iron in Early Modern England and Wales." *Economic History Review* 58, no. 1 (2005): 1-33.

Ko, Dorothy. "Pursuing Talent and Virtue: Education and Women's Culture in Seventeenth- and Eighteenth-Century China." *Late Imperial China* 13, no. 1 (June 1992): 9-39.

König, Jason, and Greg Woolf. "Encyclopaedism in the Roman Empire." In *Encyclopaedism from Antiquity to the Renaissance*. Edited by Jason König and Greg Woolf. Cambridge: Cambridge University Press, 2013. Pp. 23-63.

Koyré, Alexandre. *The Astronomical Revolution: Copernicus, Kepler, Borelli*. Translated by R.E.W. Maddison. Paris: Hermann, 1973.

Koziol, Geoffrey. *The Peace of God*. Leeds: ARC Humanities Press, 2018.

Kuran, Timur. *The Long Divergence: How Islamic Law Held Back the Middle East*. Princeton, NJ: Princeton University Press, 2011.

Kuran, Timur, and Anantdeep Singh. "Economic Modernization in Late British India: Hindu-Muslim Differences." *Economic Development and Cultural Change* 61, no. 3 (April 2013): 503-38.

Kurlansky, Mark. *Paper: Paging Through History*. New York: W.W. Norton, 2016.

Kusukawa, Sachiko. "Nature's Regularity in Some Protestant Natural Philosophy Textbooks, 1530-1630." In *Natural Law and Laws of Nature in Early Modern Europe: Jurisprudence, Theology, Moral and Natural Philosophy*. Edited by Lorraine Daston and Michael Stolleis. Farnham, UK, and Burlington, VT: Ashgate Pub., 2008. Pp. 105-22.

Landau, Peter. "The Development of Law." In *The New Cambridge Medieval History*. Volume 4: *c.1024-c.1198*, pt. 1. Edited by David Luscombe and Jonathan Riley-Smith. Cambridge: Cambridge University Press, 2004. Pp. 113-47.

Langdon, John. *Mills in the Medieval Economy: England 1300-1540*. New York: Oxford University Press, 2004.

Larner, John. "Plucking Hairs from the Great Cham's Beard: Marco Polo, Jan de Langhe, and Sir John Mandeville." In *Marco Polo and the Encounter of East and West*. Edited by Suzanne Conklin Akbari and Amilcare Iannucci. Toronto: University of Toronto Press, 2008. Pp. 133-55.

Works Cited

Larner, John. *Marco Polo and the Discovery of the World*. New Haven, CT, and London: Yale University Press, 1999.

Lederer, Herbert. "The Vienna Coffeehouse: History and Cultural Significance." In *The Thinking Space: The Café as a Cultural Institution in Paris, Italy and Vienna*. Edited by Leona Rittner, W. Scott Haine, and Jeffrey H. Jackson. Farnham, UK: Ashgate, 2013. Pp. 25–32.

Lerner, Fred. *The Story of Libraries: From the Invention of Writing to the Computer Age*. London and New York: Continuum, 2001.

Levey, Michael. *From Giotto to Cézanne: A Concise History of Painting*. London: Thames and Hudson, 1968.

Lewis, Bernard. *The Muslim Discovery of Europe*. New York: W.W. Norton & Company, 2001.

Lewis, Bernard. *What Went Wrong? Western Impact and Middle Eastern Response*. Oxford: Oxford University Press, 2002.

Li, Bozhong. "The Early Modern Economy of the Yangzi Delta in a New Perspective." *Social Sciences in China* 36, no. 1 (2015): 91–109.

Li, Bozhong, and Jan Luiten van Zanden. "Before the Great Divergence? Comparing the Yangzi Delta and the Netherlands at the Beginning of the Nineteenth Century." *Journal of Economic History* 72, no. 4 (December 2012): 956–89.

Liang, Linxia. *Delivering Justice in Qing China: Civil Trials in the Magistrate's Court*. Oxford: Oxford University Press, 2007.

Lieberman, Victor. *Strange Parallels: Southeast Asia in Global Context, c. 800–1830*. Volume 2: *Mainland Mirrors: Europe, Japan, China, South Asia, and the Islands*. New York: Cambridge University Press, 2009.

Lindberg, Carter. *The European Reformations*. 2nd ed. Oxford: Wiley-Blackwell, 2010.

Lindberg, David. *The Beginnings of Western Science: The European Scientific Tradition in Philosophical, Religious, and Institutional Context, 600 B.C. to A.D. 1450*. Chicago: University of Chicago Press, 1992.

Liu, William Guanglin. "The Making of a Fiscal State in Song China, 960–1279." *Economic History Review* 68, no. 1 (2015): 48–78.

Lloyd, G.E.R. *Greek Science after Aristotle*. New York: W.W. Norton, 1973.

Lloyd, G.E.R. *The Ambitions of Curiosity: Understanding the World in Ancient Greece and China*. New York: Cambridge University Press, 2002.

Lorge, Peter. *War, Politics, and Society in Early Modern China, 900–1795*. London and New York: Routledge, 2005.

Lowe, Roy, and Yoshihito Yasuhara. *The Origins of Higher Learning: Knowledge Networks and the Early Development of Universities*. London and New York: Routledge, 2017.

Lu, Yongxiang, ed. *A History of Chinese Science and Technology*. Volume 1. Shanghai: Shanghai Jiao Tong University Press; Heidelberg: Springer, 2015.

Lucas, Adam Robert. "Industrial Milling in the Ancient and Medieval Worlds: A Survey of the Evidence for an Industrial Revolution in Medieval Europe." *Technology and Culture* 46, no. 1 (January 2005): 1–30.

Lucas, Adam. *Wind, Water, Work: Ancient and Medieval Milling Technology*. Leiden: Brill, 2006.

Works Cited

Lux, David S., and Harold J. Cook. "Closed Circles or Open Networks?: Communicating at a Distance during the Scientific Revolution." *History of Science* 36 (1998): 179–211.

MacCormack, Geoffrey. *Traditional Chinese Penal Law*. Edinburgh: Edinburgh University Press, 1990.

MacEvitt, Christopher. "Martyrdom and the Muslim World Through Franciscan Eyes." *Catholic Historical Review* 97, no. 1 (January 2011): 1–23.

Macfarlane, Alan. *The Making of the Modern World: Visions from the West and East*. Basingstoke, UK, and New York: Palgrave, 2002.

Macfarlane, Alan. *Invention of the Modern World*. Les Brouzils, France: Odd Volumes of the Fortnightly Review, 2014.

Machamer, Peter. "Galileo's Machines, His Mathematics, and His Experiments." In *The Cambridge Companion to Galileo*. Edited by Peter Machamer. Cambridge: Cambridge University Press, 1998. Pp. 53–79.

Maddison, Angus. *Contours of the World Economy, 1–2030 A.D.: Essays in Macroeconomic History*. Oxford: Oxford University Press, 2007.

Makdisi, George. "Madrasa and University in the Middle Ages." *Studia Islamica* 32 (1970): 255–64.

Makdisi, John A. "The Islamic Origins of the Common Law." *North Carolina Law Review* 77, no. 5 (1999): 1635–1740.

Man, John. *Alpha Beta: How 26 Letters Shaped the Western World*. New York: Wiley, 2000.

Man, John. *Gutenberg: How One Man Remade the World with Words*. New York: John Wiley & Sons, 2002.

Manley, K.A. "Infidel Books and 'Factories of the Enlightenment': Censorship and Surveillance in Subscription and Circulating Libraries in an Age of Revolutions, 1790–1850." *Book History* 19 (2016): 169–96.

Mann, Charles C. *1491: New Revelations of the Americas Before Columbus*. 2nd Vintage Books ed. New York: Vintage, 2011.

Marks, Robert. *The Origins of the Modern World: A Global and Ecological Narrative*. Lanham, MD: Rowman and Littlefield, 2002.

Marks, Steven G. *The Information Nexus: Global Capitalism from the Renaissance to the Present*. Cambridge: Cambridge University Press, 2016.

Martin, Diane. "Prosecution of the Statutes of Provisors and Premunire in the King's Bench, 1377–1394." In *Fourteenth Century England*. Volume 4. Edited by J.S. Hamilton. Rochester, NY: Boydell & Brewer, 2006. Pp. 109–23.

Matar, Nabil. *Europe through Arab Eyes, 1578–1727*. New York: Routledge, 2009.

Maw, David. "Machaut and the 'Critical' Phase of Medieval Polyphony." *Music & Letters* 87, no. 2 (May 2006): 262–94.

McClaren, Anne. "Rethinking Republicanism: *Vindiciae, Contra Tyrannos* in Context." *Historical Journal* 49, no. 1 (March 2006): 23–52.

McClellan, James, III. "Scientific Organisations and the Organisation of Science." In *The Cambridge History of Science*. Volume 4: *The Eighteenth-Century*. Edited by Roy Porter. Cambridge: Cambridge University Press, 2003. Pp. 87–106.

McCloskey, Deirdre Nansen. "The Great Enrichment: A Humanistic and Social Scientific Account." *Social Science History* 40, no. 4 (Winter 2016): 583–98.

Works Cited

McCloskey, Deirdre. *Bourgeois Equality: How Ideas, Not Capital or Institutions, Enriched the World.* Chicago: University of Chicago Press, 2016.

McCloskey, Deirdre. *Bourgeois Dignity: Why Economics Can't Explain the Modern World.* Chicago: University of Chicago Press, 2010.

McDermott, Joseph. "The Ascendance of the Imprint in China." In *Printing and Book Culture in Late Imperial China.* Edited by Cynthia J. Brokaw and Kai-wing Chow. Berkeley, CA: University of California Press, 2005. Pp. 55–106.

McNeill, William H. *Keeping Together in Time: Dance and Drill in Human History.* Cambridge, MA: Harvard University Press, 1995.

McNeill, William H. *The Rise of the West: A History of the Human Community.* Chicago: University of Chicago Press, 1963.

Melton, James Van Horn. *The Rise of the Public in Enlightenment Europe.* Cambridge: Cambridge University Press, 2001.

Menzies, Gavin. *1421: The Year China Discovered America.* New York: William Morrow, 2003.

Meredith, David, and Deborah Oxley. "Food and Fodder: Feeding England, 1700-1900." *Past and Present,* no. 222 (February 2014): 163–214.

Metcalfe, Alex. *The Muslims of Medieval Italy.* Edinburgh: Edinburgh University Press, 2009.

Mikhail, Alan. "The Heart's Desire: Gender, Urban Space and the Ottoman Coffee House." In *Ottoman Tulips, Ottoman Coffee: Leisure and Lifestyle in the Eighteenth Century.* Edited by Dana Sajdi. London: I.B. Tauris, 2007. Pp. 133–70.

Miller, David Philip. "The Usefulness of Natural Philosophy: The Royal Society and the Culture of Practical Utility in the Later Eighteenth Century." *British Journal for the History of Science* 32, no. 2 (June 1999): 185–201.

Mokyr, Joel. "Institutions and the Origins of the Great Enrichment." *Atlantic Economic Journal* 44, no. 2 (June 2016): 243–59.

Mokyr, Joel. "Peer Vries's Great Divergence." *Tijdschrift voor Sociale en Economische Geschiedenis/The Low Countries Journal of Social and Economic History* 12, no. 2 (June 2015): 93–104.

Mokyr, Joel. *The Lever of Riches: Technological Creativity and Economic Progress.* New York: Oxford University Press, 1990.

Monro, Alexander. *The Paper Trail: An Unexpected History of the World's Greatest Invention.* New York: Alfred A. Knopf, 2016.

Moodie, Gavin. *Universities, Disruptive Technologies, and Continuity in Higher Education: The Impact of Information Revolutions.* New York: Palgrave Macmillan, 2016.

Moran, Bruce T. "Courts and Academies." In *The Cambridge History of Science.* Volume 3: *Early Modern Science.* Edited by Katharine Park and Lorraine Daston. Cambridge: Cambridge University Press, 2006. Pp. 251–71.

Moran Cruz, Jo Ann Hoeppner. "Popular Attitudes Toward Islam in Medieval Europe." In *Travellers, Intellectuals, and the World beyond Medieval Europe.* Edited by David R. Blanks and Michael Frassetto. New York: Palgrave Macmillan, 1999. Pp. 55–81.

Morgan, Kenneth. *Slavery and the British Empire: From Africa to America.* Oxford: Oxford University Press, 2007.

Works Cited

Morton, Nicholas. *Encountering Islam on the First Crusade*. Cambridge: Cambridge University Press, 2016.

Mote, F.W. "The Arts and the 'Theorizing Mode' of the Civilization." In *Artists and Traditions: Uses of the Past in Chinese Culture*. Edited by Christian F. Murck. Princeton, NJ: The Art Museum, Princeton University, 1976. Pp. 3–8.

Mott, Lawrence V. "A Three-Masted Ship Depiction from 1409." *International Journal of Nautical Archeology* 23, no. 1 (February 1994): 39–40.

Mun, Seung-Hwan. "Printing Press without Copyright: A Historical Analysis of Printing and Publishing in Song, China." *Chinese Journal of Communication* 6, no. 1 (2013): 1–23.

Muntersbjorn, Madeline M. "Francis Bacon's Philosophy of Science: *Machina Intellectus* and *Forma Indita*." *Philosophy of Science* 70 (December 2003): 1137–48.

Navrozov, Lev. "Assessing the CIA's Soviet Economic Indices." In *The Soviet Economy on the Brink of Reform: Essays in Honor of Alec Nove*. Edited by P.J.D. Wiles. Boston: Unwin & Hyman, 1988. Pp. 112–52.

Nederman, Cary J., and Catherine Campbell. "Priests, Kings, and Tyrants: Spiritual and Temporal Power in John of Salisbury's *Policraticus*." *Speculum* 66 (July 1991): 572–90.

Needham, Joseph, with the research assistance of Wang Ling. *Science and Civilization in China*. Volume 2: *History of Scientific Thought*. Cambridge: Cambridge University Press, 1956.

Needham, Joseph. *Science in Traditional China: A Comparative Perspective*. Cambridge, MA: Harvard University Press; Hong Kong: The Chinese University Press, 1981.

Needham, Joseph. *The Grand Titration: Science and Society in East and West*. London: Allen & Unwin, 1969.

Neem, Johann N. *Creating a Nation of Joiners: Democracy and Civil Society in Early National Massachusetts*. Cambridge, MA, and London: Harvard University Press, 2008.

Nekrasz, Carmen, and Claudia Swan. "Art." In *The Cambridge History of Science*. Volume 3: *Early Modern Science*. Edited by Katharine Park and Lorraine Daston. Cambridge: Cambridge University Press, 2006. Pp. 771–96.

Nelson, Janet. "Rulers and Government." In *The New Cambridge Medieval History*, Volume 3: *c. 900–c. 1024*. Edited by Timothy Reuter. Cambridge: Cambridge University Press, 1999. Pp. 95–129.

Newcombe, David Gordon. *Henry VIII and the English Reformation*. London: Routledge, 1995.

Nicholas, David M. *The Growth of the Medieval City: From Late Antiquity to the Early Fourteenth Century*. London and New York: Longman, 1997.

Nichols, Stephen G. "Senses of the Imagination: Pseudo-Dionysius, Suger, and Saint-Denis." *Romanistisches Jahrbuch* 61 (November 2011): 223–39.

Norberg, Johan. *Progress: Ten Reasons to Look Forward to the Future*. London: Oneworld, 2016.

North, John. *Cosmos: An Illustrated History of Astronomy and Cosmology*. Chicago and London: The University of Chicago Press, 2008.

Works Cited

Novikoff, Alex J. "Anselm, Dialogue, and the Rise of Scholastic Disputation." *Speculum* 86 (2011): 387–418.

Novikoff, Alex J. *The Medieval Culture of Disputation: Pedagogy, Practice, and Performance.* Philadelphia: University of Pennsylvania Press, 2013.

Novikoff, Alex J., ed. *The Twelfth-Century Renaissance: A Reader.* Toronto: University of Toronto Press, 2017.

Numan, Mohammed T. "Ibn Al Nafis: His Seminal Contributions to Cardiology." *Pediatric Cardiology* 35, no. 7 (October 2014): 1088–90.

O'Brien, Patrick, and Kent Deng. "Can the Debate on the Great Divergence Be Located within the Kuznetsian Paradigm for an Empirical Form of Global Economic History?" *Tijdschrift voor Sociale en Economische Geschiedenis/The Low Countries Journal of Social and Economic History* 12, no. 2 (June 2015): 63–78.

O'Callaghan, Joseph F. "The Beginnings of the Cortes in León-Castile." *American Historical Review* 74, no. 5 (June 1969): 1503–37.

O'Callaghan, Joseph F. *The Cortes of Castile-León, 1188–1350.* Philadelphia: University of Pennsylvania Press, 1989.

O'Malley, John W. *Four Cultures of the West.* Cambridge, MA: The Belknap Press of Harvard University Press, 2004.

Otis, Jessica. "'Set Them to the Cyphering Schoole': Reading, Writing, and Arithmetical Education, circa 1540–1700." *Journal of British Studies* 56 (July 2017): 453–82.

Overton, Mark. *Agricultural Revolution in England: The Transformation of the Agrarian Economy, 1500–1850.* Cambridge: Cambridge University Press, 1996.

Özbek, Nadir. "Defining the Public Sphere during the Late Ottoman Empire: War, Mass Mobilization and the Young Turk Regime (1908–18)." *Middle Eastern Studies* 43, no. 5 (September 2007): 795–809.

Pagel, Mark. *Wired for Culture: Origins of the Human Social Mind.* New York: W.W. Norton, 2012.

Pamuk, Şevket. "Institutional Change and the Longevity of the Ottoman Empire, 1500–1800." *Journal of Interdisciplinary History* 35, no. 2 (Autumn 2004): 225–47.

Pamuk, Şevket. "The Black Death and the Origins of the 'Great Divergence' across Europe, 1300–1600." *European Review of Economic History* 11, no. 3 (December 2007): 289–317.

Park, David. *The How and the Why: An Essay on the Origins and Development of Physical Theory.* Princeton, NJ: Princeton University Press, 1988.

Park, Katherine. "Masaccio's Skeleton: Art and Anatomy in Early Renaissance Italy." In *Masaccio's Trinity.* Edited by Rona Goffen. Cambridge: Cambridge University Press, 1998. Pp. 119–140.

Parker, Geoffrey. "The Limits to Revolutions in Military Affairs: Maurice of Nassau, the Battle of Nieuwpoort (1600), and the Legacy." *Journal of Military History* 71 (April 2007): 331–72.

Pedersen, Johannes. *The Arabic Book.* Translated by Geoffrey French. Edited by Robert Hillenbrand. Princeton, NJ: Princeton University Press, 1984.

Peerenboom, Randall. *China's Long March toward Rule of Law.* Cambridge: Cambridge University Press, 2002.

Penprase, Bryan E. *The Power of Stars: How Celestial Observations Have Shaped Civilization.* New York: Springer Verlag, 2011.

Works Cited

Perdue, Peter C. *China Marches West: The Qing Conquest of Central Eurasia.* Cambridge, MA, and London: The Belknap Press of Harvard University Press, 2005.

Perrett, Roy W. "History, Time, and Knowledge in Ancient India." *History and Theory* 38, no. 3 (October 1999): 307–21.

Pettegree, Andrew. *The Invention of News: How the World Came to Know about Itself.* New Haven, CT: Yale University Press, 2014.

Phillips, Kim M. "Travelers East and West." *Journal of the Economic and Social History of the Orient* 53, no. 3 (2010): 506–12.

Pipes, Daniel. *Slave Soldiers and Islam: The Genesis of a Military System.* New Haven, CT, and London: Yale University Press, 1981.

Plofker, Kim. *Mathematics in India.* Princeton, NJ, and Oxford: Princeton University Press, 2009.

Pomeranz, Kenneth. *The Great Divergence: Europe, China, and the Making of the Modern World Economy.* Princeton, NJ: Princeton University Press, 2000.

Pomeranz, Kenneth. "Ten Years After: Responses and Reconsiderations." *Historically Speaking* 12, no. 4 (September 2011): 20–25.

Principe, Lawrence M. and William R. Newman. "Some Problems with the Historiography of Alchemy." In *Secrets of Nature: Astrology and Alchemy in Early Modern Europe.* Edited by William R. Newman and Anthony Grafton. Cambridge, MA: MIT Press, 2001. Pp. 385–432.

Principe, Lawrence M. *The Secrets of Alchemy.* Chicago: University of Chicago Press, 2012.

Puttaswamy, T.K. *Mathematical Achievements of Pre-modern Indian Mathematicians.* London: Elsevier, 2012.

Qian, Wen-yuan. *The Great Inertia: Scientific Stagnation in Traditional China.* London and Dover, NH: Croom Helm, 1985.

Ragep, F.J. "Copernicus and His Islamic Predecessors: Some Historical Remarks." *History of Science* 45 (March 2007): 65–81.

Raven, Diederick. "What Needs to Be Explained about Modern Science?" *British Journal for the History of Science* 44, no. 3 (September 2011): 449–54.

Rawski, Evelyn Sakakida. *Education and Popular Literacy in Ch'ing China.* Ann Arbor: University of Michigan Press, 1979.

Raymond, Joad. *Pamphlets and Pamphleteering in Early Modern Britain.* New York: Cambridge University Press, 2003.

Reiss, Timothy J. *Knowledge, Discovery and Imagination in Early Modern Europe: The Rise of Aesthetic Rationalism.* Cambridge: Cambridge University Press, 1997.

Reynolds, Susan. "The Emergence of Professional Law in the Long Twelfth Century." *Law and History Review* 21, no. 2 (Summer 2003): 347–66.

Reynolds, Susan. *Fiefs and Vassals: The Medieval Evidence Reinterpreted.* Oxford: Oxford University Press, 1994.

Riello, Giorgio. *Cotton: The Fabric that Made the Modern World.* Cambridge and New York: Cambridge University Press, 2013.

Riley-Smith, Jonathan. *The Crusades: A History.* 3rd ed. London: Bloomsbury Publishing, 2014.

Ringmar, Erik. "Audience for a Giraffe: European Expansionism and the Quest for the Exotic." *Journal of World History* 17, no. 4 (December 2006): 375–97.

Works Cited

Rogers, Clifford J. "The Military Revolutions of the Hundred Years' War." *Journal of Military History* 57 (April 1993): 241–78.

Ronan, Colin A. *The Shorter Science and Civilisation in China: An Abridgement of Joseph Needham's Original Text.* 5 Volumes. Cambridge: Cambridge University Press, 1978–1995.

Roper, Geoffrey. "The History of the Book in the Muslim World." In *The Book: A Global History.* Edited by Michael F. Suarez and H.R. Woudhuysen. Oxford and New York: Oxford University Press, 2013. Pp. 525–52.

Rowland, Diane, and Alexandre V. Telyukov. "Soviet Health Care from Two Perspectives." *Health Affairs* (Fall 1991): 71–86.

Rubin, Edward. "Judicial Review and the Right to Resist." *Georgetown Law Journal* 96 (November 2008): 61–118.

Rudolph, Conrad. "Inventing the Exegetical Stained-Glass Window: Suger, Hugh, and a New Elite Art." *Art Bulletin* 93, no. 4 (2011): 399–422.

Runyan, Timothy. "Ships and Seafaring." In *Handbook of Medieval Culture: Fundamental Aspects and Conditions of the European Middle Ages.* 3 Volumes. Edited by Albrecht Classen. Berlin and New York: De Gruyter, 2010. 3:1610–33.

Rusnock, Andrea. "Correspondence Networks and the Royal Society, 1700–1750." *British Journal for the History of Science* 32, no. 2 (June 1999): 155–69.

Russell, Jeffrey Burton. *Inventing the Flat Earth: Columbus and Modern Historians.* Westport, CT, and London: Praeger, 1991.

Russell, Peter Edward. *Prince Henry "The Navigator": A Life.* New Haven, CT: Yale University Press, 2000.

Sarton, George. *Hellenistic Science and Culture in the Last Three Centuries B.C.* New York: Dover Publications, 1993.

Schäfer, Hans-Bernd, and Alexander J. Wulf. "Jurists, Clerics, and Merchants: The Rise of Learned Law in Medieval Europe and its Impact on Economic Growth." *Journal of Empirical Legal Studies* 11, no. 2 (June 2014): 266–300.

Schiebinger, Londa. "Women of Natural Knowledge." In *The Cambridge History of Science.* Volume 3: *Early Modern Science.* Edited by Katharine Park and Lorraine Daston. Cambridge: Cambridge University Press, 2006. Pp. 192–205.

Schiffer, Michael Brian. *Draw the Lightning Down: Benjamin Franklin and Electrical Technology in the Age of Enlightenment.* Berkeley, CA: University of California Press, 2003.

Schmitz-Esser, Romedio. "Travel and Exploration in the Middle Ages." In *Handbook of Medieval Culture: Fundamental Aspects and Conditions of the European Middle Ages.* 3 Volumes. Edited by Albrecht Classen. Berlin and New York: De Gruyter, 2010. 3:1680–1704.

Schofield, Robert E. *The Lunar Society of Birmingham: A Social History of Provincial Science and Industry in Eighteenth-Century England.* Oxford: Clarendon Press, 1963.

Sen, Tansen. "The Impact of Zheng He's Expeditions on Indian Ocean Interactions." *Bulletin of the School of Oriental and African Studies* 79, no. 3 (2016): 609–36.

Sen, Tansen. "The Travel Records of Chinese Pilgrims Faxian, Xuanzang, and Yijing: Sources for Cross-Cultural Encounters between Ancient China and Ancient India." *Education about Asia* 11, no. 3 (Winter 2006): 24–33.

Works Cited

Sesiano, Jacques. *An Introduction to the History of Algebra: Solving Equations from Mesopotamian Times to the Renaissance.* Translated by Anna Pierrehumbert. Providence, RI: American Mathematical Society, 2009.

Shackelford, Jole. *William Harvey and the Mechanics of the Heart.* Oxford and New York: Oxford University Press, 2003.

Shatzmiller, Maya. "Aspects of Women's Participation in the Economic Life of Later Medieval Islam: Occupations and Mentalities." *Arabica* 35 (March 1988): 36–58.

Shatzmiller, Maya. *Her Day in Court: Women's Property Rights in Fifteenth-Century Granada.* Cambridge, MA: Islamic Legal Studies Program, Harvard Law School, 2007.

Shatzmiller, Maya. "The Female Body in Islamic Law and Medicine: Obstetrics, Gynecology, and Pediatrics." In *Attending to Early Modern Women: Conflict and Concord.* Edited by Karen Nelson. Newark, DE: University of Delaware Press, 2013. Pp. 93–106.

Shea, William R. *The Magic of Numbers and Motion: The Scientific Career of René Descartes.* Canton, MA: Science History Publications, 1991.

Shea, William R., and Mariano Artigas. *Galileo in Rome: The Rise and Fall of a Troublesome Genius.* Oxford and New York: Oxford University Press, 2003.

Shields, Christopher, ed. *The Oxford Handbook of Aristotle.* Oxford and New York: Oxford University Press, 2012.

Shiba, Yoshinobu. "On the Emergence and Intensification of the Pattern of Rural-Urban Continuum in Late Imperial Jiangnan Society." In *The Economy of Lower Yangzi Delta in Late Imperial China.* Edited by Billy K.L. So. London and New York: Routledge, 2013. Pp. 149–207.

Short, John Rennie. *Making Space: Revisioning the World, 1475–1600.* Syracuse, NY: Syracuse University Press, 2004.

Skinner, Quentin. *The Foundations of Modern Political Thought.* Volume 2: *The Age of Reformation.* Cambridge: Cambridge University Press, 1978.

Smith, Anthony. *The Newspaper: An International History.* London: Thames and Hudson, 1979.

Smith, Pamela H. "Laboratories." In *The Cambridge History of Science.* Volume 3: *Early Modern Science.* Edited by Katharine Park and Lorraine Daston. Cambridge: Cambridge University Press, 2006. Pp. 290–305.

Sobel, Dava. *Longitude: The True Story of a Lone Genius Who Solved the Greatest Scientific Problem of His Time.* New York: Walker, 1995.

Southall, Aidan. *The City in Time and Space.* Cambridge and New York: Cambridge University Press, 1998.

Speer, Andreas. "Is There a Theology of the Gothic Cathedral? A Re-reading of Abbot Suger's Writings on the Abbey Church of St.-Denis." In *The Mind's Eye: Art and Theological Argument in the Middle Ages.* Edited by Jeffrey F. Hamburger and Anne-Marie Bouché. Princeton, NJ: Princeton University Press, 2006. Pp. 65–83.

Stasavage, David. "When Distance Mattered: Geographic Scale and the Development of European Representative Assemblies." *American Political Science Review* 104, no. 4 (2010): 625–43.

Works Cited

Stasavage, David. *States of Credit: Size, Power, and the Development of European Polities*. Princeton, NJ: Princeton University Press, 2011.

Steinberg, S.H. *Five Hundred Years of Printing*. London: British Library, 1996.

Stewart, Larry. "Other Centres of Calculation, or, Where the Royal Society Didn't Count: Commerce, Coffee-Houses and Natural Philosophy in Early Modern London." *British Journal for the History of Science* 32, no. 2 (June 1999): 133–53.

Stewart, Larry. *The Rise of Public Science: Rhetoric, Technology, and Natural Philosophy in Newtonian Britain, 1660–1750*. Cambridge: Cambridge University Press, 1992.

Strassler, Robert B., ed. *The Landmark Herodotus: The Histories*. Translated by Andrea L. Purvis. Introduction by Rosalind Thomas. New York: Pantheon Books, 2007.

Taylor, Richard C. "Ibn Rushd/Averroes and 'Islamic' Rationalism." *Medieval Encounters* 15 (2009): 225–35.

Thapar, Romila. *Early India, From the Origins to AD 1300*. Berkeley and Los Angeles, CA: University of California Press, 2002.

Tierney, Brian. *The Idea of Natural Rights: Studies on Natural Rights, Natural Law and Church Law, 1150–1625*. Atlanta, GA: Scholars Press, 1997.

Tollnek, Franziska, and Joerg Baten. "Farmers at the Heart of the 'Human Capital Revolution'? Decomposing the Numeracy Increase in Early Modern Europe." *Economic History Review* 70, no. 3 (2017): 779–809.

Touati, Houari. *Islam and Travel in the Middle Ages*. Translated by Lydia G. Cochrane. Chicago: University of Chicago Press, 2010.

Towns, Ann. "The Status of Women as a Standard of Civilization." *European Journal of International Relations* 15, no. 4 (December 2009): 681–706.

UNESCO. *Progress of Literacy in Various Countries: A Preliminary Statistical Study of Available Census Data since 1900*. Paris: UNESCO, 1953.

van Bavel, Bas, Eltjo Buringh, and Jessica Dijkman. "Mills, Cranes, and the Great Divergence: The Use of Immovable Capital Goods in Western Europe and the Middle East, Ninth to Sixteenth Centuries." *Economic History Review* 71, no. 1 (2018): 31–54.

van Gulik, Egbertus. *Erasmus and His Books*. Toronto, Buffalo, and London: University of Toronto Press, 2018.

van Zanden, Jan Luiten, and Milja van Tielhof. "Roots of Growth and Productivity Change in Dutch Shipping Industry, 1500–1800." *Explorations in Economic History* 46, no. 4 (2009): 389–403.

van Zanden, Jan Luiten, Eltjo Buringh, and Maarten Bosker. "The Rise and Decline of European Parliaments, 1188–1789." *Economic History Review* 65, no. 3 (2012): 835–61.

van Zanden, Jan Luiten. *The Long Road to the Industrial Revolution: The European Economy in a Global Perspective, 1000–1800*. Leiden: Brill, 2009.

Verhoeven, Gerrit. "'Le pays où on ne sait pas lire': Literacy, Numeracy and Human Capital in the Commercial Hub of the Austrian Netherlands (1715–75)." *European History Quarterly* 44, no. 2 (2014): 223–43.

Vogel, Hans Ulrich. *Marco Polo Was in China: New Evidence from Currencies, Salts and Revenues*. Leiden: Brill, 2013.

Works Cited

Voigtländer, Nico, and Hans-Joachim Voth. "Gifts of Mars: Warfare and Europe's Early Rise to Riches." *Journal of Economic Perspectives* 27, no. 4 (Fall 2013): 165–86.

Voogt, Gerrit. "'Anyone Who Can Read May Be a Preacher': Sixteenth-Century Roots of the Collegiants." *Nederlands archief voor kerkgeschiedenis* 85, no. 1 (2005): 409–24.

Vries, Peer. *Escaping Poverty: The Origins of Modern Economic Growth*. Vienna and Göttingen: Vienna University Press and V & R Unipress, 2013.

Wagner, Donald B. "The Administration of the Iron Industry in Eleventh-Century China." *Journal of the Economic and Social History of the Orient* 44, no. 2 (2001): 175–97.

Waines, David. *The Odyssey of Ibn Battuta: Uncommon Tales of a Medieval Adventurer*. London and New York: I.B. Tauris, and Co., 2010.

Wakeman, Frederic, Jr. "Boundaries of the Public Sphere in Ming and Qing China." *Daedalus* 127, no. 3 (Summer 1998): 167–89.

Wallace, William E. "'Dal disegno allo spazio': Michelangelo's Drawings for the Fortifications of Florence." *Journal of the Society of Architectural Historians* 46 (June 1987): 119–34.

Watson, Peter. *Ideas: A History of Thought and Invention, from Fire to Freud*. New York: HarperCollins, 2005.

West, John B. "Ibn al-Nafis, the Pulmonary Circulation, and the Islamic Golden Age." *Journal of Applied Physiology* 105, no. 6 (December 2008): 1877–80.

West, John B. "Robert Boyle's Landmark Book of 1660 with the First Experiments on Rarified Air." *Journal of Applied Physiology* 98 (2005): 31–39.

Westfall, Richard S. "The Scientific Revolution of the Seventeenth Century: The Construction of a New World View." In *The Concept of Nature: The Herbert Spencer Lectures*. Edited by John Torrance. Oxford: Clarendon Press, 1992. Pp. 63–93.

White, Lynn, Jr. *Machina ex Deo: Essays in the Dynamism of Western Culture*. Cambridge, MA: MIT Press, 1968.

Whitman, James Q. *The Origins of Reasonable Doubt: Theological Roots of the Criminal Trial*. New Haven, CT: Yale University Press, 2008.

Wiesner-Hanks, Merry E. *Women and Gender in Early Modern Europe*. 3rd ed. Cambridge: Cambridge University Press, 2008.

Wigelsworth, Jeffrey R. *Selling Science in the Age of Newton: Advertising and the Commoditization of Knowledge*. Farnham, UK: Ashgate, 2010.

Wilkinson, John, trans. and ed. *Jerusalem Pilgrims before the Crusades*. Warminster, UK: Aris & Phillip, 2002.

Wilson, Christopher. *The Gothic Cathedral: The Architecture of the Great Church, 1130–1530*. New York and London: Thames and Hudson, 1990.

Winchester, Simon. *The Man Who Loved China: The Fantastic Story of the Eccentric Scientist Who Unlocked the Mysteries of the Middle Kingdom*. New York: Harper Perennial, 2008.

Winchester, Simon. *The Map That Changed the World: William Smith and the Birth of Modern Geology*. New York: Perennial, 2001.

Witte, John, Jr. "Introduction." In *Christianity and Human Rights: An Introduction*. Edited by John Witte, Jr., and Frank S. Alexander. Cambridge: Cambridge University Press, 2010. Pp. 8–44.

Works Cited

Witte, John, Jr., and Justin Latterell. "Christianity and Human Rights: Past Contributions and Future Challenges." *Journal of Law and Religion* 30, no. 3 (2015): 353–85.

Wolfe, Alexander C. "Marco Polo: Factotum, Auditor: Language and Political Culture in the Mongol World Empire." *Literature Compass* 11, no. 7 (2014): 409–22.

Wong, R.B. "China before Capitalism." In *The Cambridge History of Capitalism*. Volume 1: *The Rise of Capitalism: From Ancient Origins to 1848*. Edited by Larry Neal and Jeffrey G. Williamson. Cambridge: Cambridge University Press, 2014. Pp. 25–64.

Wong, R. Bin. "The Political Ambiguity of Voluntary Associations in Late Imperial and Modern China: Chinese Forms of Cultural Hegemony, Coercion and Social Control in Comparative Perspective." *Global Economic Review* 31, no. 1 (2002): 27–45.

Woods-Marsden, Joanna. *Renaissance Self-Portraiture: The Visual Construction of Identity and the Social Status of the Artist*. New Haven, CT: Yale University Press, 1998.

Woodward, David, Cordell D.K. Lee, and Joseph E. Schwartzberg. "Concluding Remarks." In *The History of Cartography*. Volume 2, Book 2: *Cartography in the Traditional East and Southeast Asian Societies*. Edited by J.B. Harley and David Woodward. Chicago and London: University of Chicago Press, 1994. Pp. 843–49.

Wright, Tim. "An Economic Cycle in Imperial China? Revisiting Robert Hartwell on Iron and Coal." *Journal of the Economic and Social History of the Orient* 50, no. 4 (2007): 398–423.

Yazdani, Kaveh. *India, Modernity and the Great Divergence: Mysore and Gujarat (17th to 19th C.)*. Leiden and Boston: Brill, 2017.

Yonglin, Jiang. *The Mandate of Heaven and the Great Ming Code*. Seattle: University of Washington Press, 2011.

York, William H. *Health and Wellness in Antiquity through the Middle Ages*. Santa Barbara, CA: Greenwood, 2012.

Zaret, David. "Petitions and the 'Invention' of Public Opinion in the English Revolution." *American Journal of Sociology* 101, no. 6 (May 1996): 1497–1555.

Zeegers, Margaret, and Deirdre Barron. *Gatekeepers of Knowledge: A Consideration of the Library, the Book and the Scholar in the Western World*. Oxford, Cambridge, and New Delhi: Chandos Publishing, 2010.

Zhang, Cong Ellen. *Transformative Journeys: Travel and Culture in Song China*. Honolulu: University of Hawai'i Press, 2011.

Zhou, Gang. "Small Talk: A New Reading of Marco Polo's *Il Milione*." *Modern Language Notes* 124, no. 1 (January 2009): 1–22.

Zilfi, Madeline. "Thoughts on Women and Slavery in the Ottoman Era and Historical Sources." In *Beyond the Exotic: Women's Histories in Islamic Societies*. Edited by Amira El Azhary Sonbol. Syracuse, NY: Syracuse University Press, 2005. Pp. 131–38.

Zurndorfer, Harriet T. "The Passion to Collect, Select, and Protect: Fifteen Hundred Years of the Chinese Encyclopedia." In *Encyclopaedism from Antiquity to the Renaissance*. Edited by Jason König and Greg Woolf. Cambridge: Cambridge University Press, 2013. Pp. 505–28.

INDEX

Page references in italics refer to maps.

Aalst (Flanders), 60
Abelard, Peter, 25
Abrahamic religions, 9
Academia dei Lincei, 104
académicienne, 102
Academy of the Mysteries of Nature, 104
Adelard of Bath, 45
Afghanistan, 86
Africanus, Leo, 42
Afro-Eurasia, 7–9, *60*
    cave painting, 57
    exploration, 54, *138*
    intellectual synthesis, 87
    Islamic achievements, 32
    legal traditions, 17
    local governance, 65
    trading, 36
agricultural labor, 1, 143
agriculture, 1–2, 115
    China, 85
    China and India, 119
    Europe, 143
    Middle East early developments, 9–10
    teosinte into maize, 7
Agrigola (Bauer, Georg), 91
air pollution, 133
air pump, 95
Albert of Saxony, 88
alchemical achievements, 9
alchemical process, xiv, 4, 6
alchemical synthesis, 58, 60, 87, 146–47
alchemy and alchemists, 6–7, 12, 15, 89–90, 123, 125
alchemy metaphor, xiv, 147
Alexander V (pope), 76
Alexandria, 8, *58*
Alfonso IX (king, León), 73–74
al-Ghazali, 87, 99
Al-Hakam II, 58

al-Mas'udi, 43
alphabet, 7, 58, 60, 108, 139
alphabetization, 58, 62
al-Wazzan, al-Hasan, 42
Ambassadors, The (Holbein), 123
American War of Independence, 75
Americas, discovery, 98, *138*, 143–44
Amsterdam, 101, 109, 110, 136
Anaxagoras, 83
Anaximenes, 83
Andalusia, 45
animal-drawn mills, 134
Anselm of Canterbury, 23
Antioch, 45
Antwerp, 108
Aquinas, Thomas (Saint), 25, 47, 55, 80, 88
Arabia, 62
Arabian Sea, 38, 51
Arabic numbers. *See* Hindu-Arabic numbers
Archimedes, 84
architecture, 141
    Gothic transformation, 122
Aristarchus of Samos, 84
aristocracy, 32, 65–66, 70, 73
Aristotelian methods, 8
Aristotle, 4, 25, 86, 100
    combining with Plato's theorizing, 94
    commentaries by Ibn Rushd, 87
    geocentric theory, 84, 92–93
    law of noncontradiction, 97–98
    physics questioned, 88–89
    system of classification, 23
    theories proven false, 98
    translations, 88
art
    cave painting, 7, 57, 121
    influence on science and technology, 62, 91
    stained-glass, 122

Index

women's role, 102
See also architecture; painting
Asian mariners colonized New Guinea, 6
astronomy, study of
   Chinese advances, 83–84, 86
   Greeks, 83–84
   heliocentric theory, 84, 92–93
   Indian influences, 87
   Islamic Golden Age, 87
   laws of planetary motion, 93
   southern hemisphere observations, 95
asylum, political and religious, 79
Athens, 8
atom, theory of, 95
Augustine of Hippo (Saint), 60
Australia, 4, 6
Averroism, 56, 88, 159 n.94
Avignon, 75
Axial Age, 8
Azores, 49

Babylon, astronomical discoveries, 83
Bacon, Francis, 94, 103–4
Bacon, Roger, 49
Baghdad, x, 9, 40
Barcelona, 46, 74
Basel, 101
Bassi, Laura, 102
Batavia, 54, 105
Bauer, Georg (Agricola), 91
Bauhin, Gaspard, 91
Bayazid II, 62
bayonets, 126
Beauvais, 122
Bec (France), 23
Beijing *Gazette*, 111
Benedictine monastic order, 45, 64
Berlin, 104, 114
Berlioz, Hector, 124
Berman, Harold, 30
Bible, translation, 77
bills of exchange, 32, 87
Birmingham, 117
Bishop of Paris, 89
bishoprics, 68–69
Black Death, 36, 59, 127, 143
   labor scarcity, 115, 143
Black Sea basin, 8
Board of Longitude, 116
Bohemia, 77, 92, 102

Bologna, 105
Bombay, 54
Boston, 54
botanical gardens, 91
botany and zoology
   classification systems, 90–91
   collaboration with artists, 90–91
Boulton, Matthew, 117
Boyle, Robert, 95, 104, 113, 117
Brahe, Tycho, 92–93, 104
Brazil, 51
Brethren of the Common Life, 107
Broadberry, Stephen, 135
Brunelleschi, Filippo, 123
Buddhism, 9, 36, 86
   See also Siddhartha Gautama
Buenos Aires, 54
building cranes, 134
buildings, world's tallest, 55, 122, 141
Bulgar people, 40
Buridan, Jean, 89
Busschoff, Hermann, 105
Byron, George Gordon, Baron, 113
Byzantine Empire, 138
Byzantium, 74

Cabral, Pedro Álvares, 51
Cairo, 111
Calcutta, 54
calico craze, 95
Calicut, 51
California school, x, xii
caloric consumption, 136
Cambridge, Massachusetts, 62
Campbell, Bruce, 135
Canon (Ibn Sina), 23, 90
canon law
   compilation by Gratian, 26
   influence on secular law, 26
   Middle Ages, 20, 22
   rules on church governance, 70
Canterbury Tales, The (Chaucer), 48
Cape of Good Hope, 51, 138
Cape Town, 54
Cape Verde Islands, 49
capillaries, 94, 105
Carolingian Empire, 20, 59, 68, 73
Carthage, 45
Cartier, Jacques, 51
cartography, 8, 55, 126

Index

Casas, Bartolomé de Las, 53
Castile, 74
Catholicism. *See* Church of Rome
Catlos, Brian, 43
Cavert, William M., 133
Cayenne, 95
Central America, 10, 51, 58
ceramics industry, 106
Champagne, 70
Charlemagne, 66, 139
Charles I, 81
Charleston, 54
charters of liberty, 65, 69–70, 139
Chaucer, Geoffrey, 48
Chauvet, 121
checks and balances, 73, 75, 81, 144, 146
chemistry and alchemy
    chemical operations in India, 87
    classification systems, 89–90
    elements isolated, 96
    freestanding chemical laboratory, 92
    goal of alchemists, 6
    gunpowder, 9, 53, 85, 97, 125–27
    Islamic Golden Age, 87
    oxygen, isolation, 117
    oxygen in combustion, 95–96
China, 47–48, 141–42
    animal-drawn mills, 134
    civic initiative and Kaifeng flood, 115–16
    coal production, Northern Song China, 131–32
    disdain for science, 99–100
    early law and justice, 18–19, 30–31
    economic output, 135–36
    economic performance, x
    education system, 25
    "four great inventions," 85, 97
    Hundred Schools, 8, 85
    industrialization discontinuity, 132
    iron production, 133
    Jesuit introduction of Western mathematics, 100
    lack of consumer interest in printed books, 63
    limited commercial information, 111
    limited liability business, 33
    limited news dissemination, 111
    literacy, 107
    mathematical scientific breakthroughs, 100
    modernity, 146–47
    movable type, ceramic and wooden typeface, 58
    natural philosophy, 140
    no urban autonomy, 72, 74
    numeracy, 108
    paper, 60
    paper invention, 58, 139
    penal law, 19
    pictographic writing, 57
    political power, 66
    practical advances, 7, 9
    printing, 14
    printing, inked wood block, 58
    scholarship focus on traditional subjects, 64
    scientific advances, 85–86
    social mobility, 71
    standard of living, 2
    technical knowledge, 117–19
    understanding of nature, 83
    warfare, lack of innovations, 126–27
    woodblock book production, 63
China, governance
    civil law, 19
    civil service system, 65
    emphasis on harmony, 144
    petitions by scholar-officials, 111
    repression of discourse, 106
China, travel and travelers
    Asia-centered circuits, 37
    Buddhist clergy to India, 36
    Eurasia trade, 36, 38, 40
    geographical knowledge, 38
    giraffe gift, 50
    inward focus, 38, 40, 138
    Ming Dynasty and Asian travel, 36–39
    Mongols, fear of, 38
    treasure fleets, 38, 49
China, women
    foot binding and domestic role, 129–30
    marriage and childbearing patterns, 128–29
Christian faith, 48, 107
Christina of Sweden, 104
chthonic law, 17–18
church councils, 22, 75–76, 140
Church of Rome

215

Index

American Catholics at the American Revolution, 76
Conciliar movement and schism, 75-76
Council of Constance, 76-77
Fifth Lateran Council, papal authority, 76
Church of Rome, laws governing
 grants of royal immunity, 68
 influence on secular law, 26
 "investiture conflict," 21
 monasticism, 21-22
 restrictions on Muslim trade, 42
 secular jurisdiction, 21
Church of Rome, reform movements
 monasticism, 77
 ninety-five propositions of Luther, 77-78
circulatory system, 84, 93
Cistercian monastic orders, 64
City of God (Augustine), 60
civilization, early
 development of cities, x–xi, 4, 6
 urban centers, 7
clash of civilizations, 45
classification systems, 62
Clement VII (pope), 75
clergy, 21-22, 36, 69-70, 76, 79
clerical celibacy, 21
coastline, longest (Europe), 2
coffee houses, 140
 clienteles to specific locations, 112
 early appearance in Mecca and Cairo, 111
 in Europe, 112
 public lectures, 113
 role as libraries, 112-13
Cogito, ergo sum, 94
Collegiant movement, 79
colonialism, xiv–xv, 2, 91
Columbus, Christopher, 10, 33, 38, 51, 138
compass, mariner's, 9, 36, 48, 85, 97, 143
competition among European states
 business, 119
 culture of improvement, 64
 effect of, 144
 legal systems, 30
 military specialization, 125-26, 141
 political fragmentation, 49
conciliar movement, 65, 75-76
Concordance of Discordant Canons (Gratian), 26

concubines, 130
Confucian principles, 18-19
 business disparaged, 72
 law, 31
 practical advances, 85-86
 women's domesticity, 130
conscience, authority of, 78
conservation of charge, law of, 95
Constantine the African, 45
Constantinople, x, 122
constitutions, written
 Fundamental Constitution of the Carolinas, 81
 Fundamental Orders (Connecticut), 81
 Instrument of Government (England, Scotland, Ireland), 81
 United States Constitution, 81
contractual theory of government, 80
Cook, James, 53
Copernicus, Nicolaus, 87, 92, 104
Córdoba, 58
Corpus Juris Civilis, 20
correspondence networks
 languages, Latin and vernacular, 102
 mail delivery, 102
 Republic of Arabic Letters, 103
 travel encouraged, 103
 worldwide participants, 105
cost of borrowing, 135
craftsmen
 communication, 62
 Muslim slaves, 42
 papyrus and parchment, 58
 premodern world, 10
 shared learning, 87, 97
 travel, 103, 117, 119
 windmill design, 134
creativity of living beings, xii, 4, 7, 12-13, 141, 146
Croatia, 102
Crown-in-Parliament, 79
Crusades and Crusaders, 44-46. *See also* People's Crusade
cultural synthesis, 8, 12, 58, 137
culture of improvement, 49, 121
curricula, university, 24

da Gama, Vasco, 51
d'Ailly, Pierre, 49, 76
Damascus, 40, 43, 77

Index

Dante, Alighieri, 48
Daoism, 8, 31
Dar al-Islam, 43, 62
Darwin, Erasmus, 117
Davids, Karel, 118
decentralization of power
   law courts, 29-30
   Ottoman Empire, 71
   printing, effect of, 139
   representative assemblies, 73-75
   rights and liberties, 65-66, 68-69, 144
   warfare, effect of, 142
   written constitutions, 81
Defoe, Daniel, 103
De imitatione Christi (Thomas à Kempis), 61
De jure belli ac pacis (Grotius), 79
de Liuzzi, Mondino. *See* Mondino de Liuzzi
de Machaut, Guillaume, 124
Democritus, 84, 97
demographic catastrophe, 59, 115, 143
Deng, Kent, 136
Denmark, 92
Descartes, René, 94, 104
des Murs, Jehan, 124
dialectical (dialogic) method, 16, 23, 25, 100
Diamond, Jared, 6
di Bondone. *See* Giotto
Diderot, Denis, 117
Discourse on the Method (Descartes), 94
disease, 1, 16, 53, 87, 143
disputational method, 23
dissection, anatomical, 84, 90, 93, 123
Divine Comedy, The (Dante), 48
Dominican Friars, 46, 75
Don Juan (Byron), 113
du Châtelet, Émilie, 101
Dürer, Albrecht, 62, 100
Dutch East India Company (VOC), 134
Dutch Republic, xii, 53, 78, 102, 109, 119, 125
   See also Netherlands
Dutch Revolt, 75

early humans, 35, 121, 137
east-west axis, 10
ecclesiastical court, 29, 70
ecclesiastical hierarchy, 68
economic output, 129, 135
efflorescent economic growth, 32, 73, 127, 135, 139, 145
   factors against in Yuan Dynasty, 132
Egypt
   Alexandria library, 58
   cultural heritage, 97
   female circumcision, 130
   first civilizations, 4, 7-9
   Giraffe gift, 50
   Jerusalem reconquered, 46
   legal system, 138
   literacy rate, 107
   mathematics, development, 83-84
   papyrus and parchment, 58
   writing system, 57
Elector of Brandenburg, 79
Elements (Euclid), 45
Elman, Benjamin, 135
Elvin, Mark, 99
encyclopedias, 63, 85, 91, 117
Encyclopédie (Diderot), 117
energy and power
   coal, iron production, 131-33, 184 n.72
   fossil fuel and laborsaving devices, 146
   watermills, 133
   windmills, 134, 141
Engels, Friedrich, female emancipation, 128
England
   break with Church of Rome, 79
   caloric consumption, 136
   censorship, 109
   coal consumption, 132-33
   coffeehouses, 15, 112
   commodity price list publications, 110
   explorer Hugh Willoughby, 51
   geological survey, 117
   legal system, 29-30
   literacy, 107-8
   Magna Carta, 69
   marriage, delay, 129
   military affairs, 126-27
   modern banking, xii
   newspapers, 110
   Praemunire, 73
   religious reform, 77
   religious toleration laws, 79
   representative assemblies, 74
   rulers' role, 72
   sharing of knowledge, 116
   Statutes of Provisors, 73

Index

urban government, 70
urbanization, 115
women's role, 114
English Civil War, 75, 79, 109
English common law, 27–30
   history, 29, 138
   official royal law and popular jurisprudence, 29
   trusts, 31
   writs, or royal decrees, 29
English Glorious Revolution, 75
Enlightenment. *See* European Enlightenment
environmental deterioration, xiv, 136
Epic of Gilgamesh, The, 9, 35
Erasmus, 102
Eriugena, John Scotus, 64, 122
Euclid, 45, 84, 98
Eudoxus of Cnidus, 84
Euler, Leonhard, 12
Eurocentralism or Globalism, 1–2
Europe, achievements, 1, 4, 12, 15, 137
Europe, commerce
   business practices from Muslims, 70
   urban elites, 70
Europe, cultural unity, xii
Europe, governance
   absolutist monarchies, 74–75
   charters of liberty, 65, 69–71, 139
   counterbalance to monarchy, 73
   Curia regis, or royal council, 73–74
   expansion, 139–40
   feudalism and autonomous power, 66
   Huy, Walloon city, free urban status, 70
   liberties and immunities, 68–69, 74, 139
   Lombard League, 72
   Magna Carta, 69
   Middle Ages political divisions, 65, 67
   representative assemblies, 74
   rex infra legem, or the king under the law, 73
   Roman Empire decline, 66
   secular arguments on limiting political authority, 80–81
   urban charters, 70–71
   urban "communal movement," 68–69
   See also constitutions, written
Europe, humanists and scholars, 140
   appropriation of non-European advances, 142

intellectual centers, 101–2, 140
royal patronage, 104
women's role, 102
Europe, Renaissance, 101, 104, 145
   artists, xii, 15, 141
   geographical knowledge, 36
Europe, scholarship
   philosophical questions, 88
   translations of Greek and Islamic texts, 88
Europe, taxation rebellions
   American War of Independence, 75
   Dutch Revolt, 75
   English Civil War, 75
   English Glorious Revolution, 75
   French Revolution, 75
European bias of capital over labor, 60, 115, 127, 134, 141, 143
European civil (codified) law, 27–30, 138
   corporations as "fictive" persons, 31
   judicial torture, 29
   limited liability, 33
European Enlightenment, 145
European marriage pattern, 128–29
European Republic of Letters, 15, 140
   definition, 101
experimental philosophy, 95, 113
Eyck, Jan van, 123

fairs, commercial, 70
Federoff, Nina V., 7
female circumcision, 130
female friendly, 130
female infanticide, 131
Ferdinand and Isabella, 51, 138, 142
Ferdinand II (king of Spain), 51, 138
Fernández-Armesto, Felipe, 40
feudalism and feudal law
   contracts, 21
   manorial courts, 21
   relationship with vassals, 20–21
fiat law, 17
financial institutions, xii, 125, 135
firearms, 115, 125–27. *See also* muskets, pistols
First Opium War, 126, 142
fiscal state, 132
flintlock. *See* muskets
Florence, 59

Index

foot binding, 129
France
  architecture, xii
  artillery revolution, 125–27
  cave painting, 121
  Charlemagne, 66
  constitution, 81
  dialogic or disputational method of thinking, 23
  law of legal deposit, 62
  literacy, 107–10
  religion reform, 77
  religious freedom, 79
  rule of law, 72–75
  urbanization, 68
  voluntary associations, 114
  wine production, 70
Franklin, Benjamin, 95, 117
French Revolution, 75
Friedrich Wilhelm (Elector of Brandenburg). *See* Wilhelm, Friedrich
Fulbert, Bishop of Chartres, 23

Galen of Pergamum, 84, 90
Galilei, Galileo, 93, 98, 104
GDP. *See* per capita GDP
Geber (Paul of Taranto), 89–90
genetic engineering, 7
Geneva, 79
Genoa, 48, 68
geocentric theory, 97
Geoffrin, Marie, 114
Geographia (Ptolemy), 35, 50
geography, 116
  discovery of new lands, 98–99
  early innovation, 35
  fortuitous accidents, x
  geological survey of England and Wales, 117
  Polo's book, 47
  portolan chart, 48
  spherical world, 48
  technological innovations, 48
geography, maps
  accuracy improvements, 55
  Chinese and European central locations, 48
  gridlines, 51
  newfound lands, 54–55

Gerard of Cremona, 90
Gerbert of Aurillac, 45
Germany, 60, 66, 71, 78, 135
Gervase of Canterbury, 122
Gesner, Conrad, 91
Ghirlandaio, Domenico, 50
gift of backwardness, 32, 43, 141, 143–44
gifts of Mars, 15, 127
gifts of Venus, 15, 128
Giotto, 122
Giovanni, da Pian del Carpine, 46
Girl Spinning Wool (Giotto), 123
globalists vs. Eurocentrists, 1–2
globalization, 1–2
Glorious Revolution, 75
God as Judge and Redeemer, 24
Goldstone, Jack A., 132
Gospel, translation, 77
Gothic architecture, xii, 122
Göttingen, 105
Gratian, 26–27
gravitation, law of, 94
Great Britain, 106, 108, 110, 135
Great Divergence, x, 16, 128, 131, 145–46
  reasons for Europe, 133–35
Great Pyramid of Giza, 122
Greece, xiv, 9, 25, 98
  achievements, 7, 137
  early explorers, 35, 138
  mathematics, astronomy, medicine, 84
  pre-Socratic ideas of nature, 83
  prolific literature, 58
Greek city-states, 8
Greenland, 44
Gregory VII (pope), 45
Gresham, Thomas, 104
Gresham College, 104
Grotius, Hugo, 79
guilds, 31, 69, 72, 144
Gujarat, 72, 114
gunpowder weaponry, 53, 85, 126, 142
Gupta, Bishnupriya, 135
Gupta Dynasty, 86
Gutenberg, Johannes, 56, 60, 139

habeas corpus, 29
hadith, 32, 130
Hagia Sophia (Constantinople), 122
Halifax, 54
Halley, Edmond, 95

Index

Hammurabi, code of, 17
Han dynasty, 38
Harding, Alan, 69
Harmony of the World, The (Kepler), 93
Harrison, John, 116
Hartwell, Robert, 131–32
Harvey, William, 93
Havana, 54
Hawaii, 53
Hebrews. *See* Jewish people
heliocentric theory, 92
Hellenistic Greece, 84
    centers of culture, 8
    culture, 44
    natural philosophy, 89, 140
    physicians, 90
    travel, 35, 40
    writings, 14
Henry I (king of England), 29, 69
Henry II (king of England), 69
Henry the Navigator, 49
Henry VIII (king of England), 79
Heraclitus, 83
herbaria, 91
Herodotus, 35–36
Herophilus of Chalcedon, 84
Herzog, Warner, 121
higher education, 23, *24*
Hindu-Arabic numbers, 45, 108
Hindu law
    corporations and personhood, 153 n.45, 153 n.46
    divine revelation, 18
Historiae animalium (Gesner), 91
Histories (Herodotus), 35
Hobbes, Thomas, 79
Hodgson, James, 113, 116
Hodgson, Marshall, 71, 125
Hoffman, Philip T., 126–27
Holbein, Hans, the Younger, 123
Holland
    coffeehouses, 15
    Galileo's studies published, 98
    industrial milling, 134
    microscopes and telescopes, 92
    navy, 126
    newspapers and pamphlets, 109–10
    per capita income, 135
    personal autonomy, 128
    See also Netherlands

Holy Land, 44–46
Homer, 35
Homo sapiens, 35, 121, 138
Honan-Hopei border region, 131
Hooke, Robert, 116
Hortus Malabaricus (Rheede), 91
Huff, Toby E., 77
Hugh of Saint Victor, 64
Huguenots, 79
human capital, 71, 108, 131, 146–47
human development, theories of, 53–54
human interactions, 6, 7
Hungary, 42
"Hungry Forties," 136
Hunt, Lynn, 79
hunter-gatherers, 6
Hus, Jan, 77
Huy (Walloon city), 70
Huygens, Constantijn, 105

Ibn al-'Arabī, Abu Bakr, 40, 42
Ibn al-Nafis, 93
Ibn al-Shatir, 87
Ibn Battuta, 42, 47, 54
Ibn Fadlan, Ahmad, 40
Ibn Hayyan, Jabir, 89
Ibn Jubayr, Muhammad, 43
Ibn Rushd (Averroes), 55–56, 87–88, 143
Ibn Sina (Avicenna), 23
Ibn Tufayl, 103
Ibn Zuhr, 90
Iceland, 44
I-Ching (Book of Changes), 99
Iliffe, Robert, 116
illustration, technical, 14, 62, 91, 100, 140
Imago mundi (d'Ailly), 49
imperialism, xiv
impersonal institutions, 66
India, 147. *See also* Mughal India
    centralized political power, 144
    civilization, early, 4
    cotton print technology, 87
    early technology, 9
    females, role, 130
    flora of, 91
    legal personhood, 31
    limited liability business, 33
    literacy, 107
    mathematics, 86, 98
    merchants and political power, 72

Index

Nalanda monastery, 86
natural philosophy, 140–41
numeracy, 108
peak of scientific achievement, 86–87
travel to, 35, 48
unskilled laborers, 136
warfare, lack of innovations, 126–27
windmills and watermills, 134
women's rights, 130–31
India, Golden Age, 86
India, travel and trade, 40
destination from China, 36
destination from Europe, 49, 51
to Europe, 44
no Atlantic voyages, 50
Indian Ocean region, 38–*41*, 125, 138, 142
commerce, 36, 50
Indonesia, 51, 134
Industrial Revolution, x, 16, 131, 133–34, 145
infanticide, female, 131
inheritance law, 32
intellectual synthesis, 9, 87
intercontinental networks of exchange
circuits of exchange, *37*
correspondence, 15
epistolary exchange, 102
seafaring expeditions, 13, *52*, 54
synthesis of cultures, 137, 139
interest rates, 134–35
international law, 79, 146
Internet, 4
Invisible College, 104
Ireland, 81
Isabella I (queen of Spain), 138
Islam and Islamic lands
female circumcision, 130
Golden Age Islamdom, 36, 44, 97–98, 137
laws against printed matter, 62
limited mechanical printing, 62
no urban autonomy, 71
sharia, influence, 144
slave system, military, 65–66
women's rights, 130
Islamdom, Golden Age, 44
Muslim scholars and Afro-Eurasian intellectual synthesis, 87

Islamic lands, travel and trade
commerce with Europe, 42
commerce with India, 50
European developments, 55–56
travelers on Hajj, 40
Islamic law, 137
divine revelation, 18
Islamic sharia and divine revelation, 30
madrasahs, 25
Qur'an and commercial law, 32
waqf, unincorporated charitable endowment, 26
Israelites. *See* Jewish people
Istanbul, coffeehouses, 111
Italy
Arabic numbers, 108
Charlemagne, 66
city states, 74
civil law, xii
commerce, 71–72
Constantine the African, 45
education system, 145
Galilei, Galileo, 98
Marco Polo, 47
per capita income, 135
towns' privileges and immunities, 68
universities, early European, 23, 42
ius gentium, 19

Jabir ibn Hayyan, 89
Jakarta, 105
Janszoon, Willem, 51
Japan, 111, 115, 127, 146
warfare, halt in innovations, 127
Jaspers, Karl, 8
Jerusalem, 40, 45, 46, 48
Jewish people, 23, 42–43, 78
Jiangnan region, 136
Jin, Dengjian, 99
João II (king of Portugal), 51
John of Paris, 2, 76
John of Salisbury, 80
Jones, Eric, 134
journals, scholarly and scientific, 119
Collection Académique, 105
Journal des sçavans, 105
Philosophical Transactions of the Royal Society, 105
Julian of Norwich, 47

Index

Jurin, James, 106
Justinian, 20, 23

Kaifeng, x, 115, 132
Kepler, Johannes, 93, 95, 104
Kingston, 54
Kraków, 60
Kuran, Timur, 33

Langland, William, 48
Languedoc, 74
Lateran Councils, 76–77
Lavoisier, Antoine-Laurent, 95
law, customary
  local norms of, 19, 26
  See also chthonic law
law, early systems
  Roman civil law, 137
  university study, 138
  See also Confucian principles; Hammurabi, code of; Talmudic law
law, Middle Ages, 13
  commercial law development, 32
  corporations and trusts, 26, 153 n.45, 153 n.46
  criminal law and ordeals, 27
  "dialectical" or dialogic analysis, 23, 25
  power of rulers, 29
  reconciliation of principles, 24
  See also canon law; English common law; European civil (codified) law; feudalism and feudal law
law above all persons, idea of, 13, 19
law codes, 26–27, 137
  Ming Dynasty, 18
law of legal deposit, 62
law of nations, 31
Laws (Plato), 18
laws of motion, 94
laws of nature, 14, 31, 83, 140
laws of planetary motion, 93, 95
learned societies, 104–5
lectures, scientific, 113, 140
legal personhood, 144
Leibniz, Gottfried, 54, 94
Leiden, 101
Léon (Spain), 73–74, 139
Leonardo, da Vinci, 92, 100, 123
Lewis, Bernard, 124
Li, Bozhong, 132, 147

liberties and immunities, 68–70
library and librarians
  Alexandria library, 8, 58
  classification systems, 62
  coffeehouses, 112–13
  law of legal deposit in France, 62
  Umayyad Caliph of Córdoba, 58
life expectancy, 1–2
Lima, 54
limited government, 79, 118, 146
Lincoln Cathedral, 122
Linnaeus, 91
Lisbon, 49, 51, 60, 104
literacy and numeracy, 1, 14, 140
  censorship, 109
  growth in Europe, 139, 145
  intensive or extensive, 113
  numeracy and practical learning, 108
  signatures and literacy rates, 107
  socioeconomic levels, 106–7
literati (China), 59, 63, 106. *See also* scholar-officials (China)
Lithuania, 42
Locke, John, 79–81
logic, 8, 10, 25, 64, 84–86, 101
  study of, 85
Lollards, 79
London
  churches with high spires, 122
  coal consumption, 132–33
  coffeehouses, 95, 112–13
  intellectual center, 101–2
  laborers earnings, 136
  newspapers, 110
  printing presses in, 60
  Royal Exchange, 104
  size of, x
  See also Royal Society of London
longest coastline (Europe), 2
Louvain, 101
Lucas, Adam, 134
Lunar Society (Birmingham), 117
Luther, Martin, 77–78, 140

McCloskey, Deirdre, 117
Madeira archipelago, 49
Madhava of Sangamagrama, 86
Madison, James, 81
Madras, 54
Magellan, Ferdinand, 51

Index

mail service, 102
Mair, John, 53
Manila, 54, 62
Manuel I (king of Portugal), 51
manuscripts, 47, 56, 59, 63, 103
maps. *See* geography, maps
mariners, 10
    Asian, 6
    Chinese, 38–39, 138
    European, 48–51
    Indian, 50
    magnetic compass, 36
    Portuguese, xii, 49, 138
maritime insurance contracts, 32
Marks, Robert, x
marriage, delay, 128–29, 141
Marsilius of Padua, 76
Martin V (pope), 76
Marx, Karl, 66
    female emancipation, 128
Maryland, religious toleration laws, 79
Masonic lodges, 114
Massachusetts, 62
Mass of Our Lady (de Machaut), 124
mathematics, discoveries and advances
    algebra (*al-jabr*) and Arabic numerals, 87
    calculus, 94
    Euclidean geometry, 84, 98
    geometric proofs, 89
    Greeks, 83–84
    Indian advances, 86
    Islamic Golden Age, 87
    logarithms, 92
    Oxford and Paris Universities, 89
    premodern world developments, 10, 12
    spatial calculations, 92
    velocity and motion, 89
Maurice of Nassau, Prince of Orange, 125
Mayan people, developments, 10
Mecca, 111
mechanical philosophy, 95
Medici, Lorenzo de (the Magnificent), 50
medicine, study of, 1
    anatomical dissection, 90
    anatomy and physiology, study of, 84
    circulatory system, 93–94
    gout treatment, 105
    Greeks, 84
    Indian advances, 87
    Islamic Golden Age, 87
    medieval Europe, Islamic influence, 90
    microbes, 94
Mediterranean Sea basin, 35, 42, 48
Melton, James, 102
Mercator, Gerard, 55
merchant-warriors, 143
Merton College, 89
Mesopotamia, 4, 7, 9, 57, 83, 97
    mathematical discoveries, 83
Message from the Stars, A (Galileo), 93
methodical doubt, 94, 99
Metz, 122
Mexico, local knowledge, 7
Mexico City, 62
Michelangelo, 100, 123
migration, 35
military. *See* warfare, European
military slave system, 66
modern science
    China and India, 98–100
    discovery of new lands, 98–99
    Europe and study of nature, 96
    God's majesty, 96
    reasons for Europe, 96–97
    skepticism in premodern cultures, 99
modern world
    definition, xii
    European role, xiv
Mohist movement, 9
Mokyr, Joel, 101, 126
monasteries, *22*, 68–69
Mondino de Liuzzi, 90
Mongolia, 46
Mongols. *See also* Pax Mongolica
    conquest of Baghdad, 9
    contiguous land empire, 36
    effect on world trade, 143
monogamy, 129
Montaigne, Michel de, 54
Montesquieu, Charles de Secondat, 81, 103
Montpellier, 105
Mornay, Philippe de, 80
Morocco, 46, 49
Mozi, 8, 85
Mughal India, 63, 127, 131
music
    musical notation, 124
    polyphonic music, 124–25

223

Index

muskets, 126–27
Muslims
    effect of Qur'an on economics, 32
    European attitudes toward, 47
    European dialogic method, 23
    Hajj (religious pilgrimage), 40
    ignorance of Greek and Latin culture, 44
    lack of travel to Christian lands, 43, 138
    living in Christian lands, 42
Muslim women, public sphere, 130
Mussorgsky, Modest, 57

Nalanda, 86
Napier, John, 92
Naples, 104
natural philosophy
    Chinese advances, 85
    early developments, 83–84
    European advances, 14, 95, 140, 145
    See also astronomy, study of; botany and zoology; chemistry and alchemy; medicine, study of; physical science, study of; physics
natural philosophy, early developments
    earth as spherical, 84
    earthquakes, 83–84
    mathematics, astronomy, medicine, 84
    navigation, 51, 55. *See also* seamanship
    blue-water, xii, 138
    magnetic compass, 36
    technology, 13, 38, 142
Needham, Joseph, 30, 85, 99, 118
Netherlands, 79, 106, 107, 108
    European shipping power, 53
    haven for religious toleration, 78–79
    literacy, 107
    numeracy, 108
    price list publications, 110
    windmills for power, 134
New Astronomy (Kepler), 93
New Atlantis (F. Bacon), 104
New Bourse, 104
Newcastle, Margaret Cavendish, Duchess of, 104
Newfoundland, 44
New Guinea, 6, 51
New Organon (F. Bacon), 94
New Orleans, 54

newspapers and pamphlets, 140
    censorship, 109
    China, 111
    commercial information, 110
    developments in Germany, England and Holland, 109
    English Civil War, 109
    knowledge of the world, 109
    science information, 110
Newton, Isaac, 53, 102–3, 113
    Newtonian method, 94–96, 98–99
New York, 54
New Zealand, 53
Nicholas of Cusa (cardinal), 64
Nile Valley, 57
Nobel Prizes, 2
nobility, 40
North American colonies, 145
    newspapers, 110
    numeracy, 110
Northern Song China, xiv, 131–32. *See also* Song era (China)
northwestern Europe, European marriage pattern, 128–29
Norway, 104, 108

O'Brien, Patrick, 136
Odyssey (Homer), 35
Oldenburg, Henry, 105
Old St. Paul's (London), 122
Olympic Games, 4
On the Revolutions of the Heavenly Spheres (Copernicus), 92
On the Structure of the Human Body (Vesalius), 91
ordeal, trial by, 27
Oresme, Nicolas, 89, 96
Orléans, Philippe, duke of, 116
Ottoman Empire
    administrative decentralization, 71
    civic initiative, 116
    coffeehouses, 111–12
    lack of printed matter, 63
    military might, 142
    petitions and sharia, 111
    press freedom prohibition, 111
    Red Crescent Society, 116
    social organizations, 115
Oxford, 112
Oxford University. *See* University of Oxford

Index

Pääbo, Svante, 35
Pacioli, Luca Bartolomeo de, 92
painting, 141
    anatomical depiction, 123
    Chinese landscape painting, 121
    European art experimentation, 121–24
    linear perspective, 123
    Neanderthal cave painting, 121
    oil painting, 123
    three dimensionality, 122–23
Palestine, 46
Pamuk, Şevket, 115, 127
papal authority, 76–77
paper, 9, 139, 143
    Chinese invention, 58–59, 85, 97
    in Europe, 60
paper money, 85, 132
papyrus, 8, 58
parchment, 58
Paris, x, 122, 124
    astronomy, 95
    Averroism, 56
    learned societies, 104–5
    printing, 60
    salons, 114
    Scottish humanist teaching, 53
Parliament, 79, 109, 111
parliaments, 74
Parmenides, 84
partnership, business, 32–33
Pasquier, Étienne, 62
patent law, 32, 60, 119
pathogens, 53
Pax Mongolica, 36, 46–47
Peace and Truce of God movements, 21, 68–69
Peace of Augsburg, 78
peer review, 105, 140
Pembroke, Mary Sidney Herbert, countess of, 101
penal reform, 146
People's Crusade, 45
per capita GDP, 1, 135
Perdue, Peter C., x
Pérotin, 124
Peter the Hermit, 45
Philadelphia, 117
Philip III (king of Spain), 116
Philosophiae Naturalis Principia Mathematica (Newton), 94–95, 102

Phoenicians, 7, 57
physical science, study of
    Greeks, 83–84
    physics studied, 89
    scientific method, 94
    See also chemistry and alchemy
physics
    invisible atoms, 84
    measurements of all things, 94
    nature of electricity, 95
    projectile motion, 89
    properties of air, 95
    questioning Aristotle, 88–89
    speed of light, 95
    universal gravitation, 94
Picardy, 70
Pico della Mirandola, Giovanni, 101
Pictures at an Exhibition (Mussorgsky), 57
Piers Plowman (Langland), 48
pilgrimage, Buddhist, 36
pilgrimage, Christian
    Arabic knowledge, 44, 46
    Crusades, 45–46
    organized travel to Jerusalem, 46
pilgrimage, Muslim, 40
Pisa, 76
pistols, 127
place value, 9–10, 83, 85–86
planar graphs, 12
plantations, xv, 49
Plato, 17, 23, 94, 97
political fragmentation
    effect on creativity, 7
    in Europe, 26, 49, 98, 138, 141–42
    human rights, 54, 64
    rulers' weaknesses, 144
political power, 65
Polo, Marco, 47, 54
Pomeranz, Kenneth, x, 132
population growth and loss, 1–2, 127, 133, 136
port books, 48
portolan chart, 48
Portugal, xii, 49, 51
    passage to India, 49
    seafaring discoveries, 49
    seafaring power, 49
    slave trade, 49
postal service. *See* mail service
power barrier. *See* energy and power

Index

practical and theoretical knowledge
    chronometers and longitude, 117
    longitude, 116
    problem-solving, 116–18
Prague, 101
prehistoric cave paintings, 57
priesthood of all believers, 78, 140
Priestley, Joseph, 117
Prince-Bishopric of Liège, 70
printing
    books and learning, 58
    Chinese invention, 9, 58–59, 85, 97, 139
    in India, 63
    mechanized, 14, 55, 77, 139
    movable type, xii, 56, *60–61*, 98
    woodblock book production, 63
printing revolution, 144
    documentation, 62
    effect on Europe, 14, 59–60
    illustrations, 91–92
    output of books, 106–7
    prohibition on printed matter, 62, 111
property rights, 130
Prussia, 96
Pseudo-Dionysius the Areopagite, 122
Ptolemy, 35, 50–51, 84, 86, 92
public space, 131
public sphere, 15, 101, 109, 111–12, 146
    Muslim women discouraged, 130
    ordinary people, 140
Pythagoras, 49, 97
Pythagorians, 84

Qianlong Emperor, 106
Quebec, 54
quipus, 10
Qushji, Ali, 87

Rahimi, Ali, 147
Recht, Ben, 147
Red Sea, 38
Reformation, 79–80
    Middle Ages ideas, 80
religion and church
    American Catholics at the American Revolution, 69–70
    Anabaptists and peace movements, 78
    asylum for political and religious dissenters, 79
    Buddhism, first universal religion, 86
    Christian reform movement and literacy, 107
    condemnation of scientific questions, 89
    early developments, 8
    England's break with Church of Rome, 79
    freedom from secular lords, 69–70
    Hebrews, impact of notion of God, 9
    heliocentric theory and Inquisition, 93
    power shift to monarchy, 73
    reform movements, 77–79
    religious toleration and law, 79
    role in modern science, 96, 98, 145
    Talmudic and Islamic law, 137
    See also canon law; Church of Rome
Renaissance. *See* Europe, Renaissance
reproductive rights, 130
Republic of Letters, 15, 100–1, 103–5, 114, 118, 140
Rheede, Hendrik Adrian van, 91
rhetoric, 8
Rhode Island, religious toleration laws, 79
Ricci, Matteo, 102
Ricoldo of Monte Croce, 47
rights, 64–82, 115, 139–40, 144
    human rights, 54, 118, 145
    in medieval Europe, 14
    modern world, xiv
    political rights, 83
    property rights, 31, 130
    reproductive rights, 130
    tendency to cascade, xiv, 69, 79
river valley civilizations, 4–5, 7
Robinson Crusoe (Defoe), 103
Roger II (king of Sicily), 29
Rome, x, 42, 60, 75, 76, 104
    applied science and technology, 84–85
    civil law system, 19
    legal system influence, 19
Rømer, Ole, 95
Royal Abbey of Saint-Denis, 122
Royal Academy of Science (France), 126
royal charters to companies, 142
royal councils, 74, 139
Royal Exchange, 104
Royal Society of London, 104–6, 112, 116
rule of law, xiv, 4, 13, 30, 71
Russia's world economic ranking, 2

Index

Sachsenspiegel, 26
Safavid Empire, 63
Saint Helena, 95
Saint Petersburg, 104, 105
salon, meals and conversation, 114
Sardinia, 42
Sauma, Rabban, 44
Savannah, 54
schism, church, 75–76
scholar-officials (China), 38, 50, 65, 111, 118, 144. *See also* literati (China)
scholastic method, 23
schools
    lay schools, business and classical education, 59
    reading, arithmetic and accounting, 107–8
    scuole d'abbaco, secondary schools, 59
schooner, 48. *See also* navigation, seamanship
science. *See* astronomy, study of; botany and zoology; chemistry and alchemy
scientific lectures, 113, 140
scientific racism, xiv
scientific societies, 104–5
Scotland, 70, 79, 81, 117
scroll, 50, 58
seamanship, 138
self-government, 65, 70, 72–73
Selim I (Ottoman sultan), 62
Selim II (Ottoman sultan), 111
Senegal, 49
Seven Years' War, 126
Seville, 40
Shang period (China), 57
shareholders, 33
ship design and naval architecture. *See also* navigation, seamanship
    cannon and armaments, 50
    caravels, 48
    lateen sails, 157 n.67
    three and four masts, 48
Sic et Non (Abelard), 25
Sicily, 29, 42, 45, 74
    Muslim communities, 58
Siddhartha Gautama, 86
Sierra Leone, 51
Siger of Brabant, 56
slavery, xii, 54, 114
slave system, military, 66

slave trade, xiv, 49, 149n9
smart phones, 1, 4
Smith, Adam, 118
Smith, William, 117
social capital, 115, 129
Song era (China), xiv, 131–33, 139
Soviet Union, economy of, 2, 150 n.5
Spain, xii, 68, 90, 121, 125, 139
    Barcelona, share in governance, 74
    Cortes (royal court), 73–74
    Muslim communities, 58
    translation of Arabic works, 90
    travel to study Arabic scholarship, 45
    world explorers, 51
Spanish March, 69
spices, 36, 40, 70
sports (team), 114, 124
Sri Lanka, 134
standard of living, 4, 119, 146
    caloric consumption comparison (Europe and non-European societies), 136
    early modern Europe, 16
    Industrial Revolution, 133, 137
    northwestern Europe, 141
    prior to 1800, 1–2
    wage comparison, 135
state of nature (analytical concept), 80
Stockholm, 60
Strait of Gibraltar, 48
Strasbourg, 101
Suger, Abbot, 122
Sulawesi, 121
sulfuric acid, 90
Summa Theologica (Aquinas), 25
Sweden, 96, 107
Syria, 46, 62
Syriac-speaking Christians, 9

tabula rasa, cultural, 97, 138
tallest buildings, 55, 122, 141
Talmudic law, 18, 137
Tang era (China), 36
Tangier, 42
Tasman, Abel, 53
taxation, 75, 132
Taxila, 86
tax state, 132
team sports. *See* sports (team)
technical illustration, 100, 140

Index

technological innovations
  collaboration with artists, 100
  metallurgy, dye making and glass in India, 87
  microscopes, 92
  simple telescope, 92
  steam engine, 117
telescope, 92, 95
teosinte, 7
textiles, 9, 40, 43, 70
Thales, 83
theories of political resistance, 80–81, 140
Tiangong kaiwu, 118
Tocqueville, Alexis de, on women in America, 128
Touati, Houari, 43
tournament model of warfare, 127
trade and trade routes, 13, *37*, *39*, *41*, 142
  Chinese, 36, 38
  India, 40, 41
  Islamic, 40, 42–43
trade and trade routes, European
  Church restrictions on Muslim trade, 42
  Columbian Exchange of plants and animals, 54
  impact on Asia and Africa, 53
  technological innovations, 42
trademarks, 32
translations
  Greek and Islamic texts, 9, 23, 36, 88, 90
  religious works into the vernacular, 77, 80
transportation, 135
Transylvania, 102
travel, early. *See* China, travel and travelers; Greece; Muslims
travel and travelers, European
  admiration for Chinese monarchy, 54
  apprenticeships and tramping, 119
  Arabic knowledge, 45
  Atlantic voyages, 48
  Australia, 52
  Christian pilgrimage, 44–46
  coastline and river advantages, 3
  Crusades, 45–46
  exploration and colonization, xii, *52*, 138–39
  fascination with unfamiliar, xiv, 50
  first to Atlantic Ocean, 50
  grand European tour, 103

India by sea, 51
literature of travel, 48
Magellan circumnavigation of globe, 51
Mongolia, Court of the Great Khan, 46–47
New World discovery, 51
New Zealand, 53
Nordic exploration and settlement, 44
North American exploration, 51
ship design and naval architecture, 48
South Pacific exploration, 53
Spanish and Portuguese explorers, 51
technological innovations, 48
Willoughby Arctic exploration, 51
Travels of Sir John Mandeville, The, 47
treasure fleets, 38, 49
tribal people of New Guinea, 6
Trinity (doctrine), 25, 28
Trondheim, 104
Truce of God. *See* Peace and Truce of God movements
Two Treatises of Government (Locke), 80

ulama, 71
United States, 2, 4, 95, 128
  American Catholics at the American Revolution, 76
  constitution, 81
  Fundamental Constitution of the Carolinas, 81
  Fundamental Orders (Connecticut), 81
  Rhode Island, religious toleration laws, 79
universities, early European, 23, *24*
  academic autonomy, 24–26
  comparison to other cultures, 25
  immunity of students and faculty, 24
University of Bologna, 23, 90, 102
University of Leiden, 92
University of Oxford, 89, 112
University of Padua, 90–92
University of Paris, 89
urban charters, 70
urban councils, 69
Urban II (pope), 45
Urban V (pope), 75
urbanization, 115, 127–28

vaccines, 16
van Leeuwenhoek, Antoni, 94, 105

Index

Venice, 60
    coffeehouses, 112
Vesalius, Andreas, 91
Vienna, 114
Vietnam, 36
Vikings, 40, 44
Vindiciae, contra tyrannos (Mornay), 80
Vitoria, Francisco de, 53
Vivaldi, Vandino and Ugolino, 48
Voltaire, 54, 103
voluntary associations, xii, 15, 114–16
Vries, Peer, 146

wages, 127–28, 130, 135–36, 143
Waldo, Peter, 77
Wales, 115, 117, 133
Wang Yangming, 86
waqf, 26, 31
warfare, European, 141, 142
    artillery improvements, 125–26
    labor costs and innovation, 127
    naval investments and progress, 126
    navy expenditures, 125
    training of soldiers, 125–26
warlordism, 45, 66, 138
Washington, George, 102
watermills, 133
Watt, James, 117, 133
Wedgwood, Josiah, 106
Whiston, William, 116
White, Lynn, 64
Wilhelm, Friedrich (Elector of Brandenburg), 79
William of Orange, 78
William of Rubruck, 46–47
Williams, Reeve, 113
Williamsburg, 54
Willoughby, Hugh, 51
windmills, 119, 134
Wittgenstein, Ludwig, 12
women, labor-force participation, 141

women's status
    in China, 128–30
    female emancipation and autonomy, 128, 146
    in India, 130–31
    literacy and numeracy, 129
    marriage and childbearing patterns, 128–29
    scholarship and intellectual advancement, 15, 102
    See also marriage, delay; property rights
Wong, Roy Bin, 116
woodblock printing, 63
World Cup, 4
World War II, xiv, 2
writing systems, early, 57, 58
    China, early printing, 58–59
    Chinese invention of paper, 58
    Egypt, papyrus and parchment, 58
    Greeks, vowels added, 58
    Phoenicians, first workable alphabet, 57–58
writing systems, medieval and early modern
    Carolingian miniscule script, 59
    manuscripts copied and illustrated, 59
    moveable-type printing technology, 60
    printing presses across Europe, 60, *61*, 139
    reading and writing in lay schools, 59
    scientific and technical illustrated books, 62
Wyclif, John, 77, 79

Yangzi Delta, x, 59, 135–36, 146
    Opium Wars, 126
Yuan Dynasty, 36, 132

Zanzibar, 51
zero, concept of, 9–10, 25, 86, 98
Zheng He, 38
Zhu Xi, 86